Some recent essay collections by Isaac Asimov:
Asimov on Science Fiction, 1981
Change! 1981
The Roving Mind 1983
The Dangers of Intelligence 1986
Past, Present and Future, 1987, 1988

ASIMOV'S

GALAXY

ASIMOV'S
GALAXY

Reflections on Science Fiction

Isaac Asimov

Doubleday

NEW YORK   LONDON   TORONTO   SYDNEY   AUCKLAND

809.3876

Asi

Published by Doubleday, a division of Bantam Doubleday Dell Publishing Group, Inc., 666 Fifth Avenue, New York, New York 10103

Doubleday and the portrayal of an anchor with a dolphin are trademarks of Doubleday, a division of Bantam Doubleday Dell Publishing Group, Inc.

Library of Congress Cataloging-in-Publication Data
Asimov, Isaac, 1920–
  Asimov's galaxy: reflections on science fiction. — 1st ed.
    p. cm.
  Essays published as editorials in Isaac Asimov's science fiction magazine.
    1. Asimov, Isaac, 1920– —Authorship. 2. Science fiction—Authorship. 3. Science fiction—History and criticism. I. Title.
PS3551.S5Z463 1989   88-15909
809.3'876—dc19   CIP

BOOK DESIGN BY CAROL MALCOLM

ISBN 0-385-24120-8
Copyright © 1989 by Nightfall, Inc.
All Rights Reserved
Printed in the United States of America
January 1989
First Edition

BG

Dedicated to: Joel Davis,

Gardner Dozois,

Sheila Williams, and all the nice people at the magazine.

Table of Contents

ACKNOWLEDGEMENTS

The following essays are reprinted from *Isaac Asimov's Science Fiction Magazine,* where they appeared as editorials in the indicated issues:

"The influence of Science Fiction," August 1981; "Our Obsolete World," July 1983; "Women and Science Fiction," January 1983; "Schools and Science Fiction," November 1983; "Religion and Science Fiction," June 1984; "The Kiss of Death?" October 1986; "Shrugging It Off," August 1983; "Watch Out!" November 1981; "The Unforgivable Sin," February 1982; "Satire," March 1984; "Irony," October 1984; "Revisions," July 1982; "Plagiarism," August 1985; "Originality," April 1986; "Names," December 1984; "Dialog," April 1985; "Symbolism," June 1985; "Serials," July 1980; "Nowhere!" September 1983; "Science Fiction Poetry," March 1981; "Science Fiction Anthologies," May 1981; "What Writers Go Through," December 1981; "The Writers' Plight," January 1982; "Editors," November 1985; "Pseudonyms," January 1984; "We're Doing Well," March 1982; "Outsiders, Insiders," February 1986; "Civil War," December 1985; "Catastrophes," Mid-December 1984; "Moonshine," May 1985; "Household Robots," October 1982; "The Sun and Moon," March 1980; "The Solar System," April 1980; "What's a Galaxy?" June 1981; "Our Own Galaxy," July 1981; "Star Wars!" September 1985; "The New York *Times* Laughs Again," October 1981; "Faster than Light," November 1984; "Time Travel," April 1984; "Fantasy," February 1984; "Wish Fulfillment," June 1986; "Sword and Sorcery," January 1985; "Fairy Tales," October 1985; "Magic," March 1985; "Opinion," September 1984; "Controversy," May 1984; "Magazine Covers," September 1981; "Unreasonable!" June 1983; "Slush!" February 1985; "Book Reviews," February 1981; "Integrity," September 1986; "Nostalgia," April 1983; "Susan Calvin," December 1982; "Not an Expert," September 1982; "Violence and Incompetence," Mid-December 1982; "Family Matters," September 1980; "Persona," March 1986; "My Name," Mid-December 1983; "Bestseller," May 1983; "My Projects," October 1983; "My Autobiography," November 1980; "What Makes Isaac Run?" December 1980; "More Asimov?" February 1983; "Superstupidity," July 1985; "Autographs," December 1983; "Irritations," Mid-December 1985.

Introduction

TOWARD THE END OF 1976 THE first issue of *Isaac Asimov's Science Fiction Magazine* was published. The name is a little unwieldy and even the initials, frequently used, IASFM, strike me as not terribly convenient. I, therefore, refer to the magazine as *Asimov's* and I hope you will indulge me in this.

The magazine was not my idea. It was that of Joel Davis, the genial guiding light of Davis Publications, Inc. As far as I was concerned, I had a sneaking suspicion the magazine would not last for long, if only because dozens of science fiction magazines had been started in the previous quarter century and none had lasted long. Joel thought my name might make a difference, but I didn't think so.

There *was* a difference, to be sure, for *Asimov's* endured. It started with four issues a year and gradually rose to thirteen a year, and it will have survived its eleventh anniversary by the time you read this, and is still going strong. I still don't think it's my name that's doing it, however. Rather, it's that we've had the extraordinary good fortune to have a series of excellent editors.

There was first George Scithers, who launched it splendidly, then retired when he decided it could move on vigorously on its own. He was followed by Kathleen Moloney, who eventually left to join a book publisher. She was followed by Shawna McCarthy, who also eventually left to join a book publisher. And finally, we have Gardner Dozois, ably assisted by Sheila Williams. Behind them all was the unfailing support of Joel, and you'll notice that Joel, Gardner, and Sheila are mentioned in the dedication.

Through it all, I remained as "editorial director." That doesn't give me any editorial functions at all, I assure you. I don't have the time for that sort of thing, or the inclination, or the ability, and that's a three-way combination you just can't beat. I'm not even a "director," strictly speaking. I wouldn't dream of trying to direct an editor, and if I had showed any signs of it George (or Kathleen, or Shawna, or Gardner) would have quickly hit me with a wastepaper basket (and a full one, at that).

Of course, I have various minor functions. My name stays on the magazine. I drop in at the office once a week and cheer everyone up. I'm always available for consultations if anyone is mad enough to consult me. I go through the letters from the readers, choose those to be published, and answer them. Sometimes I even answer a few that aren't chosen to be published. I also submit a story about four times a year, and sometimes (not always) the editor accepts it.

My biggest job, however, is that of writing a fourteen-hundred-word editorial in each and every issue. In these essays, I write on any subject that pleases me. Naturally, the topic almost always touches on something of science fictional interest, but even that is not essential (see Chapter 45).

Like everything I write, my editorial essays seem to interest people* and I included about twenty of them in a book of mine entitled *Asimov on Science Fiction* (Doubleday, 1981). Since then, however, a great many more of my editorials have been published and the manuscripts are now sitting in a drawer eating their heads off.

I might as well put them to work. After all, it strikes me that a number of people have not seen the magazine and haven't read the editorials. People who do read the magazine may have missed some and may no longer possess others. And it could well be that lots of people, whether they have read them or not, would want the editorials all in one convenient place, where they can be easily cherished.

With arguments such as these, I finally persuaded myself to put together sixty-six of my essays, and here they are. (Some of them overlap slightly, by the way.) I've added afterwords where these seem to be advisable and I've tried not to be unduly wordy about that.

---

* Thank goodness I'm a modest fellow. I hate to think the excesses to which I would go were I immodest.

ASIMOV'S

GALAXY

SCIENCE
FICTION IN
GENERAL ✦

The Influence of Science Fiction

I SUPPOSE IT'S ONLY NATURAL THAT those of us who are devotees of science fiction would like to find in it something more than a matter of idle amusement. It ought to have important significance.

On many occasions in the past I have advanced arguments for supposing such significance to exist. Here is how it goes.

The human way of life has always been subject to drastic and more or less irreversible change, usually (or, as I believe, always) mediated by some advance in science or technology. Thus, life is forever changed with the invention of fire—or the wheel—or agriculture—or metallurgy—or printing.

The rate of change has been continually increasing, too, for as these changes are introduced, they tend to increase the security of the human species and therefore increase its number, thus in turn increasing the number of those capable of conceiving, introducing, and developing additional advances in science and technology. Besides that, each advance serves as a base for further advance, so that the effect is cumulative.

During the last two centuries, the rate of change has become so great as to be visible in the course of the individual lifetime. This has put a strain on the capacity of individuals, and societies, too, to adapt to such change, since the natural feeling always is that there should be no change. One is used to things as they are.

During the last thirty years, the rate of change has become so great as to induce a kind of social vertigo. There seems no way in which we can plan any longer, for plans become outdated as fast as they are implemented. By the time we recognize a problem, action must be taken at once; and by the time we take action, however quickly, it is too late: the problem has changed its nature and gotten away from us.

What makes it worse is that, in the course of scientific and technological advance, we have reached the stage where we dispose of enough power to destroy civilization (if it is misused), or to advance it to unheard-of heights (if we use it correctly).

With stakes so high and the situation so vertiginous, what can we do?

We must learn to anticipate fairly correctly and, in making our plans, take into account not what now exists, but what is likely to exist five years hence—or ten—or twenty—whenever the solution is likely to come into effect.

But how can one take change into account correctly, when the vast mass of the population simply refuses to take into account the existence of any change at all? (Thus, most Americans, far from planning now for 2000, would probably prefer to have 1955 restored.)

That is where science fiction comes in. Science fiction is the one branch of literature that accepts the fact of change, the inevitability of change. Without the initial assumption that there will be change, there is no such thing as science fiction, for nothing is science fiction unless it includes events played out against a social or physical background significantly different from our own. It is science fiction at its best if the events described could not be played out at all *except* in a social or physical background significantly different from our own.

That doesn't mean that a science fiction story should be predictive—that it should portray something that is going to happen—before it can be important. It doesn't even have to portray something that might conceivably happen.

The existence of change, the acceptance of change, is enough. People who read science fiction come, in time, to know that *things will be different.* Maybe better, maybe worse, but *different.* Maybe this way, maybe that way, but *different.*

If enough people read science fiction or are, at least, sufficiently influenced by people who read science fiction, enough of the population may come to accept change (even if only with resignation and grief) so that government leaders can plan for change in the hope of meeting something other than persistent resistance from the public. —And then, who knows, civilization might survive.

And yet this reasoning is highly tenuous, and while I accept the line of reasoning thoroughly (having, as far as I know, made it up) I can see that others might dismiss it as special pleading by someone who doesn't want the stuff he writes to be dismissed as just—stuff.

Well then, has science fiction already influenced the world? Has anything that science fiction writers have written influenced real scientists, or engineers, or politicians, or industrialists so as to introduce important changes?

What about the case of space flight, of trips to the Moon?

This has been a staple of imaginative literature since Roman times; and both Jules Verne and H. G. Wells have written highly popular stories about trips to the Moon in the nineteenth and early twentieth centuries.

Certainly, those scientists and engineers who began to deal with rocketry realistically had read science fiction and there is no question that men such as Robert Goddard and Wernher von Braun had been exposed to such things.

This is not to say that science fiction taught them any rocketry. As a matter of fact, Wells used an antigravity device to get to the Moon and Verne used a gigantic gun, and both of these devices can be dismissed out of hand as ways of reaching the Moon.

Nevertheless, the two writers stirred the imagination, as did all the other science fiction writers who flooded into the field as the twentieth century wore on and who began to write material in large masses (if not always in high quality). All of this prepared the minds of more and more people for the notion of such trips.

It followed that when the time came that rockets were developed as war weapons during World War II, there were not lacking engineers who saw them as devices for scientific exploration, for orbital flights, for trips to the Moon and beyond. And all this would not be laughed out of court by the general public, all the way down to the rock bottom of the average congressman—because science fiction had paved the way.

Even this may not seem enough—too general—too broad.

How about specific influence? How about something a specific writer has done that has influenced a specific person in such a way that the world has been changed?

That has been done, too. Consider the Hungarian physicist Leo Szilard who, in the middle 1930s, began thinking of the possibility of a nuclear chain reaction that might produce a nuclear bomb; who recognized that his thought had become a very real possibility when uranium fission was discovered in

1939; who moved heaven and earth to persuade Allied scientists to censor themselves voluntarily in order to keep information from reaching the Nazi enemy; who persuaded Einstein to persuade President Roosevelt to initiate a vast project for developing a nuclear bomb.

We know how that changed the world (whether for better or for worse is beside the point right now, but I certainly would not have wanted Hitler to get the first nuclear bomb in the early 1940s), so we can say that Leo Szilard changed it.

And how did Szilard come to have his original idea? According to Szilard himself, that idea came to him because he read a story by H. G. Wells (originally published in 1902) in which an "atomic bomb"—the phrase H. G. Wells himself used—had been featured.

Here's another case. At the present moment, industrial robots are appearing on the assembly line with increasing frequency. In Japan, whole factories are being robotized. What's more, the robots themselves are being made more versatile, more capable, and more "intelligent" very rapidly. It isn't farfetched to say that in a couple of decades this robotization will be seen to have changed the face of society permanently (assuming that civilization continues to survive).

Is there anyone we can credit for this? It is difficult to place that credit on a single pair of shoulders, but perhaps the pair that is most likely to deserve it belongs to a man named Joseph F. Engelberger, who is the president of Unimation, which manufactures one third of all the robots in use and has installed more of them than anybody else.

Engelberger founded his company in the late 1950s and how do you suppose he came to found it?

Some years before, according to his own account, when he was still a college undergraduate, he became enthusiastic about the possibility of robots when he read *I, Robot,* by Isaac Asimov.

I assure you that when I was writing my positronic robot stories back in the 1940s, my intentions were clear and simple. I just wanted to write some stories, sell them to a magazine, make a little money to pay my college tuition, and see my name in print. If I had been writing anything but science fiction, that's all that would have happened.

But I was writing science fiction—so I'm now changing the world.

✦

AFTERWORD: And in 1985, four years after the above essay was written, the first edition of *Handbook of Industrial Robotics* appeared—with an introduction by me. Why? Because the general editor, who was an Israeli, had, when young, read *I, Robot* in Hebrew and that had lured him into robotics.

The Influence of Science Fiction

2

Our Obsolete World

I WAS INTERVIEWED RECENTLY ON the telephone by a newspaper reporter and questioned on my views of science fiction. I spoke freely, as I usually do. Inevitably, I was asked about the Foundation series and I explained that it was a historical chronicle of the future. I talked about the concern of the series with the fall and rise of empires, and she at once pointed out the similarity to historical events in the past. I said, "Of course. That's deliberate."

Why, then, asked she, was it necessary to make a science fiction story out of it and place the events in the far future?

And, according to the newspaper article when it appeared, my answer was that "you can't write about the here and now; we're living in a world that is obsolete."

I don't remember saying that (I never remember what I say to reporters) but I'm sure I did because it sounds exactly like what I would say under such circumstances. After all, the world we live in *is* obsolete.

It is not an unusual situation. It seems to me that throughout history, the human world has been a patchwork of obsolescence. The human situation alters, usually as a result of the introduction of technological changes, and human social institutions and psychological attitudes do not change as fast or, sometimes, at all. When that happens, obsolescence sets in.

Any society which clings to tradition and eschews change is certain to be obsolescent and to suffer as a result at the hands of neighboring nations that do change, even if slowly. The suffering that obsolescence entails is usually military in nature, but it might be economic and be just as effective.

Nor is the resistance to change necessarily that of mere inertia or stupidity. It is sometimes the result of prolonged success and the feeling that the one way to be assured of continued success is to "not break up a winning team."

Egypt clung stubbornly to tradition after its period as the most powerful empire in the world and, as a result, it became obsolete in the thirteenth century B.C., moved into the backwater of history, and lost control of its own destiny for over two thousand years. China became obsolete in the fifteenth century when, out of self-satisfaction with its success as the largest and most advanced nation within its horizons, it refused to take advantage of its technological preeminence to develop a gunpowder-based military machine and worldwide sea exploration. (I don't judge this a morally bad attitude, merely an obsolete one.) It suffered a five-century eclipse as a result.

The ancient Greek world produced two centuries of matchless genius and success between 530 B.C. and 330 B.C., and a golden glow hovers about that period still. In part this was the result of the institution of the city-state, which introduced tremendous variety and competition, and produced an extremely complex and subtle culture through endless interplay of differing customs and attitudes under the umbrella of a common language and literature.

The competition, however, was, in part, military, and while this developed military equipment and tactics that were far in advance of the larger nations that surrounded the city-states, it also made it impossible for the city-states to unite against a common enemy. Eventually, it was inevitable that the Greek military techniques be adopted by some nearby nation that was not a city-state. The semi-Greek nation Macedon, under Philip II, was the first, and from that moment on the Greek city-states were obsolete.

Nor did the city-states recognize this. They clung to their traditional "liberties" (that is, the liberty to fight their neighbors and to indulge in civil war between such fights) and, as a result, they lost control of their own destiny and never regained it in city-state form.

Of course, it's easy to look back with the advantage of hindsight and sneer at them for not seeing the obvious facts of the situation. Yet even hindsight doesn't help, for when the occasion arises in history to take advantage of the lessons taught by the past, the chance to do so is rarely seized.

In the fifteenth century, northern Italy was a congeries of city-states which, like those of ancient Greece, produced a high culture that led the world and was, in fact, second only to that of the Greeks in their golden age. Yet they would never unite either, but clung to their separatism in the face of the growing power of the large nations about them, so that they went down to common ruin at the hands of the invading French, Germans, and Spaniards in the sixteenth century.

In the nineteenth century, Europe was the mistress of the world. On a much larger scale, the European nations were the "city-states" who fought each other endlessly and developed military techniques that left the larger, but militarily primitive, nations of what we now call the third world helpless before them.

In the twentieth century, however, European nations continued to fight each other ever more intensely and furiously, even while larger political units were developing and, in some cases, improving on European technology. After 1900, Europe was obsolete and didn't know it, and the result is that the European nations now carry on a cautious and uncomfortable existence in the shadow of the two competing "superpowers," the United States and the Soviet Union.

The danger of obsolescence has grown steadily greater through the centuries, however, for two reasons that are interrelated.

First, and basic, the changes introduced by advancing technology have become steadily more intense in nature and follow each other more rapidly. The result is that it becomes ever more difficult for social and economic institutions, to say nothing of tradition and of psychology, to match those changes. There is therefore a growing inappropriateness in the responses evoked by problems that arise.

Second, as a result of the advancing technology, the world has grown effectively smaller, more interrelated sociologically and economically, while the power of humanity to effect destruction has steadily increased. The destructive potential now far surpasses the somewhat (but by no means equally) increased power to rebuild after destruction.

When you combine the growing inappropriateness of response with the damage that such inappropriateness can do if matters come to any attempt at a military solution, it isn't hard to see that for the first time in history, we stand at the point where obsolescence can be fatal to civilization in a worldwide sense, and perhaps permanently.

In what way is our world obsolete?

First, tradition seems to blind us to the fact that it no longer makes sense to divide the world into separate nations, each of which thinks that its own "national security" justifies *any* action, no matter how dangerous to humanity as a whole. (This is analogous to the manner in which each Greek city-state considered its own interests only, without regard to Greek civilization as a whole; or Italian city-states without regard to Italy as a whole; or European nations without regard to Europe as a whole.)

Second, tradition seems to blind us to the fact that our population has grown too great, our technology too complex, to be supported by Earth alone. We think that because Earth's resources were *once* so great in comparison to human needs, those resources could be considered limitless—that they therefore still are.

As long as we possess these two traditional views, our society is not only obsolete, but dangerously so, and we stand on the brink of total disaster.

How must we change?

Clearly, we must recognize that it makes no sense for humanity to deal with the Universe in any way but as a social and economic whole. We are Earthpeople and nothing less. The fact that we feel ourselves to be Americans, Russians, Paraguayans, Nigerians, Pakistanis, etc., is irrelevant. It is a feeling we cannot indulge, but one we *must* violate for the sake of survival. Or let me put it this way: we can feel whatever local allegiances we want to, as long as it is recognized that they must bow to planetary needs, just as local rights within the United States today (my Manhattan patriotism, for instance) must bow to national needs—something all Americans casually accept.

Also, we must recognize that the human range must extend beyond Earth. We must move outward into space in search of new sources of both energy and materials, in order to release human pressures on the biosphere which are, today, steadily overweighting it and threatening the viability of the planet itself.

These two fundamental changes are interrelated since it may well be that space can be successfully conquered only through a global effort, and that only the successful establishment of a space-centered civilization will give the final impetus required for the ultimate triumph of a global consciousness.

In science fiction stories, both these changes are commonly taken for granted, and *that* is the importance of saying what I have to say in a science fictional context, rather than in the here and now.

3

Women and Science Fiction

MY EARLY SCIENCE FICTION
stories had no women in them for the most part. There were two reasons for
this: one social, one personal. The social reason first.

Prior to the public recognition in the United States that babies are not
brought by the stork, there was simply no sex in the science fiction magazines.
This was not a matter of taste, it was a matter of custom that had the force of
law. In most places, nonrecognition of the existence of sex was treated as
though it were the law, and for all I know, maybe it was indeed local law. In
any case, there were no words or actions that could bring a blush to the
leathery cheek of the local censor.

But if there's no sex, what do you do with female characters? They can't
have passions and feelings. They can't participate on equal terms with male
characters because that would introduce too many complications where some
sort of sex might creep in. The best thing to do was to keep them around in
the background, allowing them to scream in terror, to be caught and then
rescued, and, at the end, to smile prettily at the hero. (It can be done safely
then because THE END is the universal rescue.)

Yet it must be admitted that science fiction magazines showed no guts
whatever in fighting this situation. That brings us to the personal reason. In the
1930s and 1940s, the readership of the science fiction magazines was heavily
(next to exclusively, in fact) masculine. What's more, it was young and intellectually masculine. The stereotypical science fiction reader was a skinny kid
with glasses and acne, introverted and scapegoated by the tough kids who

surrounded him and who were rightly suspicious of anyone who knew how to read.

It stands to reason these skinny youngsters knew nothing about girls. By and large, I imagine they didn't dare approach girls, and if they did, were rejected by them scornfully, and if they weren't, didn't know what to do next. So why on Earth should they want this strange subspecies in the stories they read? They had not yet gotten out of the "I hate girls" stage (translation: "I'm scared of girls").

This is an exaggeration, perhaps, and no doubt there were a number of tough young men, and old young men, and girl-chasing young men who read science fiction, but by and large, I suspect it was the stereotypical "skinny intellectual" who wrote letters to the magazines and denounced any intrusion of femininity. I know. I wrote such letters myself. And in the days when I was reading and rating every science fiction story written, I routinely deducted many points for any intrusion of romance, however sanitized it might be.

At the time that I wrote and sold my first few stories, I had not yet had a date with a young woman. I knew nothing about them except what I could guess by surreptitious glances from a distance. Naturally, there were no women in my stories.

(I once received a letter from a woman who denounced me for this lack. Humbly, I wrote back to explain the reason, stating that I had been, very literally, an innocent as far as women were concerned at the beginning of my writing career. She had a good answer for that, too. She wrote back in letters of flame, that it was no excuse!)

But times change!

For one thing, society changed. The breath of liberty that was brought on by all the talk about it during World War II weakened the censor, who retreated, muttering sourly under his bad breath. The coming of the Pill heralded the liberation of women from unwanted pregnancy and marked the weakening of the double standard.

For another, people *will* grow up. Even *I* didn't remain innocent. I actually went out on a date on my twentieth birthday. I met a particular woman two years later, fell in love at first sight, and all trace of fear suddenly left me. I was married five months later and you'd be *surprised* how I changed! I have in my proud possession a plaque handed me by a science fiction convention. On the brass plate is inscribed that quality of mine that had earned me the plaque. It reads "Lovable Lecher."

And yet science fiction lagged a bit, I think. Old habits didn't change easily. My own stories, for instance, remained free of sex except where that was an integral part of the development and then only to the extent that it was, and they *still* so remain. I have gotten rid of my fear (witness my five volumes of naughty limericks), but not of my sense of decorum.

What, then, really brought on the change and brought science fiction more nearly into the mainstream of contemporary literature?

In my opinion, it was not chiefly social evolution; it was not the daring new writers.

It was the coming of women into the science fiction readership!

If science fiction readers had remained almost entirely masculine—even if the acne had cleared up and youth had withered—I think science fiction would have remained male chauvinist in the crudest possible way.

Nowadays, I honestly think that at least a third, and possibly nearly half, of the science fiction readers are women. When that is so, and when it is recognized that women are at least as articulate as men and (these days) quite ready to denounce male chauvinism and to demand treatment as human beings, it becomes impossible to continue past villainy.

Even *I* have to bow to the breath of decency. In my novel, *Foundation's Edge*, of my seven central characters, four are women—all different, all perfectly able to take care of themselves, and all formidable. (For that matter, I introduced Susan Calvin in 1941, and she strode through a man's world, asking no quarter, and certainly giving none. —I just thought I'd mention that.)

And what brought in the women readers? I suppose there are a large number of reasons, but I have one that I favor. It's Mr. Spock's ears.

There is no question in my mind that the first example of decent science fiction that gained a mass following was the television show "Star Trek," over twenty years ago. For a wonder, it attracted as many women as men. I don't suppose there is room to doubt that what chiefly served to attract those women was the unflappable Mr. Spock. And for some reason I won't pretend to guess at, they were intrigued by his ears.

Very few of the "Trekkies" leaked over into print science fiction (or all the magazines would have grown rich), but a minor percentage did and that was enough to feminize the readership of the science fiction magazines. And I think that was all to the good, too.

With so many women thumbing the magazines, women writers were naturally more welcome and their viewpoints greeted with greater reader sympathy—and women editors made more sense, too.

Don't get me wrong. There have been women writers even in the early days of magazine science fiction, and women editors, too. When I was young, some of my favorite stories were by A. R. Long and by Leslie F. Stone. I didn't know they were women, but they were. In addition, Mary Gnaedinger, Bea Mahaffey, and Cole Goldsmith were excellent editors. I never met Ms. Gnaedinger, but I did meet Bea and Cole and I hereby testify that in addition to lots of brains, character, and personality, they each happened to be beautiful. (Irrelevant, I know, but I thought I would mention it.)

Consequently, when George Scithers left us, I found it delightful that Kathleen Moloney agreed to be the new editor. It never occurred to me for an instant that a woman couldn't handle the job just because she was a woman and, as a matter of fact, Kathleen took to it with a kind of rabid delight. She introduced interesting changes and stamped her personality on the magazine.

But then, there came along the all too frequent villain in such cases, the offer-one-can't-refuse. It may have been Kathleen's performance here that aroused interest in other publishing houses and—well, one can't turn down a chance to advance in one's chosen profession, so we lost Kathleen.

And yet all is not lost, either. I have on numerous occasions mentioned the charming Shawna McCarthy, who is as sharp as a scalpel, and who is universally liked for the excellent reason that she is universally likable. *I* like her.

Shawna served faithfully as right-hand person first to George, and then to Kathleen. In the process, she learned every facet of the editing business and developed (thank goodness) the ambition to hold the top position.

So when Kathleen left, I said, "It has to be Shawna," and everyone agreed with me, especially Shawna.

And here she is. Readers—female and male—I give you Shawna!

◆

AFTERWORD: After this essay appeared, I received a number of letters from young women who insisted vehemently that they were not lured into science fiction by Spock's ears. Well, I didn't say they *all* were and, besides, that was just a joke implying that the ears were phallic symbols. I may be just a touch too subtle, at times.

4

Schools and
Science Fiction

ALL WE OLD–TIME SCIENCE
fiction people tend to swap horror stories about our early experiences as s.f.
readers.

In those days, remember, science fiction consisted exclusively of magazines which (unlike *Asimov's*) had ragged edges, blaring titles, and garish covers. What's more, they were read almost exclusively by teenage youngsters,
mostly male, and mostly introverted.

Parents were, quite understandably, suspicious of these magazines and
teachers were indignant.

And so we old-timers remember well how many times parents and
teachers would confiscate the magazines. (Property rights are never respected,
somehow, when kids are involved—perhaps even these days.) Worse yet, they
would lecture us interminably on the subject of something they called "trash."

Every once in a while, a teacher would ask a young man to write a
review of some book of his choice that he had read and liked, and the young
student might promptly write a thoughtful and penetrating review of *The
Legion of Space* by Jack Williamson. You can guess what would then happen.

In the first place, the review would come back with an F. In the second
place, the teacher, when questioned by the youngster (who had worked hard
on it and turned in a good job), would promptly explain in an insufferable
manner that the review was supposed to be of a "good book," a "work of
literature," and not of "junk."

I got inured to that kind of thing. All of us did. Even after I had begun writing and had become a successful and respected writer (to others in the field) I was hardened to not being a "real writer," to not writing "real books" —to being, in fact, a rather peculiar character.

When did it change?

In my personal case, it changed by the middle 1950s when my writing income became higher than my income as a professor. This somehow killed the humor in the jokes about my peculiar hobby. But with time, the attitude toward science fiction changed for everybody.

By the beginning of the 1970s, the *schools* had begun to take up science fiction. My personal experience in this connection came when my beautiful, blue-eyed, blond-haired daughter entered high school and promptly signed up for a course in science fiction.

I was thunderstruck. "Science fiction?" I said. "You're going to spend time in school reading science fiction for credit?"

"Sure," said Robyn. "And do you know what we're being assigned for reading? The Foundation trilogy, that's what!"

And then, a couple of months later, Robyn came home and said, a little shamefaced, "My science fiction class wants to know if you can come to school and talk to them about science fiction."

"Oh, Robyn," I said reproachfully.

"Just informally, Dad. About ten of us."

There's no way I can disappoint Robyn, so I said I would come, and on the scheduled day at the scheduled time, I walked into the school. I was promptly led into the auditorium where the entire student body was waiting for me.

I turned to glare at Robyn, and she avoided meeting my eye. Later, she explained that she had been caught by surprise herself. They had not warned her of the change in their plans.

I recovered from the shock, however, and began to consider that after all those years I had become a celebrity to the *teachers* who seemed to be smiling ingratiatingly at me. If they had had forelocks, they would have pulled them.

How did it happen?

Well, I haven't made any in-depth study of the phenomenon, but I have some notions that seem to me to make sense.

1) The students themselves seem to have been becoming more and more

interested in science fiction, and the sheer force of that increasing interest was bound to have its effects on the school system.

2) Science fiction was beginning to *look* more respectable. John Campbell pioneered a new *Astounding Science Fiction* (later *Analog Science Fiction/Science Fact)* that looked neat and sober. The ragged edges were gone even before he became editor, while he added a more restrained type style to the title, and quiet, uncluttered, even scientific-looking covers. What's more, science fiction was appearing more and more in hardcover books and in paperbacks. The magazines themselves became digest-sized and all this raised the appearance of respectability in the field.

3) The world had begun to seem a bit science fictional itself. World War II had introduced radar, jet planes, rockets, computers, and, finally, the nuclear bomb. In the immediate aftermath of the war, scientists and engineers began talking about going to the Moon, and in 1969, human beings actually stood on the soil of our satellite. There was no way that science fiction, as a field, could any longer be dismissed out of hand as idle escapism.

4) The teachers themselves had changed because they were, literally, no longer the teachers of old. They were a new generation, many of whom had read science fiction when they were youngsters, and some of whom were still reading it.

5) Most of all, however, the credit belongs to us, the older generation. We carried the flame when it wasn't easy. We wrote the material for a penny a word or less, and got the reverse of credit for it outside the field. We read the material against all the pressures from parents and teachers. And we lived to see ourselves justified.

So now, where do we stand?

The outstanding science fiction writers now receive advances in six figures; their books make the bestseller lists. These writers have even lived to see their earlier works dubbed classics and studied reverently in those same schools that would have failed any student who had dared review them when they were first issued.

It sounds, does it not, like an impossibly happy ending to a corny old rags-to-riches story.

But—there are disadvantages.

I won't talk about the loss of the old little-world of readers, when they and I were both young, and when I knew exactly what they wanted, and when their praise (not money, not fame) was all I ever dreamed of having, and all I wanted.

There are more specific disadvantages to be found in the new reputations we have in the schools, however. Very little ones, fortunately, and even amusing, in a way.

For instance— Schools have a way now of raising funds for something needed. It's called a "celebrity auction." They solicit some personal belonging from people who mean enough to a prospective audience to induce high bids, and science fiction writers are now on the list. —A manuscript, a signed book, a signed photograph, an old (but clean, I presume) sock or handkerchief.

At first, I complied. I was flattered and it was for a good cause, so I would send off signed paperbacks. —But they wore me out. So many requests began to come from schools (and churches and libraries—all good causes) every day that I finally had to quit. There were more such auctions than I had paperbacks, and there was no way in which I could pick and choose. So now I ignore them all, and I suffer agonies of guilt as a result.

There are also drives to increase reading motivation among young students. The way to do it is to give prizes. One such prize might be, for instance, a signed bookmark that a proud youngster can put into any book he manages to convince the teacher he has read. Naturally, what is needed are signatures from someone who means something to the kids, so requests are now sent to s.f. writers. For that reason, I am kept busy signing bookmarks by the dozen. So far, I have managed to keep up with that drain on my time, but if the number continues to increase, I will have to call a halt to that, too.

But these are small potatoes, really. What I dread most is the teacher who gives her students the assignment of writing letters to authors of their choice. I presume that only a small minority end up choosing me, but out of millions of youngsters even a very small minority is large in absolute numbers.

I am compelled to answer these letters (I don't want to disappoint youngsters) and what bothers me most is the artificiality of the thing. The teachers give strict instructions as to what must be written and say, apparently, "Tell him what you like about the story and what you don't like."

That's a bad idea, you see, because I don't want to be told what they don't like. However, one young man almost reconciled me to the whole business. With a fine disregard for the mutually exclusive, he wrote me a letter which I here quote in full (except for the name and address).

Dear Izic Azimov,

I like your books very much because they are interesting. I don't like your books because I don't understand them.

Your friend.

Thank you, young man. If you find my stuff interesting even though it is completely incomprehensible to you, think how great you'll think it is when you're old enough to get its meaning.

AFTERWORD: This is the first example in this book of an essay that was inspired by a letter I received from a reader. There will be a number of others.

5

Religion and Science Fiction

IN THE NOVEMBER 1983 ISSUE OF *Asimov's*, the cover story was "The Gospel According to Gamaliel Crucis" by that excellent writer, Michael Bishop. It dealt with a sensitive subject—the coming of a savior, or, in effect, the second coming of Christ.

What makes it even more effective as a science fiction story is that the savior is an extraterrestrial—and not a particularly attractive one to our human eyes since she (!) is a giant mantis. This is entirely legitimate, it seems to me, since if there is other life in the Universe, especially intelligent life, one would expect that a truly universal God would be as concerned for them as for us, and would totally disregard physical shape since it is only the "soul," that inner intellectual and moral identity, that counts.

What is more, Bishop decided to make the story more powerful by casting it into a biblical shape, dividing it into chapters and verses and making use of a touch of suitable biblical wording.

The result was a tour de force which we obviously considered quite successful, or we would not have published it. Still, we were prepared for the fact that some readers might feel uneasy with, or even offended by, the subject matter and/or style.

One letter was quite angry, indeed. The writer was "strongly displeased" and considered it "a burlesque of the scriptures" and, finding no other value to the story, considered it to have been written and published only for the sake of the burlesque.

This can be argued with, of course, but never entirely settled. If a reader sees in it only burlesque, he or she can scarcely be argued out of it. There will always be difference of opinion, often based upon emotion rather than reason, with regard to the value of any work of art.

But there is something more general here. There is the matter of how science fiction ought to deal with religion, especially *our* religion. (Few people worry very much about how some other religion is handled, since only our own is the "true" one.)

No one wants to offend people unnecessarily, and religion is a touchy subject, as we all know. In that case, might it not be best simply to avoid religious angles altogether in writing science fiction? As our angry correspondent says, "I suggest . . . that offending any substantial religious group is not the way to win friends or sell magazines."

Yes, we know that, and since we *do* want to win friends and sell magazines, we would not knowingly go out of our way to embarrass and humiliate even nonsubstantial groups of our readers just for the fun of it.

But we are also editing a serious science fiction magazine that, we earnestly hope, includes stories of literary value, and it is the very essence of literature that it consider the great ideas and concerns of human history. Surely that complex of ideas that goes under the head of "religion" is one of the most central and essential, and it would be rather a shame to have it declared out of bounds. In fact, for a magazine to censor itself out of discussing religion would be to bow to those forces that don't really believe in our constitutional guarantee of freedom of speech and press. If we were to do so, we would be, in a very deep sense, un-American.

Besides, if we were to try to avoid this very touchy subject, where would we stop? I tend to ignore religion in my own stories altogether, except when I absolutely have to have it. Well, I absolutely had to have it in some of my early Foundation stories and in "Nightfall" and so I made use of it. And, whenever I bring in a religious motif, that religion is bound to seem vaguely Christian because that is the only religion I know anything about, even though it is not mine. An unsympathetic reader might think I am burlesquing Christianity, but I am not.

Then, too, it is impossible to write science fiction and *really* ignore religion. What if we find intelligent beings on other worlds? Do *they* have a religion? Is our God universal, and is he/she/it their God as well? What do we do about it? What do they do about it?

This point is almost never taken up but, since it would certainly arise if such beings were discovered in actual fact, science fiction loses touch with reality in taking the easy way out and pretending religion doesn't exist.

Or consider time travel. I don't know how many stories have been written about people going back in time to keep Lincoln from being assassinated, but how about people going back in time to keep Jesus from being crucified? Surely that greater feat would occur to someone in actual fact if time travel were possible.

Think of the changes that could be rung on such a theme. If Jesus were rescued while on his way to the site of crucifixion, and if the rescue were made by modern technology—a helicopter or something more advanced, while the Roman soldiers were held off by rifle fire at the very least—would it not seem to the primitives of the time that supernatural forces were rescuing Jesus? Would it not seem that angels were coming to the aid of a true savior? Would it not establish Christianity as the true religion at once?

Or would it? Clearly, it was God's divine purpose (assuming the God of the Bible exists) to have the crucifixion take place in order that Jesus serve as a divine atonement for Adam's sin. Would the subversion of this plan be allowed to take place?

It's a nice dilemma, and it is within the province of legitimate science fiction. Yet who has ever considered writing such a story even though it would give us a chance to deal with what many consider the central event of history? The story would be an extremely difficult one to write, and I wouldn't feel up to it myself, but I think it is primarily self-censorship that keeps it from being written.

For that matter, what if we went back in time and found that the biblical Jesus never existed?

The mere concept of time travel makes all these speculations irresistible, so it might very well be that very religious people might object to time-travel themes, and call them blasphemous, simply because of the possibilities they give rise to.

The correspondent says in his letter, "Dr. Asimov, I know that you are an atheist—" and there may be the implication that because of this I am insensitive to the feelings of religionists, or perhaps even anxious to make them seem ridiculous.

As a matter of fact, I have frequently, in my writings, made it clear that I have never encountered any convincing evidence of the existence of the biblical God, and that I am incapable of accepting that existence on faith alone.

That makes me an atheist, but, although this may surprise some Americans, the Constitution safeguards my right to be one and to proclaim myself one.

Nevertheless, although I am an atheist, I am not a proselytizing one; I am not a missionary; I do not treat atheism as a kind of true faith that I must force on everyone. After all, I have published more than almost anyone, about 20 million words so far, and I have frequently discussed controversial problems. You are free to go through my writings and search for any sign that I ridicule religion as such. I have opposed those people who attack legitimate scientific findings (evolution, as an example) in the name of religion, and who do so without evidence, or (worse yet) with distorted and false evidence. I don't consider them true religionists, however, and I am careful to point out that they disgrace religion and are a greater danger to honest religion than to science.

And suppose I weren't an atheist. My parents were Jewish and I might have been brought up an Orthodox Jew or become one of my own volition. Might it then be argued that I would naturally favor any story burlesquing Christianity?

Or suppose I were a Methodist; would I therefore look for stories that burlesqued Judaism, or Catholicism—or atheism?

If I were in the mood to run this magazine in such a way as to offend "any substantial religious group" I wouldn't have to be an atheist. I could do it if I was anything at all, provided only that I were a bigot, or an idiot, or both.

In actual fact, I am neither, and again, I offer my collected writings as evidence. As for Shawna, she doesn't have a similar body of written works to cite but, if I may serve as character witness, I can tell you right now she is certainly not a bigot, and a hundred times certainly not an idiot.

Needless to say, I am sorry that our correspondent was upset by "The Gospel According to Gamaliel Crucis." If we lived in an ideal world, we would never publish any story that upset *anyone*. In this case, though, we had to choose. On the one hand, we had a remarkable story that considered, quite fearlessly, an important idea, and we felt that most readers would recognize this point—if not at once, then upon mature consideration. On the other hand, we had a story that might offend some of our readers.

We made the choice. We put quality and importance ahead of the chance of some offense. We hope that our angry correspondent will consider the matter again and see that the story is far more than a burlesque. He might even give Bishop points for skill and courage.

◆

AFTERWORD: This essay revealed the fact that I have not read all the science fiction stories written. Several readers wrote to tell me that Michael Moorcock in "Behold the Man" took up the very matter of a time-travel attempt to investigate Jesus that I said hadn't been done.

One more thing—In 1986, Michael Bishop published a book containing a selection of his short stories, mainly on religious themes, and got my permission to use this essay as an introduction (with some modifications). I was proud to grant the permission.

6

The Kiss of Death?

I HAVE RECEIVED A LETTER FROM David Markey of East Islip, New York, which gave me considerable reason to think. He commented on my essay "Outsiders, Insiders," which appeared in the February 1986 issue of *Asimov's* (see Chapter 27), writing:

"Although I agree wholeheartedly with your basic thrust, one thing bothers me. You used Michael Crichton's novel *The Andromeda Strain* as an example of a science fiction novel sold in the mainstream by an 'outsider' to 'the brotherhood of science fiction.' Which is true, except that when it was first published (if memory serves) the book jacket did not carry the words 'science fiction' on it. Furthermore, most books sold in the mainstream that are in fact s.f. do not carry those words anywhere in their text."

He goes on to cite books by Allen Drury and Kurt Vonnegut as further examples.

—Well, Mr. Markey, you are right. Carl Sagan's novel *Contact,* which was a runaway bestseller, is also not touted as science fiction. The publishers, in fact, are vehement about its *not* being science fiction, although it clearly is.

There are a number of well-thought-of and highly successful science fiction writers who are quite open about their desire not to be known as science fiction writers. I will name no names, but the point they make is that the phrase "science fiction" promptly puts them in a "ghetto." Reviewers will not take them seriously; what reviews they get are a paragraph long; bookstores, if they bother buying them at all, put them in odd corners behind the box in which the cat sleeps; and so on.

Other s.f. writers, who aspire to literary excellence, or who are under the impression they have already caught the virus thereof, are very haughty about the rest of us. They consider us far beneath them, are ashamed that they had to mingle with us in order to get started, and after a while refuse to remember that they ever did.

What is this, then? Is the phrase "science fiction" a kiss of death?

As I explained in my essay "The Name of Our Field" in the May–June 1978 issue of *Asimov's* (see *Asimov on Science Fiction*, Chapter 3), Hugo Gernsback invented the term "science fiction" in June 1929. The phrase was not to be found in the names of the magazines of the field, however, for quite a time. The word "science" by itself was already being used. In June 1929, Hugo Gernsback had put out the first issue of *Science Wonder Stories*. A year later, however, the first word was dropped and it became simply *Wonder Stories*.

In January 1930, Clayton Publications put out *Astounding Stories of Super Science* but with the second issue it became simply *Astounding Stories*.

It was not until March 1938 that the first issue of a magazine bearing the phrase "science fiction" in its title appeared. That was when John W. Campbell, Jr., changed *Astounding Stories* to *Astounding Science Fiction*. In fact, I was told once that it had been his intention to call the magazine simply *Science Fiction* but he found that Columbia Publications had already registered that title, so he couldn't use it. And in March 1939, Columbia did put out a magazine called *Science Fiction*.

For ten years that was it. Then, in October 1949, Mercury Press launched *The Magazine of Fantasy* which, with its second issue, became *The Magazine of Fantasy and Science Fiction*. And in October 1950, Galaxy Publishing put out the first issue of *Galaxy Science Fiction*.

After that, many magazines began to use "science fiction" in the title. Almost all of them were short-lived, but then most of the magazines that didn't use "science fiction" were also short-lived.

In February 1960, however, the name of *Galaxy Science Fiction* was changed to *Galaxy Magazine*. That puzzled me and I inquired. It was then, for the first time, that I heard that the phrase "science fiction" was a kiss of death. The editor of *Galaxy* claimed its sales were automatically limited as long as that deadly phrase was on the cover.

Well, *Galaxy*, with or without the phrase, no longer exists. There are, now, just three science fiction magazines that can be viewed as successful and prestigious. One is *Analog Science Fiction/Science Fact*, (which used to be *As-*

tounding Science Fiction). Another is *The Magazine of Fantasy and Science Fiction.* And still another is (of course) *Isaac Asimov's Science Fiction Magazine.* You will notice, I hope, that all three have that kiss-of-death phrase in the title.

Of course, it might be argued that those three magazines occupy no more than the same small corner of the publishing world that similar magazines occupied in the 1930s, and that is true. Circulations are still one hundred thousand and less. Nevertheless, omitting "science fiction" does *not* increase circulation. Rather, the omission seems to lead to the death of the magazine, so that "science fiction" would seem to be the kiss of life.

Yes, but what about science fiction writers? Aren't they stuck in a ghetto? Don't their novels tend to suffer because of that nasty phrase "science fiction" attached to it? Even if they write something else altogether—a classy mainstream novel, for instance—doesn't the stigma of "science fiction writer" cling to them? Aren't they better off if they simply leave the blasted field and pretend they were never in it? Shouldn't they go about saying, "Science fiction? Never heard of it. I write speculative fiction"?

Well, I can only speak for myself. I never thought "science fiction" was the kiss of death, and I've never found it to be so. I have written nonfiction books by the score, and have done so in every field I could manage, and no one has ever hesitated to publish me because I bore the "science fiction" stigma. Nor have the reviews dismissed me as a "science fiction writer."

I have put out fat books with such titles as *Asimov's New Guide to Science* and *Asimov's Biographical Encyclopedia of Science and Technology.* I have been responsible for a two-volume *Asimov's Guide to Shakespeare,* a two-volume *Asimov's Guide to the Bible,* an *Isaac Asimov's Treasury of Humor*—and they all do well and are accepted on their own merits. I am not in a literary ghetto, and I've never been in one.

Nor is it because I have shrewdly denied my science fiction origins. I admit that my peak science fiction production was in the 1950s and that in the 1960s and 1970s I went in heavily for nonfiction. However, I did not deny my science fiction; I didn't even abandon it. I wrote many science fiction stories in that period, when I had supposedly deserted the field, including a novel, *The Gods Themselves,* and a novelette, "The Bicentennial Man," each of which was awarded both a Hugo and a Nebula.

What's more, if, at any time in that interval, someone was to ask me what I wrote, I had my answer ready. It was "I write everything, but I am best known for my science fiction." The statement had the merit of truth, and I have always had an unaccountable feeling that I ought to tell the truth.

I was careful to maintain my connection with the science fiction fraternity. In November 1958, I accepted an invitation to write a monthly science column for *The Magazine of Fantasy and Science Fiction* (at about a tenth of the word rate I commanded for similar pieces outside the field). I have continued to do so ever since and I have now appeared in 365 issues without having missed one. Yes, I love doing them, but, in addition, I have done it with the intention of keeping myself before the eyes of the science fiction reader.

Then, too, when I was invited by Joel Davis to participate in a new science fiction magazine with my name on it, I had a number of reservations, but none of them involved any fear that the juxtaposition of "Isaac Asimov" and "science fiction" would hurt me. When my reservations were taken care of, the magazine appeared and still exists (obviously) and it has never hurt me.

In the 1980s, I returned to science fiction in a major way and have now published three new novels with a fourth in press (each novel twice as long as my novels of the 1950s).

Nor is there any pretense that the new novels are not science fiction, but are something more "respectable" (if that's the word). I admit that *Robots and Empire,* my most recent novel, does not have the phrase "science fiction" on the cover, but the very word "robots" gives it away. So does my own name on the cover, since I have always carefully and meticulously identified myself with science fiction.

And if you open the book and read the front flap-matter, here's how it starts: "Isaac Asimov's *Robots and Empire* heralds a major new landmark in the great Asimovian galaxy of science fiction." There are the fatal words and it was the publisher who wrote them, not I. Doubleday isn't afraid of the kiss of death, either; and since the book has done well, I feel "science fiction" is *not* a kiss of death.

Might I do even better without "science fiction"? I doubt it, but if I did, it would mean denying my beginnings, and I'd be ashamed to do that just in order to make more money.

7

Shrugging It Off

IN A RECENT ISSUE OF A NATIONAL magazine there was an article about science fiction which Shawna brought to my attention.

The title told one exactly what the tone would be, for it was "Destination: Void"—perfectly and logically dramatic as the title of a science fiction novel, but clearly intended to be a sneer when used as the title for an article *about* science fiction. If there were any doubt about the matter after that, there was the blurb, which read "Science fiction is to fiction as Christian Science is to science."

"I don't think I'm going to like this, Shawna," I said.

"I *know* you won't," said Shawna grimly.

And I didn't. It was a vitriolic attack on every aspect of science fiction and on all its writers and readers. So sweeping was the denunciation, in fact, that it would have been insulting to be left out, and, fortunately, I wasn't. I received only a glancing sneer, to be sure, but that was better than nothing. Referring to the Foundation series, the writer said, "In a much honored trilogy, soon to be a quartet and God knows what else . . ." (Actually, the word he was groping for, but did not know, was "tetralogy" and, beyond that, "pentalogy" and "hexology," or, simply, the general term "series," but one must not place too great a strain on a simple mind.)

My initial impulse—as always in such cases—was to write an article of equal length as a brief for the defense and try to argue the magazine into publishing it, but I didn't have to think long before I realized that this would be a foolish deed. Far better, I decided, for all of us to shrug it off and to go about our business of reading, writing, and publishing science fiction.

That decision made, I would have dismissed the whole thing from my mind, were it not that, within days, letters began to arrive that referred to this article with indignation and anger. Consequently, I suppose I had better explain the grounds for ignoring it.

In the first place, the analysis of science fiction as presented by the writer is so uniformly unfavorable that, after the initial shock, it can't help but provoke a laugh.

What? Is there *nothing* that is good in science fiction? Is there *no* piece of writing that is readable? I won't ask the writer to admit that somewhere there are a few paragraphs worthy of comparison with Tolstoy or Shakespeare—but is there nothing at all that is comparable to, say, Dorothy Sayers?

Is every science fiction writer a subliterary bungler; every novel a piece of unadulterated trash; every idea beneath contempt?

Surely nothing on Earth could be *that* bad! If we all tried very, very hard to write and publish material without a grain of redeeming virtue, we would probably fail to plumb the depths described in the article.

I could conceive of an article which, written in moderate terms, might acknowledge certain virtues of science fiction as a concept, of certain skills in some of the stories written by some of the writers, and might then point out that the flaws and demerits far outweigh the positive values, so that the field in general represents a morass that had best be avoided. This might be sufficiently convincing to place our field in a position uncomfortable enough to make a defense necessary.

But this silly stuff isn't worth more than a snicker and a yawn.

In fact, one might ask, if one is, like myself, congenitally curious about anything that is out of the ordinary, why on Earth anyone should write an article like this. It is not the kind of article anyone with even a moderate supply of common sense would write if he seriously intended to wound us. Why, then, write it at all?

It might help if we knew something about the writer of the article, but his name is utterly unfamiliar to me and to Shawna. Nor is the little bio at the foot of the first column any real help. That merely says that he "is a poet who used to write book reviews and animal features . . ."

If we accept this at face value, we have someone who could scarcely have a more microscopic set of credentials in the literary field generally, and who would seem to have none at all in science fiction.

And yet the writing is adequate and even shows a rather crude ability at handling invective, such as one would find among the teenage contributors to some of the science fiction fan magazines in the good old days of the late 1930s. (Harlan Ellison would surely have reached this level of vitriol at twelve, and I might have managed at fifteen, if I were in the mood.)

Furthermore, the writer seems to be up on all the important novels of the genre, so that it is a fair assumption that he has done a lot of science fiction reading. (One wonders, by the way, why he reads so widely in a field he despises so thoroughly. Is he an s.f. junkie who hates it but can't stay away from it? Does he swear off, knowing the damage it is doing to his brain, and does he then return to it with trembling hands, reading it by the light of a flashlight in a hidden corner of the cellar of his house? Does he curse his weakness even as he pants and drools at the sight of those book jackets?)

Given, then, his ability to turn a phrase or two, and his wide knowledge of our field, it seems reasonable to wonder if he has not tried his hand at writing science fiction. If so, he must have been rejected right and left, for certainly I know of nothing published under his name.

The trouble is, though, that Shawna and I don't know of anything submitted under his name, either. Perhaps he only longs to write science fiction but has never quite dared to commit his obscure dreams to paper, or, having done so, has never quite dared to put them to the test of editorial decision.

Either way, there is the tempting conclusion that he is writing out of wounded vanity and envious pique and, like Aesop's fox, who couldn't reach the grapes, has decided they are sour, anyway. Very sour. Excessively sour.

Poor fellow.

Or can it be, perhaps, that the unknown nature of his name is merely an illusion? Perhaps he is someone we all know who is writing under a pen name.

Frankly, I doubt that. If he is in any way prominent in our field and is striking out at it in so wholesale and nasty a manner and is, while doing so, hiding behind the shield of pseudonymity, he is no longer deserving of pity, but only of contempt. I can't think of anyone in the field who would want to strike out from ambush or, if he had the urge to do it, would run the risk of the contempt he would earn (not for exercising his right to free speech, I repeat, but for fearing to put his name to it).

And there is an allied question. Why should a national magazine of considerable prestige feel the urge to devote four pages to so uncritical and, therefore, worthless a diatribe?

Here, I think, we ought to feel rather complimented.

In the old days, when I was just beginning to try my hand at science fiction, no national magazine would have wasted four pages on denunciation of the field; or four paragraphs, either; or even four words, I think. In fact, let's face it—the editorial staff of a magazine such as the one that published the article would, back in 1938, never have *heard* of science fiction (with the possible exceptions of Jules Verne and H. G. Wells).

But now—how things have changed! The biggest blockbusters on the silver screen are science fiction movies, including *Star Wars* and *E. T.*, the biggest of them all. The top five items on this week's New York *Times* bestseller list (as I write) are either science fiction or science fiction–related and still include two of science fiction's "Big Three." (My book, *Foundation's Edge*, I am glad to report, has been on the list, at this moment of writing, for thirteen weeks and is in fourth place still.) The paperback shelves are heavy laden with science fiction and fantasy.

For goodness' sake, science fiction is *worth* denouncing these days. The editors of the prestigious magazine that published the article have heard of us, you see, and they think that enough of their readers have heard of us to make it worthwhile to devote four pages to us. They feel that perhaps additional readers, who would not otherwise bother to read the magazine, would purchase copies to read what they have to say of us.

They are, in fact, trying to get a free ride on our backs.

And what, after all, is wrong with that? My hope is that our field (especially the more carefully thought out and better-written aspects thereof) will continue to become more important and more influential on the public scene, and that its dominating ideas will become sufficiently threatening to fools and rogues to induce them all to denounce us.

AFTERWORD: To this day, I don't know who the author of the foolish article might be, but I might say it didn't harm any of us in any noticeable way at all. Science fiction continued to do as well, or better, after the article as before. The magazine, by the way, was *Harper's.* If we got no harm out of it, they got no good out of it, as far as I know.

8

Watch Out!

IN AN EARLIER ESSAY, I MENTIONED that a woman had canceled her subscription to *Asimov's* because I was a "humanist." I was rather amused at that. I was wrong, for there was nothing amusing in it at all. Let me explain why.

There is something in this world we call "modern science." It isn't terribly modern anymore since it is something like four hundred years old. Nevertheless, that is young compared to the number of years in which humanity has indulged in mythology or art or trade or agriculture or any of myriads of different human activities. Modern science is an intellectual baby in comparison.

And it's *our* baby. It's the particular enthusiasm of science fiction. The word is in the very name of our field and science fiction is inconceivable without science.

The science fiction writer doesn't have to immerse himself in science when engaging in his profession; he doesn't even have to mention it very much. Nor does he have to approve of every aspect of the social consequences of science or, for that matter, of any of them. He can be savagely satirical about science and depict a future in which the Earth is badly damaged or utterly destroyed through the agency of science.

What he cannot do, however, is to pretend that science is erroneous in basis, that scientific conclusions are worthless, that the scientific method is invalid. If he does, his writings become fantasy.

And is there anyone who casts doubt upon the validity of science?

Perhaps the usefulness or desirability of science may be in dispute, but surely not its validity.

Not so. There exists in the world a species of thinkers (if I may use that particular noun in this connection) who call themselves "scientific creationists" and who insist on accepting the literal words of the Bible.

For tactical reasons, they don't mention the Bible in their official statements since that would make their teachings religious in nature and keep it out of the schools.

Nevertheless, they believe that the Earth is, at most, only ten thousand years old. They deny the validity of evolutionary doctrine and insist that the various species of living things were separately brought into existence by a "Creator." They are careful not to name the "Creator" but does anyone suppose they mean Brahma, Zeus, or Marduk?

They have no evidence for these claims but rely for their arguments on the denial of the validity of scientific findings they don't like and on the distortion of those scientific findings they think offer them some faint hope of support.

Covering themselves with the tattered and dirty rags of denial and distortion and calling it "science," they then proceed to attack real scientists. They set up something they call "secular humanism" and define it as a religion. They claim that the concept of evolution is a "religious dogma" of secular humanism.

Note the peculiarity of this. We have a group of religious fundamentalists who can find no worse label for the people they denounce than "religion."

What do they hope to gain by this bit of semantic upside-downism—scientists as "religious" and themselves as "scientific"?

First, they arrogate to themselves pretensions to logic and reason they do not possess. Second, they make evolution (or, by similar mislabeling, anything else they decide they don't like) into something far worse than scientific error; they make it into a religious heresy.

How convenient!

A scientific error must be established as erroneous in the marketplace of science, through the laborious task of competing observations and experiments, through debate and discussion, even through arguments and polemics.

A religious heresy, on the other hand, can be summarily put down by the full power of the state and church, and I need not tell you of the kinds of methods used in the past to enforce orthodoxy in the name of an all-merciful God.

Am I going too far? Am I exaggerating?

Right now, the "scientific creationists" are moving heaven and earth to get various state legislatures to pass laws requiring their doctrines to be taught in classes whenever evolution is taught. They are calling in the power of the state right now to decide, by legislation, what is scientifically correct. And one state, Arkansas, has already passed such legislation.

Does it matter that in one rural state, or possibly a few more, a handful of legislators, terrified of losing their jobs, are willing to enforce ignorance on the children of the land? It matters not only in itself, but in the precedent it sets. Could not the same legislators also insist that "scientific storkism" be taught as one theory of childbirth, and that "scientific Santaclausism" be taught as one theory of gift giving? Why not? The level of science would be no lower.

Or perhaps you think that schools ought, after all, to teach all varieties of theories concerning matters in dispute? That this is only being open-minded and fair? Don't you think then that all creation myths ought to be taught—including those believed by hundreds of millions of Hindus, Buddhists, and animists?

Do you think that "scientific creationists" are only after a fair shake? That all they want is an equal hearing?

Can you imagine any of these Bible-wavers consenting to teach evolutionary doctrine in their churches in the name of an equal hearing? —Never!

So where's the fairness?

In the churches, they threaten the kids with eternal damnation in the roasting fires of hell if they believe anything but what they are there taught. In the homes, adults, already brainwashed, reinforce it, and so do almost all aspects of society.

The schools are the only place where evolution is as much as mentioned and even there, vigilante groups of "scientific creationists" in many parts of the nation terrify the teachers into mentioning evolution only in a whisper, or not at all.

What "scientific creationists" want is the destruction of modern science and if they win, destruction is what will follow. You cannot have any rational geology or astronomy if the Earth is viewed as only ten thousand years old; you cannot have any rational biology if evolution is squashed as heresy.

Nor can you suppose that children who are kept from science in grade school and high school will see the light in college. Even if colleges remain intellectually free, children who reach college age without having been introduced to the scientific way of thought will by then never truly learn it. They will have been intellectually ruined.

And what do you think will happen to the United States if it becomes scientifically illiterate in a scientific age, while other nations maintain scientific expertise? —Guess!

Do you think that faith in God will save us from decline and destruction? The "scientific creationists" don't think so, for one and all of them believe in a strong and overwhelming national defense. Martin Luther thought God to be a mighty fortress, but to the "scientific creationists," it takes God *plus* a mighty fortress to be a mighty fortress.

But why am I bothering you with all this in an essay in a science fiction magazine?

Well, can you recall any science fiction stories that don't assume a Universe billions of years old; that don't take evolution for granted; that don't suppose scientific findings to be essentially correct; that don't extrapolate further scientific findings that make some sort of sense in the basic structure of the Universe as we believe it to be?

Do you suppose that "scientific creationists" would be willing to allow such arrant sources of heresy as science fiction magazines to remain untouched? And even if they do, do you suppose that science fiction can survive if schoolchildren are taught, one and all, that the only legitimate source of truth rests in the literal words of the Bible and that any speculation beyond that will douse them in the undying flames?

Theodore Sturgeon once said that science fiction was the last bastion of free speech. His view was that when people as stupid as censors (and who else but stupid people would be willing to be censors?) are driven into finally detecting heresy in something as outré as science fiction, they will by then have detected it everywhere else.

So when the legions of ignorance begin putting pressure on a science fiction magazine because its editorial director believes in evolution—watch out!

✦

AFTERWORD: Since this essay was written (and even before) I have attacked the fools and knaves of creationism with all my might in many different places, including in the pages of the New York *Times Magazine.* As a result I have become the president of the American Humanist Association. I won't deny that in accepting the position I had a twinge or two as to the effect it might have on *Asimov's,* but, after all, I am scarcely going to betray my views for the sake of placating fools who, in any case, won't be placated. And, as it happens, the magazine doesn't seem to have suffered.

SCIENCE
FICTION
WRITING ✦

9

The Unforgivable Sin

MY WRITINGS ARE OCCASION-
ally controversial, and I am accustomed (though never entirely hardened) to
receiving letters of condemnation couched in bitter terms. —But then, what
the heck, I sometimes write letters of condemnation myself, and although I
like to think I use the rapier rather than the bludgeon, that may not be how it
feels to those I condemn.

So I try to be philosophical about it.

There are, however, things that penetrate the philosophical armor, be it
ever so well wrought and finely tempered.

For instance, some time ago, I received a letter from one of my peers—a
member of a university faculty—who objected to certain arguments I had
advanced, and did so, it would seem, on deeply intellectual grounds. He told
me, in his covering letter, that perhaps I had better not indulge in the process
of skating on thin ice (logically speaking) since, apparently, my reasoning
abilities were not up to the task. To bear out this sad estimate of my intelligence, he offered me a dozen pages or more of his own composition, which he
urged me to read.

With a sigh, I set about the task. On the very first page, he struck a
shrewd blow by pointing out the harm I did my readers by writing in such a
way as to make them believe they understood something when, in actual fact,
they did not. Quite gratuitously, he lumped Carl Sagan together with me in
this vile criminality. Carl, it appeared, also lured the reader into the miserable
illusion of comprehension.

I read on, and it became increasingly clear that the writer was committing what was (for a writer) the unforgivable sin. He was dull and turgid, and his style was simply impenetrable. I don't say that if I read with attention and made some shrewd guesses as to what he was trying to say, I might not have gotten some shreds of nutrition out of his essay, but, *please*, my time is reasonably valuable.

I therefore stopped and composed the following postcard:

Dear Dr. ———

Please forgive me but I have no talent whatever as a linguist, and I read only English. Without a translation, I could not manage your letter. Nevertheless, I was able to make out enough to be able to assure you that you will never fall into the Asimov/Sagan trap. No one who reads what you write will ever labor under the belief he understands something.

I admired that card for quite a while, for I felt I had neatly skewered my correspondent. Then, when the card had quite fulfilled its function of making me feel good, I tore it up and dumped it. I wrote no answer at all.

After all, why make him feel bad? Anyone who writes like that needs no additional punishment.

But why should my friend have written like that? He was undeniably intelligent. He surely knew his subject. Even granted that he had little of that intangible something called "talent," surely he could marshal his arguments logically and choose his words rationally.

Yet he is not alone in his sin. Read any scholarly paper, especially in the "soft" sciences, and you will find copious examples of unforgivably bad writing. (There are numerous exceptions, thank goodness.) Any one of you readers who has never tried to write a story may well write one that is bad, and yet you would probably not manage to write as badly as many high-IQ scholars do. Why?

In the first place, there are no economic pressures driving scholars to improve. Scholarly journals do not reject papers simply because they are badly written. It is the content that counts, muddy as that content might be. Then, too, such papers have a captive audience, since scholars *must* read papers by other scholars in their own field, however unrewarding the task.

Yet even so, should not a scholar try to write clearly for the sake of clarity itself? Is there no pleasure to be derived from the production of a luminous sentence presenting a thought with gemlike lucidity and precision? Unfortunately not. I suspect that many a scholar doubts his own intellectual capacity (for reasons which I, not being a psychiatrist, will not puzzle over) and is eager to emphasize that capacity in the only way he knows how. He uses long words, jargon which he invents and others then adopt, spavined sentences from which broken dependent clauses hang limply, and lines of thought which meander helplessly and end nowhere.

The more obscure the writing, the more the writer feels it to be the result of deep thought rather than shallow thinking, and, since he dares not proclaim that the Emperor has no clothes, he admires the obscurity of others.

Real writers, even real writers in embryo, dare not imitate this kind of writing. For instance:

1) Never be obscure unless you wish to be subtle and allusive. Writers might choose words which have poetic or multiple connotations and thus be obscure on the surface, yet present deeper meanings at the price of a little thought. This is a difficult thing to do, and for goodness' sake, don't try it, unless you have a great deal of talent or experience (or, better, both).

2) Therefore, don't use a long word when a short word will do as well; don't use a foreign word when an English word will do as well; don't use a little-known word when a common word will do as well. Sometimes, the long, the foreign, and the little-known must be used for good and sufficient reasons. For instance, in this particular essay, I am deliberately using a more extensive vocabulary and a somewhat more involuted style than I usually do, because I do not want to give the impression that I am touting simplicity out of an inability to handle anything else. The reasons for complexity occur comparatively rarely, however, and if the arcane is inserted on every occasion, it becomes wearisome and ineffective. Play it safe. Be simple.

3) Don't imagine that if a little is good, a lot would be better. If it is sometimes colorful to use an adjective as a noun, or vice versa, don't obscure the difference between the two parts of speech altogether. If hyphenating two words makes possible an economy of expression, don't hyphenate everything in sight. You may, with justice, sprinkle some salt in your soup, but surely you would not add a tablespoonful.

4) Don't overload your sentences. Don't drag them out in the belief that short sentences are childish and long sentences are "literary." Too many short sentences in a row are indeed wearisome but it takes an admixture of not very

many longer sentences to correct that, and the long sentence has to be a live one with a sturdy structure. A mere pasting together of five independent sentences by the omission of periods is repulsive.

5) Don't pile on the adjectives and adverbs because you feel that is the only way in which you can be "descriptive." The strong words are the nouns and verbs. Make them do all the work possible, and then throw in the modifiers to do whatever little is left over. Unless you are a master, or a successful poet, each modifier you include is a deadly risk.

6) I might as well add a feature of scholarly writing that will rarely tempt you. Scholars are given to the passive voice, saying, "An experiment was performed by the author that . . ." instead of saying, in a straightforward manner, "I performed an experiment that . . ." The latter is felt to be too aggressive or immodest. The passive seems to imply a greater objectivity. Well, the devil with that! If the objectivity is there, it will remain there even if you use an "I" in every sentence. If the objectivity is not there, using the passive voice won't put it there. Therefore, write strongly and directly and never be tempted to write badly just because you think it will make a good impression. The only impression it will really make is that of bad writing.

Oh well, I am growing passionate, so perhaps I had better draw to a close.

Let me tell you what I feel about good writing. It's important to be a good writer if you want to make a living writing, so good writing is important to me for that reason. It's important to be a good writer if you wish to make even an occasional sale, and George, Shawna, and I want as many of you as possible to make at least an occasional sale for the sake of the magazine, and that makes good writing important to all three of us.

But there's more to it than even that. Every one of us reads far more than he will ever write. As you all know, I write (it sometimes seems to me) every waking moment, yet even I read far more than I write. And for all of us, reading good writing is an enormous pleasure, while reading bad writing is a painful job.

What's wrong, then, with wanting to enjoy life?

AFTERWORD: It frequently happens that I reread something I have written after a long enough time to make it sound fresh and new to me. I have just reread this nearly five years after I wrote it. Doing so, I felt a glow of satisfaction. I desperately wanted to applaud, and only my well-known modesty kept me from doing so.

10

Satire

SOMETHING IS SATIRICAL WHEN
its purpose is to castigate what are perceived as the follies and vices of human
society. Satire is an ancient branch of literature and a much needed one, for
folly and vice are invariably prevalent in all societies and *should* be eliminated,
and the options for doing so are few.

The most direct method is by physical assault—by revolution. The
difficulties here are many, for folly and vice invariably support a few while
making many wretched, and it is the few who (as a result) have the money,
the power, and (most important) the support of tradition. Revolutions are
almost always bloody and violent. They rarely succeed, and when they do, the
very violence and difficulty of the process leaves the revolutionaries with an
almost paranoid need to oppress in their turn.

Nor can folly and vice be easily removed by sweet reason. As I say,
folly and vice are usually sanctified by tradition, that is, by long usage; and the
very people who most suffer under their ravages are most firm in being against
any change, even those that would clearly better their existence. In fact, it is
usually a few of those who benefit from folly and vice who, more sophisticated and better educated (and driven by guilt and shame), object to that
which benefits them. That is why revolutions, at least in their early stages, are
so frequently led by liberal and idealistic aristocrats.

What is left that is neither violent nor ineffective? Satire!

Of course, satire doesn't always do the job (after all, there is plenty of
folly and vice rampant today in every society), and it sometimes helps lead to

violence but, generally ineffective though it might be, it works better than anything else.

One proof of that is that satirists are almost always at odds with the societies they satirize. The "establishment" knows when it is stung and endangered, and responds by striking back, not with words (the deadly weapon of the satirist) but by the more immediately effective strategy of fines, imprisonment, torture, and even execution.

Since satirists are not particularly keen to experience such treatment, they generally avoid making the nature of their targets particularly clear. For that reason, they frequently make use of fantasy. Thus, Aesop's fables are a clear and direct assault on the follies and vices of humanity, but by doing this under the guise of telling little stories of talking animals, Aesop lured those who listened to him into laughing and nodding their heads wisely. By the time it occurred to them that it was they themselves who were under attack, Aesop was safely out of reach.

Well then, what is the mark of satire? When is a piece of writing a satire and when is it not?

You might, for instance, tell a straightforward story of events exactly as they happened (or might have happened) and present pure realism, eliciting only the emotions one would naturally expect from that particular tale. That is not satire.

Or, wishing to make people angry at folly and vice, a writer might deliberately distort, making the folly and vice more apparent and ridiculous than it really is, so that the target might be the more clearly visible to those who, lulled by tradition and their concentration on narrow personal matters, would not see it otherwise. That is satire.

Almost all writing has elements of satire in it. Even in nonsatirical fiction, villains are made clearly and self-consciously villainous in order to increase horror and suspense. In true satire, however, almost every element undergoes the necessary distortion, even to the point of reducing the tale to total nonrealism.

The most effective English-speaking satirists were, in my opinion, Jonathan Swift, Charles Dickens, and Mark Twain. Of those who wrote in other languages, Voltaire might well be mentioned with those three. And it is interesting that these satirists, two of whom flourished in the eighteenth century, and two in the nineteenth, all made use not only of fantasy, but of recognizable science fictional elements in constructing some of their satire.

Jonathan Swift published the book commonly known as *Gulliver's Travels* in 1726 and castigated contemporary British society under the guise of describing strange societies in unknown portions of the globe. The third part of the tale, which satirizes science itself, represents the closest approach to science fiction, and it is there that Swift describes the two satellites (as yet undiscovered) of Mars.

Voltaire, in 1752, published *Micromégas* in which two visitors, one from Saturn and one from Sirius, visit Earth and comment on its follies and vices. Voltaire also mentioned Mars' two (as yet undiscovered) satellites and, as a result, the two largest craters on the smaller satellite, Deimos, are now named Swift and Voltaire.

Among Dickens' most famous tales is *A Christmas Carol,* published in 1843, which is one of the great fantasies of all time and needs no description. Remember, though, that it contains time-travel elements. And so did Mark Twain's *A Connecticut Yankee in King Arthur's Court,* published in 1889. Both are clear satires on contemporary society.

Obviously, then, science fiction lends itself to satire. By making use of invented societies with properties that invite satirical distortion, the writer can more effectively riddle his target in the here and now.

I don't indulge in satire very often myself, being content to take each society at its own valuation and to feel that decent and reasonable human beings can make almost any society bearable. Other s.f. writers frequently write satire, however, and one such satirist who springs to mind, and whom I much admire, is Frederik Pohl.

Satire isn't easy to do. The line that separates effective demolition of a target from clumsy and offensive burlesque is a narrow one and it is up to us to select the good and reject the bad. This is difficult in itself and is made the more difficult in that the targets of the satire invariably disagree with our criteria for such selection.

One savage satire that we printed was "Soulsaver" by James Stevens, in the September 1983 issue. It was, in our opinion, a hard-hitting and effective satire on self-righteous religious hypocrisy—a target that is by no means a new one. (The most effective satire of this type ever done was Molière's *Tartuffe,* a play that was first produced in 1664 and that got Molière into a great deal of trouble.)

It was not to be expected that there would be no objection to this satire. We received a letter, for instance, which contained the following sentence:

"Although I do admit that some vocal and NOT representative Christians have helped to force that stereotype upon the general public, I feel it is the job of publications (responsible publications) to not perpetuate those stereotypes."

On the contrary, it *is* our job to strike out at folly and vice wherever we find it. If, as the reader admits, the target of the satire *does* exist, then why should we close our eyes to it? I am perfectly willing to admit that those who lend themselves to the stereotype are not representative of all, but then the more representative portions of Christianity should be bitterly offended by those nonrepresentative few who hold them up to ridicule, and should fight them vigorously. If they do *not* do so, then the job is left to us. For instance, does the reader who took the trouble to write to us to object to the story ever take the trouble to write to some of the unctuous television preachers to object to their perversion of religious principles?

The reader goes on to say, "I can understand that you and Shawna might not personally hold 'conservative' Christian beliefs, but I DO think you should exercise more sensitivity toward those of us who do possess such a faith."

That would be dangerous. If that were a proper way of behaving, then all satire would be dead. It is not only " 'conservative' Christians" who are sensitive. All human beings are, and no target of satire (including myself, for I have often been satirized in science fiction) enjoys the process.

Shall we refrain from any satire on communism or fascism because we would then be insensitive toward many people who accept such doctrines—perhaps very sincerely and idealistically? Shall we refrain from any satire on racism or on oppressive societies because there are those who sincerely believe in racism and oppression and who would feel wounded if we made sardonic fun of them?

And if we do kill satire, remember that there are elements of satire in just about everything that is written. To exercise "sensitivity" would be to institute a thoroughgoing system of censorship.

Sorry! The reader means well, but what is being asked for is totally undesirable.

11

Irony

IT IS WELL KNOWN THAT I KNOW nothing about the craft of writing in any formal way. I say so myself—constantly. Being an editorial director, however, has its demands and duties. I must answer letters from readers, for instance, and take into account any unhappiness they may have with stories and editorial policy. And that means I am sometimes forced to think about writing techniques.

That brings me to the subject at hand, the matter of the use of irony by writers.

In the previous essay, I discussed satire, and the two, satire and irony, are often lumped together and, in fact, are sometimes confused and treated as though they were synonymous. They are not!

Satire, as I explained, achieves its purpose of castigating the evils of humanity and society by exaggerating. It puts those evils under a magnifying glass with the intention of making them clearly visible.

Irony does it differently. You can get a hint from the fact that "irony" is from a Greek word meaning "dissimulation." An ironist must pretend, and the classic ironist was Socrates, who in his discussions with others would relentlessly pretend ignorance. He would ask all kinds of naive questions designed to trap an overconfident adversary into rashly taking positions that then proved to be indefensible under further naive questioning by Socrates.

Naturally, Socrates was *not* ignorant and the questions were *not* naive, and his method of procedure is known as "Socratic irony." You may well believe that those who suffered under his bland lash did not grow to love him, and I suspect he fully earned his final draught of hemlock.

Socrates set the fashion for irony for all time. He pretended to be ignorant when he was actually piercingly intelligent, and ever since then, ironists have said and pretended to believe the opposite of what they wanted the reader to understand. Instead of exaggerating the evils they are denouncing, they reverse them and call them good.

The satirist induces laughter by his exaggeration; the ironist induces indignation by his reversal. The satirist is often good-natured; the ironist tends to be savage and bitter. Satire is a comparatively mild technique whose purpose is easily grasped. Irony is a difficult technique whose point is frequently missed, and the ironist may find he is holding a two-edged sword and is himself badly gashed.

Most satirists find themselves indulging in irony sometimes, and I know exactly where I encountered irony for the first time. I was reading Charles Dickens' *Pickwick Papers* as a preteen, and in Chapter 2, I encountered Dickens' description of Tracy Tupman's "general benevolence." Said Dickens, "The number of instances . . . in which that excellent man referred objects of charity to the houses of other members for left-off garments or pecuniary relief is almost incredible."

I was astonished. I thought to myself that it wasn't very kind of Mr. Tupman to send poor people to other members instead of giving them something himself, so how could he be benevolent? And after a while, the light dawned. He *wasn't* benevolent. In fact, I decided indignantly, he was a stingy bum, and my liking for him was strictly limited for the rest of the book and ever since. I did not know that what I had just read was irony, but I understood the concept from that time on, and I eventually learned the word.

If you want a savage and prolonged bit of writing with a great deal of irony in it, I refer you to Mark Twain's *The Mysterious Stranger,* which was not published till after he was safely dead. I warn you, though, it's not pleasant reading. It certainly makes plain, however, Twain's bitter feelings about humanity and the assorted evils that seemed (to Twain, at any rate) to be inextricably bound up with it. And it may, for a time at least, embitter you with humanity, too.

Even that, however, must take second place to the all-time high in caustic irony—a pamphlet by Jonathan Swift, published about 1730, entitled *A Modest Proposal for Preventing the Children of Poor People in Ireland from being a*

Burden to their Parents or Country and for Making them Beneficial to the Public.
Swift served in Ireland and could see firsthand, and with enormous indignation, the manner in which the English brutally and callously ground the Irish into helpless and hopeless poverty.

He therefore pointed out that since the only thing the Irish were allowed to produce and keep for their own use were their children, it would supply the parents with needed money, and others with needed food, if those Irish children were sold in order to be fattened and slaughtered for sale at the butcher's. With an absolutely straight face, and with incredible ingenuity, he pointed out all the advantages that would accrue from such cannibalism.

If anything could possibly have evoked shame and even reform from those responsible for the Irish plight, that pamphlet would have done it. Undoubtedly, many of those who read the pamphlet *were* shamed; some may even have altered their attitudes and behavior. By and large, however, the exploitation of the Irish continued unchanged for nearly two more centuries and the light that casts on humanity is not a good one.

And yet, you know, not everyone has a "sense of irony," which is by no means the same as a sense of humor. I firmly believe that one can have one and not the other. It is possible to be confused by a pretense to believe the opposite of what one really believes, as I was for a few minutes by Dickens' description of Tupman as benevolent. Of course, I caught on, but if I had lacked a sense of irony, I suppose I wouldn't have.

There were, actually, good and kindly people who read Swift's pamphlet with indignation, not at the mistreatment of the Irish, but at Swift's apparently callous and immoral advocacy of cannibalism. They thought he *meant* it, and denounced him with immeasurable vehemence.

And that finally brings me to *Asimov's,* for sometimes what we publish contains irony, and if irony is hard to handle even for the absolute master of the art, good old Swift, you can understand that it is a slippery tool, indeed, for lesser mortals.

In the February 1984 issue Tom Rainbow wrote a "Viewpoint" article entitled "Sentience and the Single Extraterrestrial," that dealt with the requirements for such things as intelligence, sentience, and self-awareness. He described the kinds of extraterrestrials that might, or might not, possess such things.

From the title alone, you can tell that he is writing in the humorous mode, and indeed, when you read his essay, you will find that he is saying perfectly serious things in a deliberately funny way.

In one place, he uses irony. Having talked of the requirements of self-awareness in terms of brain/body ratios, he points out that women's brains are smaller than men's, but so are their bodies, leaving the brain/body ratio nearly the same in both sexes. (Actually, if there's an advantage it's on the side of women.) With heavy irony, he says, ". . . this reasoning leads to the somewhat startling conclusion that women must be *self-aware.*"

How can one believe that Rainbow really thinks the conclusion is "startling"? He's using ironic dissimulation. He's *pretending* to think it's startling (and italicizing "self-aware" as a typographical indication of astonishment) in order for you to understand thoroughly that this is *not* startling and that people who consider women inferior beings are ignorant, and even stupid.

And to make it even plainer, he puts himself in the ironic position of these ignoramuses and says in the next sentence, "Heck, guys, if even *girls* can be self-aware, then there's hope for Giant Dill Pickles."

The use of the adolescent term "heck," and the equally adolescent "guys," and the shift from "women" to italicized "girls" all show that he is not speaking in his own persona and that he has nothing but contempt for the attitude. He is relying, poor fellow, on his readers' having a sense of irony.

Well, they do—by and large.

But there are always exceptions, and a few women have written indignant letters to point out that this was insulting. One said that it wasn't funny or cute.

No, indeed. Swift's advocacy of cannibalism wasn't funny or cute, either, but he was trying for something else.

To be sure, Swift's entire pamphlet was aimed at his target and Rainbow was merely bringing in the matter of women's brains as a side issue, and perhaps if he were doing it again, he might decide it would be more judicious not to indulge. —But please, ladies, the man is on your side and is trying to show it by the use of that two-edged sword, irony. You may think the irony didn't work, but that doesn't make Rainbow an enemy of yours.

◆

AFTERWORD: Tom Rainbow published a number of articles of interest to science fiction readers in the pages of *Asimov's*, and Shawna McCarthy was particularly fond of his writing. She was grooming him (she said) to become "another Isaac Asimov." And then, just before his thirtieth birthday, he ran for a train, slipped, fell between two cars, and was killed.

12

Revisions

WHEN IT COMES TO WRITING, I am a "primitive." I had had no instruction when I began to write, or even by the time I had begun to publish. I took no courses. I read no books on the subject.

This was not bravado on my part, or any sense of arrogance. I just didn't know that there *were* courses or books on the subject. In all innocence, I just thought you sat down and wrote. Naturally, I have picked up a great deal about writing in the days since I began, but in certain important respects, my early habits imprinted me and I find I can't change.

Some of these imprinted habits are trivial. For instance, I cannot leave a decent margin. Poor George has tried begging and he has tried ordering, and my only response is a firm "Never!"

When I was a kid, you see, getting typewriting paper was a hard thing to do, for it required m-o-n-e-y, of which I had none. Therefore what paper I had, I saved—single-spaced, both sides, and typing to the very edge of the page, all four edges. Well, I learned that one could not submit a manuscript unless it was double-spaced and on one side of the page only, and I was *forced*, unwillingly, to adopt that wasteful procedure. I also learned about margins and established them—but not wide enough. Nor could I ever make them wide enough. My sense of economy had gone as far as it would go and it would go no further.

More important was the fact that I had never learned about revisions. My routine was (and still is) to write a story in first draft as fast as I can. Then

I go over it and correct errors in spelling, grammar, and word order. Then I prepare my second draft, making minor changes as I go and as they occur to me. My second draft is my final draft. No more changes except under direct editorial order and then with rebellion in my heart.

I didn't know there was anything wrong with this. I thought it was the way you were *supposed* to write. In fact, when Bob Heinlein and I were working together at the Navy yard in Philadelphia during World War II, Bob asked me how I went about writing a story and I told him. He said, "You type it *twice?* Why don't you type it correctly the first time?"

I felt bitterly ashamed, and the very next story I wrote, I tried my level best to get it right the first time. I failed. No matter how carefully I wrote, there were always things that had to be changed. I decided I just wasn't as good as Heinlein.

But then, in 1950, I attended the Breadloaf Writers' Conference at the invitation of Fletcher Pratt. There I listened in astonishment to some of the things said by the lecturers. "The secret of writing," said one of them, "is rewriting."

Fletcher Pratt himself said, "If you ever write a paragraph that seems to you to *sing,* to be the best thing you've ever written, to be full of wonder and poetry and greatness—cross it out, it stinks!"

Over and over again, we were told about the importance of polishing, of revising, of tearing up and rewriting. I got the bewildered notion that, far from being expected to type it right the first time, as Heinlein had advised me, I was expected to type it all wrong and get it right only by the thirty-second time, if at all.

I went home immersed in gloom and the very next time I wrote a story, I tried to tear it up. I couldn't make myself do it. So I went over it to see all the terrible things I had done, in order to revise them. To my chagrin, everything sounded great to me. (My own writing always sounds great to me.) Eventually, after wasting hours and hours—to say nothing of suffering spiritual agony—I gave it up. My stories would have to be written the way they always were—and still are.

What is it I am saying, then? That it is wrong to revise? No, of course not—anymore than it is wrong not to revise.

You don't do *anything* automatically, simply because some "authority" (including me) says you should. Each writer is an individual, with his or her own way of thinking, and doing, and writing. Some writers are not happy unless they polish and polish—unless they try a paragraph this way and that way and the other way.

Once, Oscar Wilde, coming down to lunch, was asked how he had spent his morning. "I was hard at work," he said.

"Oh?" he was asked. "Did you accomplish much?"

"Yes, indeed," said Wilde. "I inserted a comma."

At dinner, he was asked how he had spent the afternoon. "More work," he said.

"Inserted another comma?" was the rather sardonic question.

"No," said Wilde, unperturbed. "I removed the one I had inserted in the morning."

Well, if you're Oscar Wilde, or some other great stylist, polishing may succeed in imparting an ever higher gloss to your writing and you *should* revise and revise. If, on the other hand, you're not much of a stylist (like me, for instance) and are only interested in clarity and straightforward storytelling, then a small amount of revision is probably all you need. Beyond that small amount you may merely be shaking up the rubble.

I was told last night, for instance, that Daniel Keyes (author of the classic "Flowers for Algernon") is supposed to have said, "The author's best friend is the person who shoots him just before he makes one change too many."

Let's try the other extreme. William Shakespeare is reported by Ben Jonson to have boasted that he "never blotted a word." The Bard of Avon, in other words, would have us believe that, like Heinlein, he got it right the first time, and that what he handed in to the producers at the Globe Theatre was first draft. (He may have been twisting the truth a bit. Prolific writers tend to exaggerate the amount of nonrevision they do.)

Well, if you happen to be another Will Shakespeare, or another Bob Heinlein, maybe you can get away without revising at all. But if you're just an ordinary writer (like me) maybe you'd better do *some*. (As a matter of fact, Ben Jonson commented that he wished Will had "blotted out a thousand," and there are indeed places where Will might have been—ssh!—improved on.)

Let's pass on to a slightly different topic.

I am sometimes asked if I prepare an outline first before writing a story or a book.

The answer is: no, I don't.

To begin with, this was another one of those cases of initial ignorance. I didn't know at the start of my career that such things as outlines existed. I just wrote a story and stopped when I finished and if it happened to be one length it was a short story and if it happened to be another it was a novelette.

When I wrote my first novel, Doubleday told me to make it seventy thousand words long. So I wrote until I had seventy thousand words and then stopped—and by the greatest good luck, it turned out to be the end of the novel.

When I began my second novel, I realized that such an amazing coincidence was not likely to happen twice in a row, so I prepared an outline. I quickly discovered two things. One, an outline constricted me so that I could not breathe. Two, there was no way I could force my characters to adhere to the outline; even if I wanted to do so, they refused. I never tried an outline again. In even my most complicated novels, I merely fix the ending firmly in my mind, decide on a beginning, and then, from that beginning, charge toward the ending, making up the details as I go along.

On the other hand, P. G. Wodehouse, for whose writings I have an idolatrous admiration, always prepared outlines, spending more time on them than on the book and getting every event, however small, firmly in place before beginning.

There's something to be said on both sides, of course.

If you are a structured and rigid person who likes everything under control, you will be uneasy without an outline. Then, too, if you are an undisciplined person with a tendency to wander all over the landscape, you will be better off with an outline even if you feel you wouldn't like one.

On the other hand, if you are quick-thinking and ingenious, but with a strong sense of the whole, you will be better off without an outline.

How do you decide which you are? Well, try an outline, or try writing without one, and find out for yourself.

The thing is: don't feel that any rule of writing must be hard and fast, and handed down from Sinai. By all means try them all out but, in the last analysis, stick to that which makes you comfortable. You are, after all, an individual.

13

Plagiarism

To THE ANCIENT ROMANS, A *plagiarius* was what we call a kidnapper, and to steal children is certainly a heinous crime. It appears to those who work with their minds and imaginations, however, that to steal one's brainchildren is almost as heinous a crime, and so "plagiarism," in English, has come to mean the stealing of ideas, forms, or words by someone who then puts them forth as his or her own.

A scientist's formulas, an artist's paintings, an inventor's models, a philosopher's thoughts might all be the subject of plagiarism, but common usage has come to apply the term, specifically, to the theft of a writer's production.

Plagiarism is a horrid nightmare to writers in several different ways; and it is much more serious than nonwriters may realize.

If a writer, for any reason, commits plagiarism, copying some already published material, and if he gets away with it to the extent of getting the plagiarized material republished, he is bound to be caught sooner or later. Some reader, somewhere, will notice the theft. In that case, even if the plagiarist isn't sued or punished in any way, you can be sure that no editor who knows of the plagiarism will buy anything from that writer again. If the plagiarist has a career, it is permanently ruined.

You may think that such a literary thief deserves a ruined career, and certainly I think so, but copying an already published item word for word is such a surefire failure that only an idiot or a complete novice would do it. What about the case where someone simply makes use of the central idea of the story, the series of events it contains, the climax, the emotional milieu, and so on, but does *not* repeat it word for word? What if he uses his (or her) own words entirely, changes the incidents in nonessential details, uses a different setting, and so on?

In that case, it becomes more difficult to decide whether plagiarism has taken place. After all, it *is* possible to get the same ideas someone else has had.

Thus, Ted Sturgeon once wrote a story which he sent to Horace Gold of *Galaxy* and which was accepted. I wrote a story which I sent to Horace Gold while Ted's story was still unpublished. There was no chance of communication between us; we lived in different cities and had not exchanged phone calls or letters in months, nor had either of us discussed our stories with anyone. Nevertheless, not only did we both center our stories about a double meaning in the word "hostess," but two of my characters were Drake and Vera, and two of his were Derek and Verna.

It was the purest of coincidences, for except for the double meaning and the character names that we shared, the stories were miles apart. Nevertheless, even the *appearance* of plagiarism must be avoided. I had to make enough changes in my story (because it was the later one received) to destroy the appearance. To do so spoiled the story in my opinion, but it had to be done anyway.

In the same way, when I am writing a story, I must be conscious that there have been other stories dealing with similar ideas or similar characters or similar events, and I must make every effort to dilute that similarity. Once when I wrote a story called "Each an Explorer," I never for a moment forgot John Campbell's "Who Goes There?" and spent more time trying to avoid his story than trying to write my own. In the same way, when I wrote "Lest We Remember" (published in *Asimov's*) I had to steer a mile wide of Keyes' "Flowers for Algernon." It's part of the game.

But I haven't read every story ever written and many that I have read, I have completely forgotten, at least consciously. What if I duplicate important elements of stories I have never read or have forgotten? It's possible. I once wrote a short-short which ended with a certain dramatic climax in the last sentence. Eventually, I received a letter from another writer whose story had been published before I wrote my story and who had made use of the same dramatic climax in his last sentence. What's more, I had his story in an anthology in my library. I did not remember reading it, but I had had the opportunity to do so. The two stories, except for the climaxes, were completely different, but I promptly wrote the other author and told him that although he had my word that there was no conscious imitation, I would withdraw the story from circulation and it would never again appear in any anthology, any collection, any form whatever—and it never has.

Fortunately, the other writer accepted this, but what protection have I (or has any other writer) against the accusation of plagiarism over what is a bit of unconscious recall, or, for that matter, an outright coincidence?

Actually, very little. I rely, to a large extent, on my prolificity and my unblemished record. No one as prolific as I should have to depend on someone else's ideas, and my own mental fertility is obvious to all. Secondly, I am cautious enough never to discuss my stories before they are published, nor will I listen to others who might want to discuss *their* stories. In fact, I won't even read unsolicited manuscripts sent me by strangers. They go back at once, unread.

Even so, every established writer lives under an eternal Damoclean sword of possible accusation of plagiarism. A casual reference, a small similarity, a nonessential duplication may be enough to produce a suit. Such a suit, however unjustified, however certain of being thrown out of court, can be hurtful to an innocent writer. It is, after all, an expense. Lawyers must be paid, time must be lost, and, invariably, one is urged to "pay off the kook."

But what if *you*, the established writer, have been plagiarized? That has never happened to me to the extent of publication—that I know of. To be sure, there have been pastiches of me—deliberate imitations of my robot stories, or my Black Widowers mystery stories, and so on. These come under the heading of "fun." The writer who turns them out makes no secret of it, and the editor knows that it's a pastiche. Sometimes, the editor sends the manuscript to me to ask if I have any objection. I have always given permission. Then, too, there are stories that are bound to be similar to mine in some benign way. The *Star Wars* movies have some distant similarities to my Foundation stories, but, what the heck, you can't make a fuss about such things.

Unpublished plagiarism is more common. An English professor once sent me a story written by a student in first-year English. It didn't seem to her likely that the kid could have written that good a story and there were things in it that seemed reminiscent of me—such as the Three Laws of Robotics. I went over the story and it was my "Galley Slave" word-for-word. I returned it to the professor and told her to (a) punish the student appropriately, and (b) not let me know anything about it. (I'm softhearted.)

And what if you're an editor and get stuck with some material that might conceivably have been plagiarized? In the first place—is it? A completely original, nonreminiscent story is possible, but very rarely met up with. Similarities with some particular published story are almost unavoidable. However, the more similarities there are with the same previously published story, the greater the possibility of plagiarism. Nevertheless, it is difficult to establish certainty if the copying isn't word-for-word.

Should an editor refuse a story, however good, if there are too many similarities? Of course! Remember that I said even the appearance of plagiarism must be strictly avoided.

There is, however, a catch. An editor has not read every story that has been published. Sometimes an editor, being human, has not even read every *famous* story ever published. Or an editor has read many stories but some of them have completely gone from her mind. Such an editor may, in all innocence, therefore publish a doubtful story. She (or he) is then a *victim* and not an accomplice.

Just as honest, established writers must live, constantly, with the fear of being accused of plagiarism, or of themselves being plagiarized, so must honest, established editors live, constantly, with the fear of being victimized by having published a doubtful story.

What does one do in such a case? One can't entirely ignore the matter. For one thing, the similarity between the new story and an older story is sure to be seen by some readers. Even if the older story is very obscure, someone will have read it and remembered it. If it is a well-known story, letters will come in heaps.

One can ask the writer of the doubtful story for an explanation. If the explanation seems unconvincing, one can avoid buying stories from the writer again. One might warn other editors in the field to be careful. And one can try hard not to let it happen again—knowing full well that there is no way of stopping *every* piece of literary prestidigitation.

It is comforting to know, however, that if an editor lets something suspicious get into print, the fact will not remain unreported for long. We can be sure, then, that if no indignant reader has written within two weeks of the appearance of an issue, we have probably committed no ghastly mistakes of this nature in that particular issue.

◆

AFTERWORD: Naturally, this essay was written because Shawna McCarthy had accepted and published a story which was recognized by a number of readers to be a plagiarism (though not a word-for-word one). I carefully refrained from naming the story or the author (though we will never buy a story from him again). When a reader wrote to us indignantly that this response was insufficient, I had to explain that it would be tricky to try to *prove* plagiarism in court, and that there might well be a countersuit for libel. Life can be hard, I'm afraid.

14

Originality

HAVING PUBLISHED THE PREVI-
ous essay on plagiarism, I now wish to look at the other side of the coin. After all, if plagiarism is reprehensible, total originality is just about impossible.

The thing is that there exists an incredible number of books in which an enormous variety of ideas, and an even more enormous variety of phrases and ways of putting things, have been included. Anyone literate enough to write well has, as a matter of course, read a huge miscellany of printed material and, the human brain being what it is, a great deal of it remains in the memory at least unconsciously, and will be regurgitated onto the manuscript page at odd moments.

In 1927, for instance, John Livingstone Lowes (an English professor at Harvard) published a six-hundred-page book entitled *The Road to Xanadu,* in which he traced nearly every phrase in *The Rime of the Ancient Mariner* to various travel books that were available to the poet, Samuel Taylor Coleridge.

I tried reading the book in my youth but gave up. It could only interest another Coleridge scholar. Besides, I saw no point to it. Granted that the phrases already existed scattered through a dozen books, they existed for everybody. It was only Coleridge who thought of putting them together, with the necessary modifications, to form one of the great poems of the English language. Coleridge might not have been 100 percent original but he was original *enough* to make the poem a work of genius. You can't overrate the skills involved in selection and arrangement.

It was this that was in my own mind, once, when I was busily working on a book of mine called *Words of Science* back in the days when I was actively teaching at Boston University School of Medicine. The book consisted of 250 one-page essays on various scientific terms, giving derivations, meanings, and various historical points of interest. For the purpose I had an unabridged dictionary spread out on my desk, for I couldn't very well make up the derivations, nor could I rely on my memory to present them to me in correct detail. (My memory is good, but not *that* good.)

A fellow faculty member happened by and looked over my shoulder. He read what I was writing at the moment, stared at the unabridged, and said, "Why, you're just copying the dictionary."

I stopped dead, sighed, closed the dictionary, lifted it with an effort, and handed it to my friend. "Here," I said. "The dictionary is yours. Now go write the book."

He shrugged his shoulders and walked away without offering to take the dictionary. He was bright enough to get the point.

There are times, though, when I wonder how well any story of mine would survive what one might call the "Road to Xanadu" test. (There's no point in offending fellow writers by analyzing *their* originality, so I'll just stick to my own stuff.)

The most original story I ever wrote in my opinion was "Nightfall," which appeared back in 1941. I had not quite reached my twenty-first birthday when I wrote it and I have always been inordinately proud of the plot. "It was a brand-new plot," I said, "and I killed it as I wrote it, for no one else would dare write a variation of it."

To be sure, it was an Emerson quote that began the story—"If the stars would appear one night in a thousand years, how would men believe and adore; and preserve for many generations the remembrance of the City of God"—and it was Campbell who presented me with the quote and who sent me home to write the reverse of Emerson's thesis.

Allowing for that, the development and details of the story were mine —or were they?

In 1973, I was preparing an anthology of my favorite stories of the 1930s (the years, that is, before John Campbell's editorship, so that I named the book *Before the Golden Age*) and I included, of course, Jack Williamson's "Born of the Sun," which had been published in 1934 and had, at that time, fascinated my fourteen-year-old self. I reread it, naturally, before including it and was horrified.

You see, it dealt in part with a cult whose members were furious at scientists for rationalizing the mystic tenets of the believers. In an exciting scene, the cultists attacked the scientists' citadel at a very crucial moment and the scientists tried to hold them off long enough to get their task done.

I can't deny having read that story. After all, I still remembered it with pleasure forty years later. Yet only six and a half years after reading it, I wrote "Nightfall" which—

—dealt in part with a cult whose members were furious at scientists for rationalizing the mystic tenets of the believers. In an exciting scene, the cultists attacked the scientists' citadel at a very crucial moment and the scientists tried to hold them off long enough to get their task done.

No, it wasn't plagiarism. For one thing, I wrote it entirely differently. However, the scene fit both stories and having been impressed by it in Jack's story, I drew from memory and used it in my own story automatically—never for one moment considering that I wasn't making it up out of nothing but had earlier read something very like that scene.

I suppose that any thoroughgoing scholar who was willing to spend several years at the task could trace almost every quirk in "Nightfall" to one story or another that appeared in the science fiction magazines in the 1930s. (Yes, I read them all.) Naturally, he could do the same for any other story written by any other author.

Here's something even more curious. In a note dated 27 June 1985, a reader sent me an enclosure—a Xerox of a short article from the October 1937 issue of the magazine *Sky* (now known as *Sky and Telescope,* I believe).

The article is entitled "If the Stars Appeared Only One Night in a Thousand Years." It begins with the Emerson quotation and it is by M. T. Brackbill. The author describes what it might be like if *the* night on which the stars appeared were coming. There might be "pro-stellarists" who believe the stars are coming, and "anti-stellarists" who dismiss the whole thing as a fable. And then the night comes and everyone stares entranced at the stars and finally watches them disappear with the dawn, sadly realizing that for a thousand years they will never be seen again.

It's rather touching, and about the only thing Brackbill misses, that I could see, was the certainty that on that particular night there was bound to be a heavy nightlong overcast in various parts of the world, so that millions of people would invariably be disappointed.

The person who sent me the Xerox accompanied it with this note:

"Dear Mr. Asimov— I happened to spot this article. I wonder if it was an inspiration for one of the greatest short stories ever written!"

Just an "inspiration"? If the article and "Nightfall" were carefully studied and compared, how many events and phrases in the story might seem to have been inspired or hinted at in the article? I haven't the heart to do this myself and I hope no one else does.

Unfortunately, neither the name nor the address of the person who sent me the Xerox was on the note, and the envelope the whole thing had come in had not been saved. (Please, everyone, if you want an answer, put your name and return address *on your letter* and not just on the envelope. I frequently discard envelopes without glancing at them except to make sure they are addressed to me.)

In any case, I couldn't answer him. So I must use this essay as the only way of reaching him.

The truth is that I never saw the article, never had a hint that it existed until the day I received the note and enclosure from my unknown correspondent. It had not the slightest iota of direct influence on my story.

But John Campbell presented me with the Emerson quote and the request that I reverse it only three years after the article had appeared. Had *he* seen it?

I wouldn't be surprised if he had, and if, as soon as he had come across it or had had it drawn to his attention, he copied down the quote and then waited for the first unwary science fiction writer to cross his threshold. (How thankful I am that it was I.)

Were he still alive (he would only be seventy-five today, if he were), I would ask him about it. I am quite sure, though, what his answer would be. It would be "What difference does it make?"

So there arises the question: if it is impossible to be completely original, how can you tell permissible influence from plagiarism?

Well, it depends on the extent and detail of the borrowing. Based on that, it is possible to tell! It may not always be provable in a court of law, but, believe me, it is possible to tell!

15

Names

WE RECEIVED AN INTEREST-
ing letter some time ago from Greg Cox of Washington State. It is short and I
will take the liberty of quoting its one sentence in full:

"I enjoyed very much the Good Doctor's story in the May 1984 issue
["The Evil Drink Does"], but I *have* to ask: How did a young lady from such
an allegedly puritanical background end up with the unlikely (if appealing)
name of *Ishtar Mistik???"*

It's a good question, but it makes an assumption. In the story, Ishtar
remarks, "I was brought up in the strictest possible way. It is impossible for me
to behave in anything but the most correct manner."

From that you may suppose that Ishtar's family were rigidly doctrinaire
Presbyterians, or superlatively moral Catholics, or tradition-bound Orthodox
Jews, but if you do it's an assumption. I say nothing about Ishtar's religious
background.

To be sure, Ishtar is the Babylonian goddess of love, the analog of the
Greek Aphrodite, and it is therefore odd that such a name should be given a
child by puritanical parents, if the puritanism is Christian or Jewish in origin.
But who says it is? The family may be a group of puritanical druids (even
druids may have strict moral codes, and probably do) who chose "Ishtar" for
its sound.

But let's go into the matter of names more systematically. Every writer
has to give his characters names. There are occasional exceptions, as when a
writer may refer to a limited number of characters, in puckish fashion, as "the

Young Man," "the Doctor," "the Skeptic," and so on. That is artificial and is usually used in rather lighthearted stories.

Sometimes that sort of thing is limited to one person. Thus, P. G. Wodehouse, in his golf stories, refers to the narrator as "the Oldest Member" and never gives him a name. He only need be referred to for a few paragraphs at the start, however, and then he remains in the background as a disembodied voice. In my own George and Azazel stories, the first-person character to whom George speaks in the introduction, and whom he regularly insults, has no name. He is merely "I." Of course, the perceptive reader may think (from the nature of George's insults) that I's name is Isaac Asimov, but again that is only an assumption.

Allowing for such minor exceptions then, writers need names.

You might think that this is not something that bothers anyone but apparently it does. I have received numerous letters (usually from early teenagers) who seem to be totally unimpressed by the ease with which I work up complex plots and ingenious gimmicks and socko endings but who say, "How do you manage to decide what names to give your characters?" *That* is what puzzles them.

In my attempts to answer, I have had to think about the subject.

In popular fiction intended for wide consumption, especially among the young, names are frequently chosen for blandness. You don't want the kids to stumble over the pronunciation of strange names or to be distracted by them. Your characters, therefore, are named Jack Armstrong or Pat Reilly or Sam Jones. Such stories are filled with Bills and Franks and Joes coupled with Harpers and Andersons and Jacksons. That is also part of the comforting assumption that all decent characters, heroes especially, are of Northwest European extraction.

Naturally, you may have comic characters or villains, and *they* can be drawn from among the "inferior" races, with names to suit. The villainous Mexican can be Pablo; the comic black, Rastus; the shrewd Jew, Abie; and so on.

Aside from the wearisome sameness of such things, the world changed after the 1930s. Hitler gave racism a bad name, and all over the world, people who had till then been patronized as "natives" began asserting themselves. It became necessary to choose names with a little more imagination and to avoid seeming to reserve heroism for your kind and villainy for the other kind.

On top of this, science fiction writers had a special problem. What names do you use for nonhuman characters—robots, extraterrestrials, and so on?

There have been a variety of solutions to this problem. For instance, you might deliberately give extraterrestrials unpronounceable names, thus indicating that they speak an utterly strange language designed for sound-producing organs other than human vocal cords. The name Xlbnushk is a good one, for instance.

That, however, is not a solution that can long be sustained. No reader is going to read a story in which he periodically encounters Xlbnushk without eventually losing his temper. After all, he has to look at the letter combination and he's bound to try to pronounce it every time he sees it.

Besides, in real life, a difficult name is automatically simplified. In geology, there is something called "the Mohorovičić discontinuity" named for its Yugoslavian discoverer. It is usually referred to by non-Yugoslavians as "the Moho discontinuity." In the same way, Xlbnushk would probably become Nush.

Another way out is to give nonhuman characters (or even human characters living in a far future in which messy emotionalism has been eliminated) codes instead of names. You can have a character called 21MM792, for instance. That sort of thing certainly gives a story a science fictional ambience. And it can work. In Neil R. Jones' Professor Jameson stories of half a century ago, the characters were organic brains in metallic bodies, and all of them had letter-number names. Eventually, one could tell them apart and didn't even notice the absence of ordinary names. This system, however, will work only if it rarely occurs. If all, or even most, stories numbered their characters, there would be rebellion in the ranks.

My own system, when dealing with the far future, or with extraterrestrials, is to use names, not codes, and easily pronounceable names, too—but names that don't resemble any real ones, or any recognizable ethnic group.

For one thing, that gives the impression of "alienism" without annoying the reader. For another, it minimizes the chance of offending someone by using his or her name.

This is a real danger. The most amusing example was one that was encountered by L. Sprague de Camp, when he wrote "The Merman" back in 1938. The hero was one Vernon Brock (not a common name) and he was an ichthyologist (not a common profession). After the story appeared in the December 1938 *Astounding,* a thunderstruck Sprague heard from a real Vernon

Brock who was really an ichthyologist. Fortunately, the real Brock was merely amused and didn't mind at all, but if he had been a nasty person, he might have sued. Sprague would certainly have won out, but he would have been stuck with legal fees, lost time, and much annoyance.

Sometimes I get away with slight misspellings: Baley instead of Bailey; Hari instead of Harry; Daneel instead of Daniel. At other times, I make the names considerably different, especially the first name: Salvor Hardin, Gaal Dornick, Golan Trevize, Stor Gendibal, Janov Pelorat. (I hope I'm getting them right; I'm not bothering to look them up.)

My feminine characters also receive that treatment, though the names I choose tend to be faintly classical because I like the sound: Callia, Artemisia, Noÿs, Arcadia, Gladia, and so on.

I must admit that when I started doing this, I expected to get irritated letters from readers, but, you know, I never got one. My system of naming began in wholesale manner in 1942 with the first Foundation story, and in the forty-plus years since, not one such letter arrived. Well, Damon Knight once referred to Noÿs in a review of *The End of Eternity* as "the woman with the funny name," but that's as close as it got.

Which brings me to the George and Azazel stories again. There I use a different system. The George and Azazel stories are intended to be humorous. In fact, they are farces, with no attempt or pretense at realism. The stories are outrageously overwritten on purpose. My ordinary writing style is so (deliberately) plain that every once in a while, I enjoy showing that I can be florid and rococo if I choose.

Well then, in a rococo story, how on Earth can I be expected to have characters with ordinary names, even though the stories are set in the present and (except for Azazel) deal only with Earthpeople, so that I can't use nonexistent names?

Instead I use real names but choose very unusual and pretentious first names. In my George and Azazel stories, characters have been named Mordecai Sims, Gottlieb Jones, Menander Block, Hannibal West, and so on. By associating the outlandish first name with a sober last name, I heighten the oddness of the first. (On second thought, I should have made Ishtar Mistik, Ishtar Smith.)

None of this is, of course, intended as a universal rule. It's just what *I* do. If you want to write an s.f. story, by all means make up a system of your own.

16

Dialog

MOST STORIES DEAL WITH people, and one of the surefire activities of people is that of talking and of making conversation. It follows that in most stories there is dialog. Sometimes stories are largely dialog; my own stories almost always are. For that reason, when I think of the art of writing (which isn't often, I must admit) I tend to think of dialog.

In the Romantic period of literature in the first part of the nineteenth century, the style of dialog tended to be elaborate and adorned. Authors used their full vocabulary and had their characters speak ornately.

I remember when I was very young and first read Charles Dickens' *Nicholas Nickleby.* How I loved the conversation. The funny passages were very funny to me, though I had trouble with John Browdie's thick Yorkshire accent (something his beloved Matilda, brought up under similar conditions, lacked, for some reason). What I loved even more, though, was the ornamentation—the way everyone "spoke like a book."

Thus, consider the scene in which Nicholas Nickleby confronts his villainous Uncle Ralph. Nicholas's virtuous and beautiful sister, Kate, who has been listening to Ralph's false version of events, which make out Nicholas to have been doing wrong, cries out wildly to her brother, "Refute these calumnies . . ."

Of course, I had to look up "refute" and "calumny" in the dictionary, but that meant I had learned two useful words. I also had never heard any seventeen-year-old girl of my acquaintance use those words, but that just showed me how superior the characters in the book were, and that filled me with satisfaction.

It's easy to laugh at the books of that era and to point out that no one *really* talks that way. But then, do you suppose people in Shakespeare's time went around casually speaking in iambic pentameter?

Still, don't you want literature to improve on nature? Sure you do. When you go to the movies, the hero and heroine don't look like the people you see in the streets, do they? Of course not. They look like movie stars. The characters in fiction are better-looking, stronger, braver, more ingenious and clever than anyone you are likely to meet, so why shouldn't they speak better, too?

And yet there are values in realism—in making people look, and sound, and act like real people.

For instance, back in 1919, some of the players on the pennant-winning Chicago White Sox were accused of accepting money from gamblers to throw the World Series (the so-called "Black Sox scandal") and were barred from baseball for life as a result. At the trial, a young lad is supposed to have followed his idol, the greatest of the accused, Shoeless Joe Jackson, and to have cried out in anguish, "Say it ain't so, Joe."

That is a deathless cry that can't be tampered with. It is unthinkable to have the boy say, "Refute these calumnies, Joseph," even though that's what he means. Any writer who tried to improve matters in that fashion would, and should, be lynched at once. I doubt that anyone would, or should, even change it to "Say it isn't so, Joe."

For that matter, you couldn't possibly have had Kate Nickleby cry out to her brother, "Say it ain't so, Nick."

Of course, during much of history most people were illiterate and the reading of books was very much confined to the few who were educated and scholarly. Such books of fiction as existed were supposed to "improve the mind" or risk being regarded as works of the devil.

It was only gradually, as mass education began to flourish, that books began to deal with ordinary people. Of course, Shakespeare had his clowns and Dickens had his Sam Wellers, and in both cases, dialog was used that mangled the English language to some extent—but that was intended as humor. The audience was expected to laugh uproariously at these representatives of the lower classes.

As far as I know, the first book which was written entirely and seriously in substandard English and which was a great work of literature nevertheless (or even, possibly, to some extent *because* of it) was Mark Twain's *Huckleberry Finn,* which was published in 1884. Huck Finn is himself the narrator, and he is made to speak as an uneducated backwoods boy *would* speak—if he happened to be a literary genius. That is, Twain used the dialect of an uneducated boy, but he put together sentences and paragraphs like a master.

The book was extremely popular when it came out because its realism made it incredibly effective—but it was also extremely controversial, as all sorts of fatheads inveighed against it because it didn't use proper English.

And yet, even so, Mark Twain had to draw the line, too, as did all writers until the present generation.

People, all sorts of people, use vulgarisms as a matter of course. I remember my days in the Army when it was impossible to hear a single sentence in which the common word for sexual intercourse was not used as an all-purpose adjective. Later, after I had gotten out of the Army, I lived on a street along which young boys and girls walked to the local junior high school in the morning, and back again in the evening, and their shouted conversations brought back memories of my barracks days with nauseating clarity.

Yet could writers reproduce that aspect of common speech? Of course not. For that reason, Huck Finn was always saying that something was "blamed" annoying, "blamed" this, "blamed" that. You can bet that the *least* he was really saying was "damned."

A whole set of euphemisms was developed and placed in the mouths of characters who wouldn't, in real life, have been caught dead saying them. Think of all the "dad-blameds," and "goldarneds," and "consarneds" we have seen in print and heard in the movies. To be sure, youngsters say them as a matter of caution, for they would probably be punished (if of "good family") by their parents if caught using the terms they had heard said parents use. (Don't let your hearts bleed for the kids, for when they grow up they will beat up *their* kids for the same crime.)

For the last few decades, however, it has become permissible to use all the vulgarisms freely and many writers have availed themselves of the new freedom to lend an air of further realism to their dialog. What's more, they are apt to resent bitterly any suggestion that this habit be modified or that some nonvulgar expression be substituted.

In fact, one sees a curious reversal now. A writer must withstand a certain criticism if he does *not* make use of said vulgarisms.

Once when I read a series of letters by science fiction writers in which such terms were used freely and frequently, I wrote a response that made what seemed to me to be an obvious point. In it, I said something like this:

Ordinary people, who are not well educated and who lack a large working vocabulary, are limited in their ability to lend force to their statements. In their search for force, they must therefore make use of vulgarisms which serve, through their shock value, but which, through overuse, quickly lose whatever force they have, so that the purpose of the use is defeated.

Writers, on the other hand, have (it is to be presumed) the full and magnificent vocabulary of the English language at their disposal. They can say anything they want with whatever intensity of invective they require in a thousand different ways without ever once deviating from full respectability of utterance. They have, therefore, no need to trespass upon the usages of the ignorant and forlorn, and to steal their tattered expressions as substitutes for the language of Shakespeare and Milton.

All I got for my pains were a few comments to the effect that there must be something seriously wrong with me.

Nevertheless, it is my contention that dialog is realistic when, and only when, it reflects the situation as you describe it and when it produces the effect you wish to produce.

At rather rare intervals, I will make use of dialect. I will have someone speak as a Brooklyn-bred person would (that is, as I myself do, in my hours of ease), or insert Yiddishisms here and there, if it serves a purpose. I may even try to make up a dialect, as I did in *Foundation's Edge,* if it plays an important part in the development of the story.

Mostly, however, I do not.

The characters in my stories (almost without exception) are pictured as being well educated and highly intelligent. It is natural, therefore, for them to make use of a wide vocabulary and to speak precisely and grammatically, even though I try not to fall into the ornateness of the Romantic era.

And, as a matter of quixotic principle, I try to avoid expletives, even mild ones, when I can. —But other writers, of course, may do as they please.

◆

AFTERWORD: There is a top-ranking science fiction writer who seems consti-
tutionally incapable of not using vulgarisms, even when this makes serious
trouble for him with important businessmen he is dealing with. I once tried to
make peace on his behalf by saying, "When he says to you ——— ———
———, that's just his way of saying, 'Hello, how are you?' " The person I was
talking to, however, refused to be appeased.

17

Symbolism

To A CHILD, A STORY IS A STORY, and to many of us, as we grow older, a story remains a story. The good guy wins, the bad guy loses. Boy meets girl, boy loses girl, boy gets girl. We don't want anything beyond that—at least to begin with.

The trouble is that if that's all there is, one is likely to grow weary eventually. Children love to play ticktacktoe, for instance, but it's such a limited game that, after a while, most children don't want to play it any more. In the same way, children, as they grow older, may stop wanting to read stories that are only stories.

Since writers get as tired of writing stories that are only stories as readers get tired of reading them, it is only natural that writers begin to search for new and different ways to tell a story—for their own mental health, if nothing else.

A writer can try to find a new kind of plot, or he can indulge in stylistic experimentation, or he can strive for events that are ambiguous and conclusions that are inconclusive, or he can blur the distinction between good and evil, or between dream and reality. There are many, many things he can do and the one thing all these attempts have in common is that they annoy those readers who still are in the stage of wanting stories that are only stories.

Mind you, I don't sneer at such readers. For one thing, I myself still write stories that are primarily stories, because that's what *I* like. In my stories, there is a clear beginning, a clear middle, and a clear end, the good guy usually wins, and so on.

Nevertheless, you can't blame writers and readers for wanting something more than that, and those of us (I include myself, please note) who are suspicious of experimentation and fancy tricks ought to make some effort to understand what's going on. We may fail to grasp it entire, but we may at least see just enough to avoid an explosion of unreasonable anger.

One game that writers very commonly play is the one called symbolism. A story can be written on two levels. On the surface, it is simply a story, and anyone can read it as such and be satisfied. Even children can read it.

But the simple characters and events of the surface may stand for (or symbolize) other, subtler things. Below the surface, therefore, there may be hidden and deeper meanings that children and unsophisticated adults don't see. Those who can see the inner structure, however, can get a double pleasure out of it. First, since the inner structure is usually cleverer and more convoluted than the surface, it exercises the mind more pleasantly. Second, since it is not easy to detect, the reader has the excitement of discovery and the pleasure of admiring his own cleverness. (You can easily imagine what fun the writer has constructing such symbolic significance.)

I suppose the best example of something written on two levels is the pair of books popularly known as *Alice in Wonderland*. On the surface, it's a simply written fantasy, and children love it. Some adults reading it, however, find themselves in an intricate maze of puns, paradoxes, and inside jokes. (Read Martin Gardner's *The Annotated Alice*, if you want to increase your pleasure in the book.)

Or take J. R. R. Tolkien's *The Lord of the Rings*. On the surface, it is a simple tale of a dangerous quest. The small hobbit Frodo must take a dangerous ring into the very teeth of an all-powerful enemy and destroy it—and, of course, he succeeds. On a second, deeper level, it is an allegory of good and evil, leading us to accept the possibility that the small and weak can triumph where the (equally good) large and powerful might not; that even evil has its uses that contribute to the victory of the good; and so on.

But there is a third level, too. What *is* the ring that is so powerful and yet so evil? Why is it that those who possess it are corrupted by it and cannot give it up? Is such a thing pure fantasy or does it have an analog in reality?

My own feeling is that the ring represents modern technology. This corrupts and destroys society (in Tolkien's views) and yet those societies who gain it and who are aware of its evils simply cannot give it up. I have read *The Lord of the Rings* five times, so far, and I have not yet exhausted my own symbolic reading of it. I do not agree with, and I resent, Tolkien's attitude and yet I get pleasure out of the intricacy and skill of the structure.

There is an important point to be made concerning symbolism.

A writer may insert it without knowing he has done so; or else, a clever interpreter can find significance in various parts of a story that a writer will swear he had no intention of inserting.

This has happened to me, for instance. The middle portion of my novel *The Gods Themselves,* with its intricate picture of a trisexual society, has been interpreted psychiatrically and philosophically in ways that I *know* I didn't intend, and in terms that I literally don't understand. My Foundation series has been shown, by apparently careful analysis, to be thoroughly Marxist in inspiration, except that I have never read one word by Marx, or about Marx either, at the time the stories were written, or since.

When I complained once to someone who worked up a symbolic meaning of my story "Nightfall" that made no sense to me at all, he said to me haughtily, "What makes you think you understand the story just because you've written it?"

And when I published an essay in which I maintained that Tolkien's ring symbolized modern technology, and a reader wrote to tell me that Tolkien himself had denied it, I responded with "That doesn't matter. The ring nevertheless symbolizes modern technology."

Sometimes it is quite demonstrable that an author inserts a deeper symbolism than he knows—or even understands. I have almost never read a layman's explanation of relativity that didn't succumb to the temptation of quoting *Alice* because Lewis Carroll included paradoxes that are unmistakably relativistic in nature. He did not know that, of course; he just happened to be a genius at paradox.

Well, sometimes this magazine publishes stories that must not be read only on the surface, and, as is almost inevitable, this riles a number of readers.

I am thinking, for instance, of the novella "Statues" by Jim Aikin, which appeared in our November 1984 issue, and which various readers objected to strenuously. There were statements to the effect that it wasn't science fiction or even fantasy, that it had no point, that it was anti-Christian, and so on.

To begin with, the story, taken simply as a story, is undoubtedly unpleasant in spots. I winced several times when I read it, and I tell you, right now, that I wouldn't, and couldn't, write such a story. But I'm not the be-all and the end-all. The story, however difficult to stomach some of its passages may be, was skillfully and powerfully written. Even some of those who objected had to admit that.

And it was indeed a fantasy. Aikin made it clear toward the end that the statues were not pushed about, and that their apparent movement was not a delusion. They were on the side of the heroine and were cooperating with her, trying to rescue her from her unhappy life.

But that is only the surface. A little deeper and we see that it is a case of the old gods trying to save the young woman from the new. It is a rebellion against the rigid pharisaic morality of some aspects of the Judeo-Christian tradition and a harking back to the greater freedom of some aspects of paganism. The story is in the spirit of that powerful line of A. C. Swinburne in his "Hymn to Proserpine"—"Thou hast conquered, O pale Galilean; the world has grown gray from thy breath."

Looked at this way, the story is not anti-Christian (surely the "Christian" characters in the story are not all there is to Christianity) but is against hypocrisy-in-the-name-of-religion, which I imagine no one favors, least of all Christians.

But if you go deeper still, you will find the story is one more expression of the longing for the old. In this story it is expressed by contrasting the frowning new god with the kindly old ones. In *The Lord of the Rings* it is expressed by contrasting the evil technology of the Dark Lord, Sauron, with the pastoral life of the simple hobbits. (Of course, it is much safer to make of the enemy a devil figure than a God figure, so Tolkien got into no trouble at all.)

You can see the value of symbolism when you compare either of these with Jack Finney's famous "The Third Level," where he demonstrates his longing for the old by a straightforward contrast between 1950 and 1880. It leaves nothing to discover and, in my opinion, therefore, is a weak story.

But "Statues"—like it or not—is a *strong* story that makes an important point with great skill.

AFTERWORD: I can never escape from the clever critics. When *Publishers Weekly* reviewed my novel *Foundation and Earth* (Doubleday, 1986), the reviewer said, "He has, however, found an ingenious way around his clumsiness with novelistic narrative by employing a formal fairy tale structure in which . . ." I read this to my dear Janet in order to denounce the idiot reviewer for accusing me of clumsiness of any kind. Janet dismissed that and said, "Did you employ a formal fairy tale structure?" I responded, "Who? Me?"

18

Serials

WHEN IS A WRITER NOT A WRITER?

When he is asked to write outside his specialty.

Writing is not a unitary matter. A person who is a skilled science writer, or who can turn out fascinating popular histories, may be hopeless when it comes to writing fiction. The reverse is also true.

Even a person such as myself who is adept at both fiction and nonfiction and ranges over considerable variety in both subdivisions is not a universal writer. I can't and won't write plays, whether for the theater, motion pictures, or television. I don't have the talent for it.

It is surprising, in fact, how thinly talent can be subdivided. The functions, advantages, and disadvantages of fiction differ so with subject matter that every writer is more at home in one kind of fiction than in another. I can do science fiction and mysteries but I would be madly misjudging myself if I tried to do "mainstream" novels or even "new-wave science fiction."

Oddly enough, even length counts. You might think that if someone is writing a story, it can be any length. If it finishes itself quickly, it is a short story; if it goes on for a long time, it is a novel; if it is something in between, it is a novelette or a novella.

That's just not so. Length is not the sole difference. A novel is not a lengthy short story. A short story is not a brief novel. They are two different species of writing.

A novel has space in which to develop a plot leisurely, with ample room for subplots, for detailed background, for description, for character development, for comic relief.

A short story must make its point directly and without side issues. Every sentence must contribute directly to the plot development.

A novel is a plane; a short story is a line.

A novel which is too short and thus abbreviates the richness of its development would be perceived by the reader as skimpy and therefore unsatisfactory. A short story which is too long and allows the reader's attention to wander from the plot is diffuse and therefore unsatisfactory.

There are writers who are at home with the broad swing of the novel and are not comfortable within the confinement of the short story. There are writers who are clever at driving home points in short stories and who are lost in the echoing chambers of the novel. And of course there are writers who can do both.

A magazine such as ours is primarily a vehicle in which the short story is displayed. It is important we fulfill this function for a variety of reasons:

1) Short stories are worth doing and worth reading. They can make concise points that novels cannot, in ways that novels cannot.

2) A group of short stories which, in length, takes up the room of one novel offers far more variety than a novel can, and there is something very pleasant about variety.

3) Those writers who are adept at the short story need a vehicle.

4) Beginning writers need a vehicle, too, and beginners are well advised to concentrate on short stories at the start. Even if their true skill turns out to be in the novel, initial training had better be in the short story, which requires a smaller investment in time and effort. A dozen short stories will take no more time than a novel and offer much more scope for experimentation, and "finding oneself."

When George, Joel, and I began this magazine, we were aware of all these points and were determined to make it a magazine devoted to the short story exclusively. And we are still so determined.

Yet it is not easy to be rigid. It is perhaps not even desirable to be rigid under all circumstances. There are times when the best of rules ought to be bent a little.

What are the forces, for instance, that drag us in the direction of length? To begin with, there are (rightly or wrongly) more literary honors and monetary rewards for novels than for short stories, so that if a writer can handle any length, he usually finds himself gravitating toward the novel.

Naturally, since a novel requires a great investment of time and effort, it is the experienced writers of tried quality who are most likely to move in that direction. And once they've done that, they're not likely to want to let go. It becomes difficult, in fact, to persuade them to take time out from their current novel in order to write a short story.

As long as we stick rigidly to short stories, therefore, we tend to lose the chance at picking up the work of some of the best practitioners in the field. Newcomers, however worthy, tend to have less experience and their writing tends to be less polished.

For the most part, this does not dismay us. We *want* the newcomers, and the freshness of concept and approach is quite likely to make up for what clumsiness of technique comes from inexperience. The clumsiness, after all, will smooth out with time—and at that point, the new talent will almost inevitably begin to write novels.

Occasionally, then, we bend. If a story comes along by an established writer that is unusually good but is rather long, we are tempted to run it. We have indeed run stories as long as forty thousand words in a single issue.

There are advantages to this. If you like the story, you can get deeply immersed in it and savor the qualities that length makes possible and that you can't get otherwise. And there are disadvantages. If you don't like the story and quit reading it, you have only half a magazine left and you may feel cheated.

The editor must judge the risk and decide when a long story is likely to be so generally approved of that the advantages will far outweigh the disadvantages.

But what do we do about novels? Ignore them?

Most novelists do not object to making extra money by allowing a magazine to publish part or all of the novel prior to its publication *as* a novel. And most magazines welcome the chance of running a novel in installments.

Consider the advantages to the magazine. If the first part of a serial is exciting, is well written, and grabs the reader, it is to be expected that a great many readers will then haunt the newsstands waiting for the next issue. If many serials prove to have this grabbing quality, readers will subscribe rather than take the chance of missing installments.

Magazine publishers do not object to this. Even Joel wouldn't.

There are, however, disadvantages. Some readers actively like short stories and dislike novels. Others may like novels but bitterly resent being stopped short and asked to wait a month for a continuation. They may also resent having to run the risk of missing installments.

We are aware of these disadvantages and also of our own responsibility for encouraging the short story, so we have sought a middle ground.

These days there are so many novels and so few magazines that there isn't room to serialize them all. Still, some good novels are available for early publication of a portion only—some portion that stands by itself. We have been deliberately keeping our eyes open for this.

It's not always easy to find a novel-portion that stands by itself. The fact that something goes afterward or comes before (or both) is likely to give the reader a vague feeling of incompleteness. Sometimes, then, we try to run several chunks, each of which stands by itself or almost does. This comes close to serialization, but if the second piece can be read comfortably without reference to the first, then it's not. Again, George must use his judgement in such cases.

But then, every once in a long while, we are trapped by our own admiration of a novel and find ourselves with a chunk we would desperately like to publish, but that is too long to fit into a single issue and that can't conveniently be divided into two independent chunks.

—Then, with a deep breath, if we can think of no way out, we serialize. We hate to do this, and we hardly ever will. But hardly ever isn't never!

When there's no other way out, rather than lose out on something really first-class, we will have to ask you to wait a month.

But hardly ever.

AFTERWORD: The readers can't say I'm not honest. In the January 1986 issue of *Asimov's,* five and a half years after the above essay was written, with Gardner Dozois newly at the helm, we ran the first part of a three-part serial. Gardner thought the quality made it worth doing. There was some objection from the readers, inevitably, but we didn't suffer unduly. And we don't plan on doing it often.

19

Nowhere!

IN 1516, THE ENGLISH SCHOLAR Thomas More (1478–1535) published a book (in Latin), with a long title—as was the fashion in those days—that was also in Latin. When it finally appeared in its first English edition in 1551, the title was given as *A fruteful and pleasaunt Worke of the beste State of a publyque Weale, and of the newe yle, called Utopia.* We refer to the book simply as *Utopia.*

In the book, More described the workings of what he considered an ideal human society, as found on the island nation of Utopia, a nation that was governed entirely by the dictates of reason. His description of such a society is *so* noble and rational that it would seem enviable even today.

More was under no illusions as to the real world, however. The word "utopia" is from the Greek *ou* ("not") and *topos* ("place"), so that it means "nowhere." More realized, in other words, that his ideal existed nowhere on Earth (and still doesn't). In fact, his book, in describing his ideal society, served also, by clear contrast, to excoriate the actual governments of his day, particularly that of his native England which, of course, he knew the best.

An easy mistake was made, however. Since Utopia, as described, was such a wonderful place, it could easily be imagined that the first syllable was from the Greek prefix *eu*, meaning "good," so that "utopia" might mean not "nowhere" but the "good place."

The word "utopia" entered the English language, and the other European languages as well, as "an ideal society." The adjective "utopian" refers to any scheme that has what seems a good end in view, but that is not practical and cannot be carried through in any realistic sense.

We might speak of "utopian literature"—written accounts in which ideal societies are described, with More's as the classic, but not the earliest, example. Plato's *The Republic* was a description, nineteen centuries earlier than *Utopia*, of an ideal state dependent upon reason. Earlier still were accounts of ideal states in mythological or religious literature, in the form of past golden ages or of future messianic ones. The Garden of Eden is a well-known example of the former, and the Eleventh Chapter of Isaiah of the latter.

The production of utopian accounts has not fallen off since the time of More, either. The most influential recent examples have been *Looking Backward*, published in 1888 by Edward Bellamy (1850–1898), which described the United States of 2000 under an ideal socialist government, and *Walden Two*, published in 1948 by B. F. Skinner (1904–   ), which described an ideal society based on Skinner's own theories of social engineering.

All such utopias are not convincing, however. Unless one accepts the conventions of religion, it is difficult to believe in golden or messianic ages. Nor can one easily suppose that sweet reason will at any time dominate humanity.

In the course of the nineteenth century, however, something new entered the field of utopianism. The possibility arose that scientific and technological advance might impose a utopia from without, so to speak. In other words, while human beings remained as irrational and imperfect as ever, the advance of science might supply plenty of food, cure disease and mental ailments, track down and abort irrational impulses, and so on. A perfect technology would cancel out an imperfect humanity. The tendency to take this attitude and to paint the future in glowing technological colors reached the point where what we call "science fiction" is called, in Germany, "utopian stories."

As a matter of fact, however, it isn't at all likely that the average writer is going to try to write a truly utopian story. There's no percentage in it. All you can do is describe such a society and explain, at great length, how good it is, and how well it works, and how it manages not to break down. There can't be any drama in it—no problems, no risks, no threat of catastrophe, no pulling through by the merest squeak. Clearly, if such things were possible the utopia would be no utopia. It follows that utopian stories are, by their very nature, dreadfully dull. The one utopian novel I've actually managed to read was

Looking Backward, and although it was a bestseller in its times and still has its enthusiasts, I tell you right now that if dullness could kill, reading it would be a death sentence.

So dull are utopian books that they fail to fulfill their function of pointing out the errors and faults of the societies that really exist. You can't grow indignant over these faults if you fall asleep in the process.

There developed, therefore, the habit of attacking societies in a more direct fashion. Instead of describing the good opposite, one described the evil reality, but exaggerated it past bearing. Instead of a society in which everything was ideally good, one described a society in which everything was ideally bad.

The word coined for a totally bad society is "dystopia," where the first syllable is from the Greek prefix *dys-* meaning "abnormal" or "defective." Dystopia is the "bad place," so you know what "dystopian literature" would be.

Dystopias are intrinsically more interesting than utopias. Milton's description of his dystopian hell in the first two books of *Paradise Lost* is far more interesting than his description of utopian heaven in the third book. And in *The Lord of the Rings,* not much can be told about the stay of the Fellowship in the utopian elfland of Lorien, but how the story intensifies and grows more interesting as we approach the dystopian Mordor.

But can there be dystopias today with science and technology advancing as they do?

Certainly! You need only view science and technology as *contributing* to the evil (which is not difficult to do).

And yet *pure* dystopian tales are as dull and as unbearable as pure utopian ones. Consider the most famous pure dystopian tale of modern times, *1984* by George Orwell (1903–1950), published in 1948 (the same year in which *Walden Two* was published). I consider it an abominably poor book. It made a big hit (in my opinion) only because it rode the tidal wave of cold-war sentiment in the United States.

The pure utopian tale can only hit the single note of "Isn't it wonderful —wonderful—wonderful—." The pure dystopian tale can only hit the single note of "Isn't it awful—awful—awful—." And one cannot build a melody on the basis of a single note.

Well then, what is a science fiction writer supposed to do if both utopian and dystopian stories are dull?

Remember, they are poor only if they are pure, so avoid the extremes. Milton's hell was made interesting because of his portrait of Satan, courageous even in the ultimate adversity, feeling pangs of remorse even when immersed in ultimate evil. Milton's heaven was past saving because there was no way of introducing danger in the face of an omnipotent, omniscient God. His dystopia was not pure; his utopia was.

The evil of Mordor was made bearable by the courage and humanity of Frodo, and the story would have remained interesting and successful even if Frodo had failed in the end. It was his courage and humanity, not his victory, which really counted.

The essence of a story is the struggle of one thing against another: a living thing against the impersonal Universe; a living thing against another living thing; one aspect of a living thing against another aspect of himself.

In each case, you have to make it possible for the reader to identify with at least one side of the struggle, so that his interest and sympathy is engaged. I say "at least" one side, because if you are skillful, you can cause him to identify with both sides and be emotionally torn.

The side or sides with whom you identify must carry on the struggle with courage, intelligence, and decency—or, at least, learn to do so. The story won't be effective if you are ashamed of the side you make your own.

Both sides must have a fair chance to win. It is tempting to pile the odds up against your side so as to make his ultimate victory the more unexpected, exciting, and triumphant, but in that case you must be sure that your side *does* end up victorious. You can't make it David versus Goliath unless David wins, and as one becomes more and more experienced and sophisticated in reading, that may come to seem too obvious and even too unrealistic.

It seems to me, then, that the best you can do is to present your story as a struggle between sides which are both mixtures of good and evil (thus placing it somewhere between the extremes of utopia and dystopia), and don't make the odds overwhelming in either direction. You can then proceed to make your point without being *forced* into a happy ending and under conditions of maximum excitement and reader uncertainty. The reader will not only be uncertain as to how his side will win, but *if* it will win, or even, perhaps, which is truly his side.

I don't say this is easy, of course.

✦

AFTERWORD: I also don't say the readers will like it. We are all conditioned into black-and-white by our early reading. In children's stories it is Jack versus the giants; Hansel and Gretel versus the witch; St. George versus the dragon; good guys versus the bad guys, with no doubt whatever as to which is which. And some of us (including me, at times) don't completely grow up.

20

Science Fiction Poetry

WHEN SOMEONE WRITES AS much as I do on as many subjects as I do, the impression is bound to arise that I know everything. Not so. I freely admit to areas of ignorance and incomprehension, and one of these areas is that of modern poetry.

Nevertheless, I am bound, by my own understanding of my job as editorial essayist, to discuss every facet of the science fiction field at one time or another, and we do publish occasional poetry. Not much poetry, to be sure, but then no one willingly publishes much poetry these days. —So I'll give my thoughts on the matter, asking you to remember my admitted lack of expertise.

Why do we publish poetry? Why not?

Surely science fictional themes and emotions can be expressed in poetic form now and then. Consider, for instance, the most remarkable example of science fiction poetry (in my opinion) that has ever been written. It was published in 1842 and here it is:

> *For I dipped into the future, far as human eye could see,*
> *Saw the Vision of the world, and all the wonder that would be;*
>
> *Saw the heavens fill with commerce, argosies of magic sails,*
> *Pilots of the purple twilight, dropping down with costly bales;*
>
> *Heard the heavens fill with shouting, and there rained a ghastly dew*
> *From the nations' airy navies grappling in the central blue;*

Far along the world-wide whisper of the south-wind rushing warm,
With the standards of the peoples plunging through the thunder-storm;

Till the war-drum throbbed no longer, and the battle-flags were furled
In the Parliament of man, the Federation of the world.

Aerial commerce and aerial warfare (the "ghastly dew" might even be an unconscious foreshadowing of radioactive fallout) culminating in a world government are foreseen. Not bad for 1842!

The chances are you are familiar with the passage, which is a measure of its success, for it has been quoted and requoted endlessly. It is from "Locksley Hall" by Alfred, Lord Tennyson. Concerning its quality I have nothing to say; I am no judge. However, it scans perfectly and it rhymes, too.

Scansion, rhyme, together with other devices such as alliteration, assonance, and so on grew up in English poetry out of the needs of an illiterate society. When people can only tell a long story from memory, rhythm and rhyme are an enormous help. It is for this reason that the epic poem is as old as history, while the prose novel is a creature of modern times and a literate society.

Thanks to the rhythm and rhyme, the passage I quoted can be easily memorized and is pleasant to recite. Tennyson also supplies us with colorful phrases that are impossible to forget, once read. (The same poem contains the line "In the spring a young man's fancy lightly turns to thoughts of love.")

Then, too, the content is science fictional beyond cavil. Indeed, later in the poem is a couplet that states what I might call the central dogma of science fiction, and does so in a way that, in my opinion, cannot be improved:

Not in vain the distance beckons. Forward, forward let us range;
Let the great world spin for ever down the ringing grooves of change.

And yet all those poetic devices that make poetry quotable, however useful in an illiterate society, are irritatingly confining once the society grows literate. The poet finds that the restrictive rules of such poetry, the endless jigging alternation of stresses, the deadly repetition of final syllables and initial letters force him into saying what he wants to say in second or third best fashion, because first best won't fit. It forces him into archaisms, inversions, elisions, and other artificialities. It wears him out to no purpose.

Nowadays, therefore, rigid scansion and careful rhyme are confined, almost entirely, to light verse and to sentimental ballads. In the former case, the jigging and repetition are strong elements in the humor being sought for; in the latter case, they help the words fit the music and let the singer remember how it goes.

There's nothing essentially wrong with light verse, of course. Most of what we print is light verse, which is usually short, straightforward, comprehensible, and, often, humorous. The three contests I have set up, involving acrostic sonnets, double dactyls, and limericks, all involved light verse. In each of the three cases, the output was judged on mechanical perfection and on wit; in no case did I try to judge poetic content.

But if you take away rhyme and meter and all those other devices, what's left? Haven't you abolished poetry?

Not really. We're so used to the appurtenances, we mistake them for the real thing. It's like imagining that if males and females stripped, the first removing their shirts and pants and the latter their blouses and skirts, it would then become impossible to tell the sexes apart.

The central core of poetry is compression and combination. The trick is to say a great many things in short space by the clever use of words not only for their literal meanings, but for their fringe-shades, their connotations and associations—and by combining words in such a way that together they take on more and deeper meaning than either word would if it stood separately.

Furthermore, modern poetry seems to be largely autobiographical. That is, the poet talks chiefly about the self, its experiences and emotions, and through the poetry we can come to know the poet deeply. Whereas a long, reasoned, logical essay might, like the steady, calm light of the Sun, gloss over a person's character and show the surface only, a heartfelt piece of poetry under a hundred words long might illuminate a person's character in a flash of X rays, showing an uncertain glimpse of something not otherwise visible at all. And if we come to understand one person, the poet, more deeply than is possible in flat prose, we might, by that fact, understand ourselves and all humanity more deeply as well.

That sounds like a huge advantage to be gained by shaking oneself free of the artificial shackling of syllables-by-order, but there are disadvantages:

1) It is hard to do. Because there are no artificial rules and it is all a matter of well-chosen words in well-arranged juxtaposition, it seems to the amateur that anyone can do it. And everyone tries. The result is that most

modern poetry is, I suspect, simply awful. But then we know, by Sturgeon's Law, that most of anything is simply awful.

2) It is intellectual. The meaning is not on the surface; it can't be. There isn't *room* on the surface, and some of the meaning has to be underneath—in layers under layers if the poem is good enough and rich enough. This means that the reader must work at it and think about it and consider subsidiary meanings of words, and the association of various words in combination. It's not easy. Most people aren't equipped to do it because they don't know the language subtly enough or the poet deeply enough. Some people who *are* equipped to do so have other things to do and don't want to "waste their time" at the job. (In this latter category, I am afraid that I myself am included.)

3) It isn't quotable. The absence of rhythm and rhyme; the juxtaposition of words not for beauty of sound but for depth of meaning—makes the poem hard to memorize, hard to recite, and hard to listen to. While none of this diminishes the essential value of the poem, it does diminish the casual pleasure in it.

4) It isn't immediately moving. When there was talk of decommissioning the USS *Constitution* ("Old Ironsides") as hopelessly obsolete, a twenty-one-year-old medical student, Oliver Wendell Holmes, wrote a poem that began "Ay, tear her tattered ensign down" that was printed in a newspaper and that brought a lump to the throat of every reader. (It *still* does, at least to mine). Millions of people were moved to protest against the action, and into contributing money to save the ship. Even schoolchildren brought in their pennies. And the ship was *saved*. It still exists and no one would ever dream of decommissioning it. I don't know of any modern poem that could possibly achieve such a result.

Such disadvantages are important from the standpoint of a magazine such as ours, which must please its readers. We can print modern poetry if it strikes us as unusually good, but we can never expect a majority of our readers to approve—so we can't do it often. We therefore stick, for the most part, to light verse—old-fashioned in its structure, but easy, pleasurable, and usually eliciting a smile.

AFTERWORD: I suppose you have heard of the village idiot who found a donkey that the rest of the village had looked for in vain. When asked how he did it, the village idiot said, "I said to myself, 'Suppose you were a donkey, where would you go?' Then I went there and there he was."

Well, when I am dealing with a subject I know nothing about, such as poetry, I say to myself, "Suppose you were a poet, what would you say?" Then I go ahead and say it. After this essay appeared, I met a woman from the neighborhood who said she taught poetry in school and had just read the above essay. I said at once (defensively), "I don't really know much about poetry." But she said, "You could have fooled me. That was a wonderful essay." I didn't really dare believe her, but I loved her for saying it.

21

Science Fiction Anthologies

I HEAR IT SAID NOW AND THEN that the short story is a lost literary art form; that the magazines and various outlets that fostered the short story are dead and gone; that fiction today concentrates on the novel.

That would be too bad if it were true, but, of course, it isn't entirely true. In the field of science fiction, at least, the short story absolutely flourishes and the reader simply can't get enough of it. Indeed, any good science fiction story can count on periodic resurrection in the form of items in author collections and in multiauthor anthologies. Some of my stories have been anthologized up to thirty times and I by no means hold the record for such things. I suspect that both Ray Bradbury and Harlan Ellison (to name but two) can cite stories of their own that have seen far more repetitions than any of mine have.

And there you have something that is oddly characteristic of science fiction—the vast number and varying nature of anthologies in the field. I have the impression that there is no precedent in literature for this.

Why is it so? Why should science fiction, rather than some other subsection of popular literature, spawn an unending series of anthologies of enormous variety?

I suspect that, in part at least, what is responsible is the unusual fervor of the devoted science fiction reader. Particular stories strike such a reader with the force of a sledgehammer. Combine this with the fact that magazine science fiction tends to be ephemeral. Few young readers save the magazines for long. Even if they start a collection, after a few years there comes college or marriage or other interests generally, and the collection falls apart, drifts away, vanishes.

Yet the memory of those particularly good stories lingers and a glow of glory builds about them. I have long lost count of the number of letters I have received from readers who tell me that once, when the world was young, they read a story about thus-and-so. They can't remember the title, the author, where it appeared, or anything more than thus-and-so, but could I tell them what the story was and how they could go about finding it again?

Sometimes I remember the story from the small clues they present and can give them the missing information. More often I cannot.

You see, then, that anthologies offer a second chance. They sometimes bring back for readers stories once loved and then lost. Once I deliberately devised an anthology *(Before the Golden Age,* Doubleday, 1974) in order to present some stories that I myself had loved and lost.

Sometimes such stories are better not found, for they don't, in actual fact, bear the prismatic colors that fond memory lends them; but sometimes they do. When I reread "Tumithak of the Corridors" during the preparation of my 1974 anthology, I found it to be a time machine that restored me to my teenage years for an hour or two.

The first anthology of magazine science fiction appeared in 1943. It was *The Pocket Book of Science Fiction* edited by Donald A. Wollheim. Among the stories it contained was Stanley G. Weinbaum's "A Martian Odyssey," which I had never read, having missed the issue in which it first appeared. I was able to enjoy it for the first time when I bought the anthology, and that is another service such books offer. They allow you to recover stories you never knew you had lost.

In 1946, there appeared the first *hardcover* anthology of magazine science fiction, *The Best of Science Fiction* edited by Groff Conklin. It was an anthology of almost painfully intense interest to me, for it was the first to contain a story of mine—"Blind Alley." That was never one of my own favorites; in fact, I considered it then, and now, too, as rather second-rate. Still, I discovered eventually that Groff's opinions of quality could usually be relied on, so perhaps I underestimate "Blind Alley."

In any case, *Astounding,* the magazine in which "Blind Alley" had originally appeared, bought all rights in those days, but John Campbell insisted that anthology income go to the authors involved. It was in this way that I made the great discovery that the same story could be paid for twice and, therefore, by extension, any number of times. (It is only this fact that makes it possible for a science fiction writer to earn a living, so this was by no means a nonsignificant discovery.)

Later in that same year, the most successful science fiction anthology ever to appear was published. It was *Adventures in Time and Space* edited by Raymond J. Healey and J. Francis McComas. It was a large, thick volume, with stories drawn almost entirely from the Golden Age of *Astounding,* and it contained my story "Nightfall." That was my introduction to the strange notion that one of my own stories was already considered a classic.

The success of the Healey-McComas anthology opened the floodgates. I haven't the faintest idea how many anthologies have been published since, but I am quite certain that there isn't an issue of any science fiction magazine that hasn't been carefully picked over to see if any gems have remained undiscovered—nor any gem or even semi-gem that hasn't been discovered and rediscovered and re-rediscovered.

Lately, I myself have joined the parade. I'm not entirely a novice at the anthologists' game, for I edited *The Hugo Winners* (Doubleday, 1962) along with successor volumes in 1971 and 1977, all of which were quite successful.

However, I never let myself get too involved in such matters because every anthology entails a great deal of tedious scut work—selection, obtaining of permissions, the making out of payments, and so on. The result was that through 1978, I edited only nine anthologies, which is very few for a person of my own wholesale proclivities who considers nothing worth doing that isn't worth doing *a lot.*

With my ninth anthology, however, *One Hundred Great Science Fiction Short-Short Stories* (Doubleday, 1978), I made the marvelous discovery that my friend Martin Harry Greenberg—tall, a little plump, intelligent, conscientious, hardworking, and good-humored—found a peculiar perverted pleasure in doing all those things, such as getting permissions and taking care of payments, that I hated to do.

Then the two of us discovered Charles G. Waugh, also tall, hardworking, intelligent, and conscientious, but less plump and much more grave than either Martin or I. It turned out he knew every science fiction story ever published, remembered all the statistics and plots, and could put his hand on any of them instantly. Ask him for a story about extraterrestrials from Uranus who reproduce by binary fission and I imagine he would have three different sets of Xeroxes in your hand the next day.

That changed everything. In 1979 and 1980, I helped edit no fewer than twelve anthologies and, at the moment of writing, there are six in press and more in preparation. (Not all are with Martin and Charles; a couple are with Alice Laurance, who has an attribute that the first two lack to an enormous degree—beauty; and one is with J. O. Jeppson, to whom I am closely related by marriage.)

Very often these recent anthologies have had my name blown out of proportion on the covers for crass commercial reasons, and over my protests, since I contribute no more than my fair share.

On the other hand I contribute no less than my fair share either and it chafes a little when someone takes it for granted that I am merely collecting money for the use of my name. I would overlook the slur on my integrity involved in this, since all great men suffer calumny, but I hate to lose credit for all the work I do.

Charles, Martin, and I constantly consult each other by mail and phone and we each dabble in every part of the work, but there is division of labor, too. Charles works particularly hard at locating stories and Xeroxing. Martin works particularly hard at the business details.

And as for me— Well, all the stories descend on me and I read them all and do the final judging (what I throw out is thrown out). I then write the introduction or the headnotes or (sometimes) both. And since I'm the one who lives in New York, I tend to do the trotting round to various publishers when that is necessary.

The net result is that each of the three of us does what he best likes to do, so that preparing the anthologies becomes fun for all of us. To be sure, I labor under the steady anxiety that something might happen to Martin or Charles but, under my shrewd questioning, both Sally Greenberg and Carol-Lynn Waugh have made it clear that each entirely understands the importance of keeping her husband in good functioning order, and I rely on them with all confidence.

◆

AFTERWORD: My interest in anthologies has continued, I might say. At the moment of writing this, it is over seven years since the above essay appeared and I have now over a hundred anthologies under my belt, most of them with Martin and Charles.

Since the essay was written, I am sorry to have to say that Sally Greenberg has passed on, which was a sad loss, for it was a very happy marriage. Marty, however, with the good fortune that is deservedly his, has found a worthy successor, and Rosalind Greenberg has now taken over the job (enthusiastically) of preserving Marty for my anthological needs.

22

What Writers
Go Through

EVERY ONCE IN A WHILE I GET A
letter that strikes a chord. Jeanne S. King of Marietta, Georgia, suggested that I
write an essay on what writers go through. Her tender heart bled for writers
and I think she has a point.

First, let me make it clear what I mean by "writers." I don't want to
confine the word only to those who are successful, who have published bestselling books, or who crank out reams of published material every year (if not
every day), or who make a lavish living out of their pens, typewriters, or
word processors, or who have gained fame and adulation.

I also mean those writers who just sell an occasional item, who make
only a bit of pin money to eke out incomes earned mainly in other fashions,
whose names are not household words, and who are not recognized in the
street.

In fact, let me go further and say I even mean those writers who never
sell anything, who are writers only in the sense that they work doggedly at it,
sending out story after story, and living in a hope that is not yet fulfilled.

We can't dismiss this last classification as "failures" and not "real" writers. For one thing, they are not necessarily failures forever. Almost every
writer, before he becomes a success, even a runaway, supernova success, goes
through an apprentice period when he's a "failure."

Secondly, even if a writer is destined always to be a failure, and even if
he is never going to sell, he remains a human being for whom all the difficul-

ties and frustrations of a writer's life exist and, in fact, exist without the palliation of even an occasional and minor triumph.

If we go to the other extreme and consider the writer whose every product is an apparently sure sale, we find that the difficulties and frustrations have not disappeared. For one thing, no number of triumphs, no amount of approval, seems to have any carrying power at the crucial moment.

When even the most successful writer sits down before a blank piece of paper, he is bound to feel that he is starting from scratch and, indeed, that the Damoclean sword of rejection hangs over him. (By the way, when I say "he" and "him," I mean to add "she" and "her" every time.)

If I may use myself as an example, I always wince a little when anyone, however sincerely and honestly, assumes that I am never rejected. I admit that I am rarely rejected, but between rarely and never is a vast gulf. Even though I no longer work on spec and I write only when a particular item is requested, I *still* run the risk. The year doesn't pass without at least one failure. It was only a couple of months ago that *Esquire* ordered a specific article from me. I duly delivered it, and they, just as duly, handed it back.

That is the possibility all of us live with. We sit there alone, pounding out the words, with our heart pounding in time. Each sentence brings with it a sickening sensation of not being right. Each page keeps us wondering if we aren't moving in the wrong direction.

Even if, for some reason, we feel we *are* getting it right and that the whole thing is singing with operatic clarity, we are going to come back to it the next day and reread it and hear only a duck's quacking.

It's torture for every one of us.

Then comes the matter of rewriting and polishing; of removing obvious flaws (at least, they seem obvious, but are they really?) and replacing them with improvements (or are we just making things worse?). There's simply no way of telling if the story is being made better or is just being pushed deeper into the muck and the time finally comes when we either tear it up as hopeless, or risk the humiliation of rejection by sending it off to an editor.

Once the story is sent off, no amount of steeling oneself, no amount of telling oneself over and over that it is sure to be rejected, can prevent one from harboring that one wan little spark of hope. Maybe— Maybe—

The period of waiting is refined torture in itself. Is the editor simply not getting round to it, or has he read it and is he suspended in uncertainty? Is he going to read it again and *maybe* decide to use it—or has it been lost—or has it been tossed aside to be mailed back at some convenient time and has it been forgotten?

How long do you wait before you write a query letter? And if you do write a letter, is it subservient enough? Sycophantic enough? Groveling enough? After all, you don't want to offend him. He might be just on the point of accepting and if an offensive letter from you comes along, he may snarl and rip your manuscript in two, sending you the halves.

And when the day comes that the manila envelope appears in the mail, all your mumbling to yourself that it is sure to come will not avail you. The sun will go into eclipse.

It's been over forty years since I've gone through all this in its full hellishness, but I remember it with undiminished clarity.

And then even if you make a sale, you have to withstand the editor's suggestions, which, at the very least, mean you have to turn back to the manuscript, work again, add or change or subtract material, and perhaps produce a finished product that will be so much worse than what had gone before that you lose the sale you thought you had made. At the worst, the changes requested are so misbegotten from your standpoint that they ruin the whole story in your eyes, and yet you may be in a position where you dare not refuse, so that you must maim your brainchild rather than see it die. (Or ought you to take back the story haughtily and try another editor? And will the first editor then blacklist you?)

Even after the item is sold and paid for and published, the triumph is rarely unalloyed. The number of miseries that might still take place are countless. A book can be produced in a slipshod manner or it can have a repulsive book jacket, or blurbs that give away the plot or clearly indicate that the blurb writer didn't follow the plot.

A book can be nonpromoted, treated with indifference by the publisher, and therefore found in no bookstores, and sell no more than a few hundred copies. Even if it begins to sell well, that can be aborted when it is reviewed unsympathetically or even viciously by someone with no particular talent or qualifications in criticism.

If you sell a story to a magazine, you may feel it is incompetently illustrated, or dislike the blurb, or worry about misprints. You are even liable to face the unsympathetic comments of individual readers who will wax merry, sardonic, or contemptuous at your expense—and what are *their* qualifications for doing so?

You will bleed as a result. I never met a writer who didn't bleed at the slightest unfavorable comment, and no number of favorable or even ecstatic remarks will serve as a styptic pencil.

In fact, even total success has its discomforts and inconveniences. There are, for instance—

People who send you books to autograph and return, but don't bother sending postage or return envelopes, reducing you to impounding their books or (if you can't bring yourself to do that) getting envelopes, making the package, expending stamps, and possibly even going to the post office.

People who send you manuscripts to read and criticize. ("Nothing much, just a page-by-page analysis, and if you think it's all right, would you get it published with a generous advance, please? Thank you.")

People who dash off two dozen questions, starting with a simple one like "What in your opinion is the function of science fiction and in what ways does it contribute to the welfare of the world, illustrating your thesis with citations from the classic works of various authors? (Please use additional pages, if necessary.)"

People who send you a form letter, with your name filled in (misspelled), asking for an autographed photograph, and with no envelope or postage supplied.

Teachers who flog their class of thirty into sending you thirty letters telling you how they liked a story of yours, and send you a sweet letter of her own asking you to write a nice answer to each one of the little dears.

And so on—

Well then, why write?

A seventeenth-century German chemist, Johann Joachim Becher, once wrote "The chemists are a strange class of mortals, impelled by an almost insane impulse to seek their pleasure among smoke and vapor, soot and flame, poisons and poverty; yet among all these evils I seem to live so sweetly, that may I die if I would change places with the Persian King."

Well, what goes for chemistry, goes for writing. I know all the miseries, but somewhere among them is happiness. I can't easily explain where it is or what it consists of, but it is there. I know the happiness and I experience it, and I will not stop writing while I live—and may I die if I would change places with the President of the United States.

♦

AFTERWORD: I admit that it is decades since I experienced most of the tortures I described in the above essay, but I have an excellent memory and I remember the first three years of my travels along the writers' trail. And even if I had forgotten, my dear wife, Janet, is a writer (with a number of published works—even books—under her belt) and, compared to me, she's a beginner, so that I have the chance of watching once again what a writer must go through. In fact, I'll continue the sad tale in the next essay.

23

The Writers' Plight

SOME TIME AGO, I RECEIVED A rather sorrowful letter from a science fiction writer pointing out that inflation had raised the price of s.f. magazines rapidly in recent years but that the word rates commanded by writers for those magazines had not gone up correspondingly.

I passed the letter on to Joel, and we each replied, rather apologetically, that the price increases had been forced on us by increasing cost of paper, printing, etc., etc., etc., and that publishers' profits (what there might be of them) had not gone up, either.

I have, however, been thinking about the subject and perhaps I have done Joel wrong.

Back in 1938, when I was just making my first sales, my stories went to *Amazing Stories* and *Astounding Science Fiction,* each of which retailed, at that time, at 20 cents an issue. (I am not depending on memory here and on the glow of nostalgia. I took out the respective issues and looked at them.) The payment for the stories, in each case, was 1 cent a word. This meant I had to sell twenty words to buy a copy of the magazine.

Now let's shift to 1981 (when this essay was first written). In the previous couple of weeks, I sold two stories. One was to *Asimov's* (and no, that wasn't as easy a job as you might think—I sent George two, and he rejected one of them). The other story, which was a fantasy and therefore unsuitable for this magazine, I sent to *F & SF,* which took it but rejected the same story that George had rejected. (Stupid editors!)

Accepting my own word count on the stories as accurate, *F & SF* paid me 4.5 cents a word and *Asimov's* paid me 6.8 cents a word. Both magazines now sell for $1.50 an issue. This means I must sell thirty-three words to buy a copy of *F & SF* and twenty-two words to buy a copy of *Asimov's*.

Conclusion: *Asimov's* payments to writers has just about kept up with the inflationary trend of the last forty years as represented by the price of science fiction magazines. *F & SF* is a little behind, but it is a smaller magazine and has always paid slightly lower rates. I can't criticize it for that.

Nevertheless, this doesn't mean that the writers' plight, generally, is a financially happy one. It isn't how much you get for each word that alone counts; it's also how many words you sell. Considering how long it takes to write each word, and how many times you have to rewrite each word, and how freely and casually editors can reject each word, you can end up selling very few words indeed, and even a reasonably high word rate won't help, in that case.

In my first eleven years as a writer—and as a "successful" writer, who was selling almost every word he wrote, with very little revision involved— my total income, for all eleven years put together, was $7,700.

Of course, those years spanned the 1940s, when prices were lower than they are now and when I paid no income tax to speak of, so that the figure isn't quite as bad as it sounds—but it's bad enough.

It was because of my minuscule earnings as a writer that I continued with my education, got my degrees and academic status, which turned out to be a Very Good Thing. Had I begun to make "big" money those first eleven years, I might have been tempted to abort my education and become a professional writer at once and that would have been a Bad Thing, so I don't complain about my slow start. Quite the reverse.

But what is the situation now? A survey was conducted, a few years ago, of a considerable number of writers who might well be considered as successful. At least, all those in the survey had published a minimum of one book, and to many earnest writers pounding their typewriters, even one published book would be an El Dorado dream.

And what was the annual income of all those successful writers, on the average? It turned out that the average was something like $4,700 a year. That's with this year's prices and this year's tax bite. And that's the average! Half of them (perhaps a little more than half, since a few high earners may disproportionately skew the average upward) make *less* than $4,700. Not exactly a living wage!

Now I admit I'm a fat cat. I won't pretend to coyness since it's all frankly spread out in my autobiography. It's been three decades since I made that little, or, for the most part, anywhere near that little. And yet, as readers of these essays know, I have never forgotten my early years and my identification with the struggling writer is complete. So I blanched when I saw the headline (on the front page of the New York *Times* yet) and felt myself fill with rage at a world in which that could happen.

What's more, I read later, in the same newspaper, that reduced royalties are becoming the thing with book publishers. Expenses are going up and the publishers must shoulder rising wages for people working in paper mills, printing establishments, their own offices, and so on. One can't blame the wages for rising, considering inflationary pressure. Still, the publishers must find places to economize to keep book prices from going through the roof and book sales from going through the basement—so they ask writers to accept less.

But are there not inflationary pressures on writers, too? Don't writers have to pay rent, buy food, take care of the kids? Why must they, *and they alone*, take less so that others can take more, when it is the writer on whom the entire publishing industry depends, and it is the writer, and the writer alone, that gives it meaning?

Why? There must be a reason.

Let's compare the position of a writer with, say, a person laboring in a paper mill.

The product of the paper mill is paper. It is produced in reasonably uniform quality and, if a particular quantity of a particular type and grade is ordered, precisely that quantity is received, and all of it is suitable for the purposes for which it is bought, and all of it is used. There is no "rejection" to speak of.

What's more, the various people in the paper mill are faceless nonindividuals as far as the product is concerned. No one looking at a particular batch of paper knows which laborer, or which group of laborers, is responsible, or would think of wondering, or could conceivably care. Even if some laborers are less good at their work than others, it would scarcely show up in the paper. Even if papermaking is a skilled craft, it is not a *talented* craft. A basic amount of skill is all that is needed.

How different from writing! Here material floods unmaskèd into the publisher's offices in quantities a hundred, or even a thousand, times as much as he requires. He can pick and choose, and he ends up rejecting far more than he takes. You can see how this weakens the writers' economic clout and why the publisher can casually ask sacrifices of the writer where he can only smile winsomely at the paper-mill laborer.

What's more, writing is a *talented* craft. Even among writers with the same basic skills (writers who can all handle a typewriter and who all know how to spell words) some have that little undefinable extra that turns out a particularly good book and some do not. Those with that extra are much more likely to end up accepted than those who are not. If those few winners are subtracted, the mass of writers who remain have an economic clout that is virtually zero.

But wait; all is not dark. There is another side. A laborer in a paper mill may well care nothing for his work, except as a means of earning a living. He may live for the workday end, especially on Friday. Most of his life may be waiting for tedium to pass. Why not? What's paper to him, or he to paper? His name's not on it.

A writer, on the other hand, is turning out more than a piece of writing. The writing has his name on it. It is *peculiarly* his. Others can write, but no one can write *precisely* as he does. He would like to earn a living, yes, but he also has a dream—that of seeing his name on a published story or book—that of receiving personal praise for a personal product—that of perhaps hitting the big time of fame and wealth. (There's very little chance of the last, of course, but a laborer in a paper mill has no chance at all, in the way of his job.)

However needful the money, it is the dream that is the motive force—that keeps a writer going all hours and all days, despite disappointment after disappointment.

And (to get back to that survey) things aren't so bad. Generally, writers who make very little money writing have other sources of income: a job of their own that they work at; or, possibly, a working spouse. None of them is starving.

Besides which, they were all asked what, in view of their low incomes, they planned to do in the future, and each one answered, "Keep on writing!"

And so, Gentle Reader, if you are a struggling writer, don't let this essay discourage you. The dream remains, and lightning *does* sometimes strike, and it *may* strike you. Besides, no matter what anyone says or does—you will keep on writing. (Just don't give up your job, or your working spouse.)

◆

AFTERWORD: In those years when I was averaging $700 a year, my parents took care of my basic needs at first, and then I eked out small sums first from the National Youth Administration and then from the GI Bill of Rights. Even after my writing income began to creep upward I worked for nine years on the faculty of Boston University School of Medicine. It was not until I was thirty-eight years old and had been a professional writer for twenty years that I dared let go and let my writing do the entire job of supporting me. So, believe me, I've been there.

24

Editors

SOMETIMES WRITE ESSAYS BASED on strongly disapproving letters we receive, but, of course, we get the other kind, too, and sometimes one of them is worth an essay.

For instance, we received a very nice letter from Malcolm K. McClintick of Indianapolis, which is not appearing in the letter column, because I want to discuss it here. In fact, I'm writing this essay precisely because he asked me to do so in a paragraph that goes as follows:

". . . in a future editorial I wish you'd address this question: If writers have so much trouble getting started, if fiction (good fiction) is that difficult, if so few submissions are close to the mark, then exactly what magical gift is it that editors have? Why is it that Eleanor Sullivan, Cathleen Jordan, Shawna McCarthy, etc. etc. can recognize a salable story but writers can't? And if they know what a salable story is, why aren't they getting rich writing such stories, books, etc., instead of editing them? How and why did they become editors in the first place, and what qualified them to do so?"

I haven't made a deep study of the subject; I have no scholarly knowledge of editors and what makes them tick. However, I have thoughts on the subject (as I have on most subjects) and I am willing to spread them out for your consideration.

Naturally, I must begin with a bit of introspection. When this magazine was first proposed to me by Joel Davis nearly a decade ago, I'm sure he imagined that I would be the editor. I repelled that notion with such firmness and with such an obvious horror that it was mentioned only once and then never again.

Why? There are some financial reasons, of course. An editor's job is full-time. Even when she (by which I mean "he or she," please) is not in the office forty hours a week, she probably fills out the time at home and she is a rare editor indeed if she doesn't spend considerably more than forty hours a week at the job. I simply cannot spend that much time at editing because editing would deprive me of that time for writing, and editing is a notoriously underpaid job while my writing is a notoriously overpaid one. I couldn't take the financial loss.

But that is not germane. Even if editorial work were to represent a financial gain to me, I would repel it with the same fervor. Writing and editing are two *different* professions and require two *different* personalities. I am a true writer in that I would much rather write than edit (or than almost anything, actually—and I stick in that "almost" only to avoid the obvious witticisms), so that even if I were a reasonably competent editor, I would stick to writing. In the same way, there are some who find such satisfaction in editing that they would rather edit than write, even if they were reasonably competent writers. (And all three women mentioned in the letter are competent writers who have been published.)

But, as a matter of fact, I would *not* be a reasonably competent editor; I would, in my opinion, be in the running for the world's worst editor. (Yes, I know I help edit a lot of anthologies but I confine my work to helping select stories from those already published and therefore already known to be good, and to writing introductions and headnotes.) It is not just that I don't know the machinery of putting magazines together and the routine of running them. I presume I can learn that, given a little time. It is that I *have no way of telling a good story from a bad one.*

Or, to use Mr. McClintick's phrase, I cannot "recognize a salable story." Sure, I can tell when a story is illiterate, stupid, or unreadable, but I can't tell a nearly good story from a very good one.

How is that possible? Don't I write good stories as a matter of course and every once in a while don't I write a very good story? Don't I almost never write a bad story? Then how is it I can't tell a good story from a bad one?

Because I'm lucky. I just happen to write good ones, without knowing how or why. When I do write an occasional story that's not so good, I don't recognize it as such. I hand it in to editors with the same silly smile I wear on my face when I bring in my good ones. Or, to put it another way, I present my good ones with the same hidden misgivings I present my not so good ones.

Other good writers may not be as hopelessly ignorant as I am but I'll bet a great many of them are not literate enough in the editorial sense to be trusted in the editorial chair for two minutes.

But now let's look at it from the other side. The beauteous Shawna can tell a good story from a bad one. I'm afraid we must accept that as indisputable. She took the Hugo as best editor in 1984, and in 1985 no fewer than seven stories that she had selected for this magazine were also selected for Nebula nominations.

And although Shawna is paid about as much as the magazine can afford to pay her, my personal feeling is that she is worth much more money and can probably use much more, too. Well then, if she has such a sure knowledge of what a good story is, why doesn't she write good stories and make a lot more money?

Well, as it happens (forgive me, Shawna dear), knowing what makes a good story does not necessarily mean that you can sit down and think up an idea of your own, and devise a scheme of your own for putting that idea into effective story form, and then get all the necessary events into the right order and express them with just the right words. Knowing and doing don't necessarily fit into the same head (though they might, I know).

And even if Shawna *could* write a good story if she chose, she might simply *hate* to go through all the work involved. I have known enough writers to know that the process of writing can be torture, even for good, competent writers, and I have read articles that maintained that alcoholism is an occupational hazard of writers for that reason. I'm lucky. It isn't hard work for me and I can stay at the typewriter all day, caroling old English madrigals as I write, but Shawna might well think that she would rather edit for a pittance than plunge into unending misery for a dubious pot of gold at the end of the rainbow.

You might say that there are people who are both good editors and good writers, and I agree. John Campbell, Horace Gold, and Tony Boucher, all grade-A editors, were also grade-A writers, but all three of them, once they became editors, just about stopped writing. They preferred being editors.

Occasionally, you get someone who is so evenly balanced that he keeps oscillating. Consider Fred Pohl who, for many years, alternated between some years as an editor and some years as a writer, top-notch in both respects. I suspect, though, the alternation produced high tension, and that he was very relieved when he finally toppled over, once and for all, on the writer's side.

But "how and why did they become editors . . . and what qualified them to do so?"

To begin with, you have to want to be an editor. That means you must like the subject matter of a magazine and be ready to read incredible quantities of stories of that kind. Shawna, for instance, had, all through her childhood, devoured science fiction, and when she found out that George Scithers was looking for an assistant, and that she might have a chance to read science fiction *for money,* she applied for the job at once.

Second, you have to learn how to be an editor, just as you have to learn anything else. Before George hired her, Shawna had obtained a job as editorial assistant at *Firehouse,* a magazine for firemen. Because the editor resigned, she took his place and learned the mechanics of putting out a magazine. It was hard work, but she had a talent for it.

Then, when she got the job with George, she learned how to do the kind of work one had to do in a science fiction magazine. She spent years working under the direction of two different editors, and finally she became editor herself with the January 1983 issue.

At any moment during this apprentice period, if she had shown any serious defect, she would have been released.

George Scithers had done editorial work a-plenty before he became founding editor of this magazine. He has a small publishing house of his own, but it is large enough to have taught him the trade. Eleanor Sullivan spent many years as managing editor under Fred Dannay, before becoming editor in her own right. Cathleen Jordan worked at Doubleday as an editor before coming to *Hitchcock,* and before that she had worked under a very good editor named Larry Ashmead, who had himself first worked under a very good editor named Dick Winslow.

There are exceptions, of course. John Campbell had no editorial experience whatever when he became the greatest editor science fiction has ever seen. —But he was a genius, and there are no rules for that.

AFTERWORD: In 1966, Joseph Ferman, publisher of *The Magazine of Fantasy and Science Fiction,* needed a new editor. I had been writing a regular column for the magazine for six years and so he asked me for my recommendations. I had come to know Joe's son, Ed, and it seemed to me he was a quiet, intelligent fellow who had been working along in secondary positions on the magazine, so I said, "Why not your son, Joe?" Joe seemed astonished but thought it over and decided I was right. Ed stepped into the position and is still there twenty-two years later. No one would dream of saying he does anything less than a first-class job.

It was also I who first suggested that George Scithers edit *Asimov's* to begin with and I insisted on Shawna when Kathleen Moloney left. It may be, then, that even though I'm no judge of good stories, I may possibly be a judge of good editors.

SCIENCE
FICTION
WRITERS ✦

25

Pseudonyms

IT WAS QUITE FASHIONABLE, IN earlier times, to refrain from putting one's name to things one had written. The writer could leave himself unnamed ("anonymous"—from Greek words meaning "no name"), or else he could use a false name ("pseudonym"—from Greek words meaning "false name"). So common was the practice that a pseudonym is often referred to as a "pen name," or, to give it greater elegance by placing it in French, a "nom de plume."

There were a variety of reasons for this. In most places in the world and at most times, it was all too easy to write something that would get you in trouble. The corruption, venality, and cruelty of those in power cried out for exposure, and those in power had the strongest objections to being exposed. For that reason, writers had to expect all sorts of governmental correction if caught—anywhere from a fine to death by torture.

The best-known example of this type of pseudonym was Voltaire, the eighteenth-century French satirist, whose real name was François-Marie Arouet.

A second major reason was that any nonscholarly writing was considered rather frivolous, and a decent person guilty of concocting such material might well be looked askance upon by society. A pseudonym, therefore, preserved respectability. This was especially true of women, who were widely considered subhuman in mentality (by men) and who would have shocked the world by a too open demonstration of the possession of brains. Mary Ann

Evans, therefore, wrote under the name of George Eliot, and Charlotte Brontë wrote under the name of Currer Bell, just at first.

One would think that neither reason would hold for the world of modern American science fiction. Why should anyone fear punishment for writing science fiction in our free land, or why should anyone fear the loss of respectability if convicted of the deed? And yet—

It is conceivable, particularly in the early days of magazine science fiction, that people in the more sensitive professions, such as teaching, would not have cared to have it known that they wrote "pseudoscientific trash" and so would protect themselves from lack of promotion, or outright dismissal, by the use of a pseudonym. I don't know of such cases definitely, but I suspect some.

It is even more likely that in the bad old days before the women's movement became strong, women who wrote science fiction concealed their sex from the readers (and even, sometimes, from the editors). Science fiction was thought to be a very masculine pursuit at the time and I know two editors (no names, please, even though both are now dead) who insisted on believing that women *could not* write good science fiction. Pseudonyms were therefore necessary if they were to sell anything at all.

Sometimes, women did not have to use pseudonyms. Their first names might be epicene, and that would be protection enough. Thus, Leslie F. Stone and Leigh Brackett were women but, as far as one could tell from their names, they might have been as masculine as Leslie Fiedler and Leigh Hunt. Editors and readers at first believed they were.

Or women might simply convert names to initials. Could you tell that A. R. Long owned up to the name of Amelia, or that C. L. Moore was Catherine to her friends?

There were other reasons for pseudonyms in science fiction. In the early days of the magazines many of the successful writers could only make a living by writing a great deal just as fast as they could, for a variety of pulp markets. They might use different names for different markets, creating separate personalities, so to speak, that wouldn't compete with each other. Thus Will Jenkins wrote for the slicks under his own name but adopted the pseudonym Murray Leinster when he wrote science fiction.

Sometimes, even within the single field of science fiction, particular writers wrote too many stories. They were so good that editors would cheerfully buy, let us say, eighteen stories from them in a particular year in which they only published twelve issues of their magazines. This meant (if you work out the arithmetic carefully) that it would be necessary to run more than one story by them in a single issue now and then, and editors generally have a prejudice against that. Readers would feel they were cheated of variety, or suspect that editors were showing undue favoritism, or who knows what. Therefore some of the stories would be put under a pseudonym.

The pseudonyms might be transparent enough. For instance, Robert A. Heinlein at the height of his magazine popularity wrote half his stories under the name of Anson MacDonald, but Bob's middle initial A. stood for Anson, and MacDonald was the maiden name of his then wife. Similarly, L. Ron Hubbard wrote under the name of René Lafayette, but the initial L. in Hubbard's name was Lafayette, and René was a not too distant version of Ron. Still, as long as the readers were led to believe that not too many stories of one author were included in the inventory, all was well.

Sometimes, an author is so identified with a particular type of story that when he writes another type of story, he doesn't want to confuse the reader by false associations—so he adopts a new name. Thus, John W. Campbell was a writer of superscience stories of cosmic scope, and one day he wrote a story called "Twilight" which was altogether different. He put it under the name of Don A. Stuart (his then wife's maiden name was Dona Stuart, you see) and rapidly made that name even more popular than his own.

Sometimes, an author simply wants to separate his writing activities from his nonwriting activities, if they are of equal importance to him. Thus, a talented teacher at Milton Academy who is named Harry C. Stubbs writes under the name of Hal Clement. He's not hiding. Hal is short for Harry, as all Shakespearian devotees know, and the C. in his full name stands for Clement.

Again, my dear wife has practiced medicine for over thirty years as Janet Jeppson, M.D. As a writer she prefers J. O. Jeppson. The earnings fall into two different slots as far as the IRS is concerned and that makes it convenient for her bookkeeping.

In my own case, I have eschewed pseudonyms almost entirely; I am far too fond of my own name, and far too proud of my writing to want to sail under false colors for *any* reason. And yet, in one or two cases—

Thus in 1951, I was persuaded to write a juvenile science fiction novel in the hope that it would be sold as the beginning of a long-lived television series. (Those were early days, and no one understood how television was going to work.) I objected, very correctly I think, that TV might ruin the stuff and make me ashamed of having my name associated with it. My editor said, "Then use a pseudonym."

I did, plucking Paul French out of the air for the purpose, and eventually wrote six novels under that name. (Some people, with little knowledge of science fiction, assumed from this that *all* my s.f. was written as Paul French, a suggestion that simply horrified me.)

As soon as it was clear that TV was not interested in my juveniles, I dropped all pretense and made use of the Three Laws of Robotics, for instance, which was a dead giveaway. Eventually, when it was time for new printings, I had my own name put upon it.

Again, in 1942, I wrote a short story for an editor who wanted it done under a pseudonym in order to give the impression that it was by a brand-new author. (The reason is complicated and I won't bore you with it. You'll find it in my autobiography.) I wrote it, reluctantly, under the name George E. Dale but eventually included it in my book *The Early Asimov* as a story of my own.

Also in 1942, I sold a story to the magazine *Super Science Stories* which printed it under the pseudonym H. B. Ogden for reasons I no longer remember. (Even my memory has its limits.) So little did I care for the story, and so unhappy was I over the nonuse of my name, that I totally forgot about it, until nearly forty years later when I was going over my diary carefully in order to prepare my autobiography.

I was shocked to find there was a story of mine that I had forgotten and didn't own in printed form. Fortunately, with the help of Forrest J Ackerman I got the issue and reprinted the story in the first volume of my autobiography, *In Memory Yet Green,* acknowledging it as my own.

In 1971, I was persuaded to write a book entitled *The Sensuous Dirty Old Man,* in which I gently satirized sexual how-to books such as *The Sensuous Woman.* Since the latter book was written by a writer identified only as J, my editor felt the joke should be carried on by having my book written by Dr. A. Even before publication day, however, it was announced that I was the author and my identity was never a secret.

At the present moment, then, absolutely none of my writing appears under anything but my own name.

✦

AFTERWORD: In the United States, ethnic names are sometimes converted into insipid Anglo-Saxon to cater to the prejudices of the public or to place on marquees or for ease of pronunciation. I was dreadfully afraid, when I was trying to become a writer, that I would be asked to change my name to something as bland as (to select a name at random) Arthur Clarke. I would have refused, of course, but, fortunately, I was never asked.

26

We're Doing Well

I HAVE ALWAYS LOOKED UPON THE science fiction writing fraternity as a family, and, as it happens, I am proud of that family. We are doing well.

There was a time when to be a science fiction writer was to be part of a group that elicited smiles at best and contempt at worst. We had to huddle together against the vast enemy outside and that was, in my opinion, the cause of the birth of the strong family feeling we now all have. I don't feel bad about that; I think it was worth it. What we gained was ample repayment for what we thought we suffered.

The time of huddling is gone, however. The science fiction writer is no longer looked down upon merely by virtue of his occupation. He is, instead, accorded a measure of respect as a person of imagination and as a futurist. Once his work begins to be acknowledged outside the field, he is considered an authority. What's more, the taint of science fiction does no damage.

Let me give you a personal example. The New York *Times Sunday Magazine* asked me to write an article on my views on "creationism," which I was delighted to do. I wrote the article, and it was published on 14 June 1981. Before its appearance, the *Times* called to ask me what to put in the one-sentence identification of the author that they run with every article.

I gave them the current number of my books and the topics they dealt with, as well as my academic title and affiliation.

Then, in a sudden access of caution, I said, "And listen, perhaps you had better not use the phrase 'science fiction.' I am fighting an active, insidious force that will stop at nothing to further its ends and I don't want to give them a free stick with which to strike at science. I don't want to give them the chance of writing letters that begin: 'It is significant that a cheap science fiction writer would support evolutionary doctrine which is strictly science fiction to begin with.'"

"Nonsense," said the *Times*. "You are best known as a science fiction writer and that goes in."

So it came about that the identification read: "Isaac Asimov, a professor of biochemistry at Boston University School of Medicine, is the author of 232 books, including science fiction, books on literature, history, science, mathematics and the Bible."

Science fiction, you will note, took pride of place. It didn't bother the *Times* and, to my astonishment, it was not mentioned in the numerous indignant letters from creationists that reached me after the article appeared. —I had underestimated the respectability of the field.

Nor am I the only science fiction writer in the public eye.

Consider Harlan Ellison, who is, to my way of thinking, the most colorful personality the field has ever produced.

He is a much sought-after lecturer, and his off-the-cuff performances (which I have heard on a number of occasions) are invariably bravura examples of his ability to hold an audience transfixed for several hours at a time. His comments range over a wide variety of subjects. He supports, with the utmost vigor, such causes as feminism, gun control, pluralism, and so on.

Now I strongly agree with Harlan on all these matters, and on many others. In fact, the only time I ever felt that we were on opposite sides of the fence was when I maintained the importance of science in science fiction. As many of you know, I insist that even when there is no overt science in a science fiction story, the writer *must* have a reasonable understanding of modern science in order that he avoid making scientific errors.

Here, I felt, Harlan might disagree with me, for his stories rarely involve science directly. In fact, he prefers not to have them categorized as science fiction. They are nothing more or less than "Ellison fiction," for no one else writes exactly as he does.

Imagine, then, my delight, when I came across the following passage in Harlan's column in the September 1981 issue of *Future Life*. He said:

"Look: One of the basic tenets of *good* science fiction has always been that it has an intellectual content that sets it apart from and above the usual sprint of merely entertainment diversions. While we'll suspend our disbelief to allow James Bond or Burt Reynolds to jump a car in a way that we know defies gravity and the laws of impact or whiplash, we balk at permitting that kind of mickeymouse stunt in a SF film, because we know that science fiction deals with the laws of the known universe and its accepted physics."

Good for you, Harlan! I'm proud of you.

Or consider Ben Bova, first an editor of *Analog* and later editorial director of *Omni*. He was, and still is, a science fiction writer, and, in his role as editor, he has done much to encourage good science fiction writing by others.

But he is doing more. He is becoming one of the outstanding spokesmen in the United States for the advance into space.

I have heard him talk on the subject, and I have read what he has written on the subject. He is calm, he is knowledgeable, he is persuasive. In particular, he has published a book called *The High Road* (Houghton Mifflin, 1981) which I recommend to all of you. In it, he discusses every facet of the coming space-age technology, and I would like to quote from his introductory page:

A new space race has begun, and most Americans are not even aware of it.

The race is not merely between two nations jockeying for political prestige or military power. This new race involves the whole human species in a contest against time. All of the people of Earth are in a desperate race against global disaster . . .

To save the Earth we must look beyond it, to interplanetary space . . .

This new space race, in reality, is a crucial struggle against human-kind's ancient and remorseless enemies: hunger, poverty, ignorance, and death.

We must win this race, for one brutally simple reason: survival.

There! That's saying it as it is, in plain, forceful English. And what it makes clear is that all the arguments against going out into space are arguments against survival—neither more nor less.

Good for you, Ben! I'm proud of you.

There are others of the science fiction fraternity who make their voice felt in the outside world, speaking loudly in favor of science, of technological advance, of a viable future, of *human survival*. And they are all listened to with respect.

Included, for instance, are Arthur Clarke, Jerry Pournelle, Larry Niven, Poul Anderson, Fred Pohl— I don't always agree with all their views from a political or economic standpoint, but that's not important. I do agree with their technophile views and that *is* important.

Even Ray Bradbury, who is somehow the epitome of all there is in science fiction that does not involve science, and who is much more a poet than a scientist, is a powerful and respected voice in favor of space exploration and use.

And no one derides any of us as "mere science fiction writers."

So we're doing well.

Of course, it might seem to you that a science fiction writer only becomes respectable once he manages to crawl out of the pages of his stories and makes a name for himself outside.

Not so! In fact, the reverse is to be found. There are well-known cases of scientists who have attempted to write science fiction, sometimes successfully, and who have published under their own names—making no effort whatever to hide their shame, because there is no shame connected with it. The well-known astronomer Fred Hoyle has been, until recently, the most spectacular example of this.

But now we have someone else. Right now, the best-known scientist in the world is the astronomer Carl Sagan. He has written numerous articles on science for the general public and has been a firmly outspoken opponent of such exercises in pseudoscientific nonsense as Velikovskian catastrophes, von Däniken-ish extraterrestrial visitations, and Ufological kidnappings.

He has written bestselling books such as *The Cosmic Connection* and *The Dragons of Eden* (the latter winning a Pulitzer Prize). He has become a remarkable television personality first, with his appearance on nationally syndicated talk shows and then with his spectacular television series "Cosmos." Following that, he put his "Cosmos" performance into book form and it became a runaway sales phenomenon.

And in order to top all this, what is he doing?

Why, he is writing a science fiction novel!

Good for you, Carl! I'm proud of you.

◆

AFTERWORD: It took a while, but Carl Sagan's novel was finally finished and published under the name of *Contact*. It was, as we all expected it to be, a bestseller.

Outsiders, Insiders

I AM A GREAT BOOSTER OF "THE brotherhood of science fiction." I wrote an essay on the subject, with just that title, which appeared in *Asimov on Science Fiction*. I delight in thinking of us ardent writers and readers of science fiction as a band of brothers (and sisters, of course) fond of each other, and supporting each other.

Unfortunately, there are aspects of such a situation that are not entirely delightful. Let's consider these unfavorable aspects, because if the field of science fiction is to remain as ideal as we all want it to be, we have to see the dangers. We may not be able to defeat those dangers even if we see them, but we certainly can't if we *don't* see them.

For instance, if we are truly a small and intimate band (as I remember us being in the Golden Age of Campbell, though perhaps that may only be the consequence of nostalgia) then there is a danger that we might close our ranks, unfairly and petty-mindedly, against outsiders.

I remember, for instance, when Michael Crichton wrote *The Andromeda Strain* and it hit the bestseller lists. In those days, it had not yet become common for science fiction and fantasy to be actual bestsellers, and here was an "outsider" who had accomplished it. What made him an outsider? Well, he hadn't sold to the magazines. He didn't show up at conventions. He wasn't one of *us*.

There followed reviews in various science fiction prozines and fanzines and it seemed to me, at the time, that they were uniformly unfavorable. I can't judge how justified those reviews might have been, for I never read the book (perhaps because I, too, felt he was an outsider), but there did appear, in my opinion, an extra helping of venom beyond what I usually noticed in unfavorable reviews.

Was that fair? No, it wasn't. Crichton, a person of great talent, went on to be very successful both in his later books (some of them not science fiction) and in movies as well. Our objections to him did not hurt him and he doesn't need us. In retrospect, we might conclude that some of us were petty.

Nor am I trying to preach from some high moral position, implying that I am myself above such things. Not at all.

I went through a period soon after World War II in which I reacted badly (though entirely within myself), and I look back on that period in shame.

When one is part of a small and comparatively insignificant clique, warming oneself in its closeness and camaraderie, what happens if one of the clique suddenly rises and becomes famous in the wide world outside?

Thus, in the 1940s, Robert Heinlein was quickly accepted as the best science fiction writer of us all (and in the opinion of many, he still is *the* grand master) and I accepted that, too. I was not envious, for I was just a beginner and I knew that many writers were better than I was. Besides, I liked Bob's writing a great deal. And most of all, he was one of *us,* writing for the same magazines, going to the same conventions, corresponding with us, first-naming us and expecting us to first-name him, and so on.

But then, soon after World War II, Bob Heinlein was involved with a motion picture, *Destination Moon.* It wasn't a very good motion picture; it didn't make the hit that the later *2001: A Space Odyssey* or *Star Wars* did. But it was the first motion picture involving one of *us,* and while I said not a word, I was secretly unhappy. Bob had left our group and become famous in the land of the infidels.

To make it worse, he had published "The Green Hills of Earth" in *The Saturday Evening Post* and it had created a stir. It was a real science fiction story and it was in the slicks—not only in the slicks, but in the greatest and slickest slick of them all. We all dreamed of publishing in the *SEP* (I, also) but that was like dreaming of taking out Marilyn Monroe on a date. You knew it was just a dream and you had no intention of even *trying* to make it come true. And now Bob had done it. He hadn't just tried, he had *done* it.

I don't know whether I simply mourned his loss, because I thought that now he would never come back to us, or whether I was simply and greenly envious. All I knew was that I felt more and more uncomfortable. It was like having a stomachache in the mind, and it seemed to spoil all my fun in being a science fiction writer.

So I argued it out with myself—not because I am a noble person but because I hated feeling the way I did, and I wanted to feel better. I said to myself that Bob had blazed new trails, and that it didn't matter *who* did it, as long as it was done. Those new trails had been opened not for Robert Heinlein, but for *science fiction* and all of us who were in the business of writing or reading science fiction could be grateful and thankful, for we would sooner or later experience the benefit of Bob's pioneering.

And that was true. Because Bob made science fiction look good to people who did not ordinarily read science fiction, and who despised it when they thought of it at all, it became more possible for the rest of us to have our stuff published outside the genre magazines—even in the *SEP*. (I had a two-part serial published in that magazine myself eventually, but that was when it was long past its great days.)

The result of my working this out meant I was free of sickness on later occasions. When my first book, *Pebble in the Sky*, appeared under the Doubleday imprint, it was followed in a matter of months by *The Martian Chronicles* by Ray Bradbury. I don't have to tell you that Ray's book far outshone mine. It didn't bother me, for it seemed to me that the better Ray's book did, the more people would read science fiction in book form, and some of them would be sure to look for more of the same and stumble over mine. And they did. *Pebble* is still earning money, thirty-eight years later.

And however annoying it might be that Michael Crichton could enter our field straight out of medical school, move right up to the novel level, and land on the bestseller list, and have everyone drooling over him, where's the harm? He did it (unintentionally, perhaps) for *us*. He added to the respectability of science fiction among those who found us unrespectable, and made it easier for the rest of us to get on the bestseller list occasionally.

Far from snarling, we should have been cheering.

—Another point. A band of brothers (and sisters) is at its best when there is nothing much to compete for. As long as we were all getting no more than one and two cents a word (as we did in that wonderful Golden Age of Campbell) with no chance at book publication, foreign sales, and movies; as long as the only kudos we could get was first place in the Analytical Laboratory which meant a half cent a word bonus; as long as no one outside our small field had ever heard of any of us under any circumstances—what was there to compete for? The most successful of us were almost as permanently impecunious as the least, so there was no reason to snarl and bite.

Now, however, times have changed. There are many more of us, and some of us write bestsellers. In fact, the greatest bestseller of the 1980s, Stephen King, is, after a fashion, one of us. It's no longer a few thousand bucks that's at stake; it's a few million. And that brother bit fades, bends, and crumples under the strain.

I don't write reviews, but I do read them, and I'm beginning to see the venom again as one writer discusses the work of another member of the brotherhood. What's more, the annual award of the Nebulas, which are determined by vote among the members of the Science Fiction Writers of America, seems to rouse hard feeling and contentiousness every year. The stakes are simply too high.

Thus, a young member of the brotherhood (to *me* he seemed a child) complained to me the other day that the "young writers" (young to *him*) were ferocious in their competitiveness. There was none of the friendliness, he said, that there was in *our* day (meaning his and mine, though I was a published writer when he was born).

I suppose he's right, though.

In a way, I can't ache to return to the good old days when we were all impoverished together. It seems a glamorous time in my mind now, but I remember Sophie Tucker's immortal dictum: "I've tried poor, and I've tried rich, and rich is better."

But is there a price we must pay for it? Must the camaraderie be gone? Must the friendly back-and-forth be over?

Why not remember that science fiction is still a relatively specialized field; that s.f. writers have to know a great deal more, and develop more unusual skill, than is needed by ordinary writers; that s.f. readers, too, demand more because they need more? Can we remember that we're all in this together? That those in front pave the way for those behind? That at any time someone can appear from the strange land of outside, or the stranger land of youth, and carve out new territory for all of us, and that they should be welcomed gladly?

Let's be friends. There are endless worlds of the mind and emotions to conquer, and we can advance more surely if we support—not fight—each other.

♦

AFTERWORD: It was the reference to Crichton's *The Andromeda Strain* in the above essay that elicited a letter from a reader that, in turn, elicited my essay "The Kiss of Death?" which appears as Chapter 6 in this book.

28

Civil War

S CIENCE FICTION WRITERS HAVE
always disagreed among themselves over issues of the day, including issues
both in and out of science fiction itself. Why not? They are thinking people
and thinking people are bound to disagree on this or that. What is more, they
tend to be creative, articulate, and, in many cases, cantankerous people, and the
disagreements can be loud and boisterous.

On controversial issues within science fiction, I remember some particularly grim disagreements. I'm thinking of John Campbell's last decades when
he took up such peculiar causes as psi powers, dianetics, the Dean drive, the
Hieronymus machine, and so on. There was always the possibility that the
Campbell market (the best in science fiction) might be harder to crack for a
writer if his opposition to these bits of curiosa were too loud, but that didn't
stop a number of writers from speaking up in opposition to Campbell's views.

However, these disagreements interested only science fiction people and
the tempests, however stormy, were in an invisibly small teapot as far as the
rest of the world was concerned.

There were, of course, disagreements on world issues, too, among science fiction writers and readers. During the 1930s, there were, I am sure,
science fiction writers who were more anti-Fascist than anti-Communist, some
who were more anti-Communist than anti-Fascist, and some who were isola-
tionist and bade the rest of the world go to Hades. In 1938, New York City
fandom was riven in two and a portion of the science fiction society was
evicted for being too vocally anti-Fascist. The expelled portion promptly

formed a group commonly referred to as "the Futurians," and it became the most unusual science fiction fan club in history. The majority of its members went on to become important names in the world of professional science fiction. (Yes, I was an early member, though I joined after the expulsion had taken place.)

Perhaps the most divisive issue afflicting the field, among those issues that had nothing to do with science fiction itself, came in the 1960s. The Vietnam War, which tore apart the American people more bitterly than anything since the Civil War, tore apart science fiction writerdom as well. Why not? We, too, are the people.

It went so far that, at one time, one of the science fiction magazines ran two competing full-page advertisements: one calling for an end to the Vietnam War and the withdrawal of all American troops, and one calling for the vigorous prosecution of the Vietnam War to victory. Each was signed by a long list of science fiction writers, and I was on the side of withdrawal.

My own point of view was a simple one. I harked back to the statement of the shrewd (if unprincipled) Joseph Fouchet, who headed Napoleon's secret police, and who said of the illegal execution of the Duc d'Enghien, carried through at Napoleon's order, "It was worse than a crime, it was a blunder." So I said, in a letter I wrote at the time, "I am against the Vietnam War, not because it is an unjust and immoral war, something that is always a matter of dispute; but because it is a *stupid* war, something that is beyond dispute." Almost everyone agrees with me *now*, but that is cold comfort.

At the time, however, no one outside the science fiction field took notice of our own Homeric struggle. No one cared. After all, we were just a bunch of science fiction writers.

But now we are making headlines.

Some time ago, the New York *Times* ran an article on the fact that science fiction writers disagreed on Reagan's "Star Wars" project. I was quoted against it and Jerry Pournelle was quoted for it and both of us had our photos prominently displayed. What followed rather took me aback—for I didn't expect it. I began to be called by reporters who wanted to interview me on Star Wars, by publications who wanted me to write on Star Wars, and so on.

I was eventually interviewed by Peter Rowe of the San Diego *Union*, who crossed the continent to do it, and in the Sunday edition of 21 April 1985, there was a prominent article headlined THE DIZZYING STAR WARS DEBATE with the subheadline "ANGRY SCI-FI [*sic*] WRITERS ARGUE—and there is my photograph, with me looking as handsome as a movie star. I am quoted extensively, with Arthur Clarke on my side and with Jerry Pournelle, Robert Heinlein, and others on the other side.

The disagreement seems to be as deep and emotional as it was over the Vietnam War, but this time the civil war among science fiction writers is making headlines and is being featured prominently in the press. Why?

Two reasons. First, and more generally, science fiction writers have been growing more newsworthy steadily over the years. We are no longer laughable little people writing for obscure magazines with peculiar names. A number of us, such as Heinlein, Clarke, Frank Herbert, Anne McCaffrey, and others—even I—have been turning out bestsellers and have been sweeping in big bucks, and that impresses the public far more than the fact that each of us is full of brains and beauty.

Secondly, Reagan's Star Wars seems to be peculiarly science fiction in origin. According to the article in the San Diego *Union* an organization headed by Jerry Pournelle and called The Citizens Advisory Council for National Space Policy sent Reagan a communication in 1981, a year and a half before his Star Wars speech, calling for space-based antimissile defenses. The article doesn't say that Reagan derived his idea from this communication, but it strikes me that he might have been influenced by it.

If so, I can only hope that this won't be held against us when the Star Wars madness finally collapses (as, in my opinion, it eventually must).

Now we come to the part that really bothers me. Until now, none of the disagreements over issues, whether science fiction in nature or not, has seemed to become personal. I bitterly disagreed with Campbell over his fringe enthusiasms but remained his close personal friend to the end of his life. I have disagreed with Heinlein and Poul Anderson on political views for forty years now, but this has not affected my friendship, during all those decades, with either one. An essay by Pournelle in this magazine goaded me into an answering essay (see Chapter 55), as did one by Anderson (see Chapter 36). I can't easily imagine how I could disagree with anyone more intensely and emotionally than I disagree with Pournelle, but when I meet Jerry we greet each other amicably.

I think this is important. In any civilized society, disagreements must be talked out, not beaten out. The disagreement is with the *views,* not with the person. The aim is to persuade, not to destroy.

But now blood is being drawn. According to the *Union* article, Arthur

Clarke argued against Star Wars at a meeting of Pournelle's council and was shouted down. He was told that it was presumptuous for him to try to tell the United States what to do when he was not an American citizen.

That was a horrible thing to say for a number of reasons.

1) Arthur is one of *us*, and who can be aware of the importance of viewing humanity as a whole if science fiction people do not? It is we who are forever speaking of "Earthmen" and "Terrans." Is it for us now to deify the little splinter groups that separate us into suspicious, hating, warring factions?

2) Arthur has specifically been asked his opinion on space matters. More than once he has testified before committees of the Congress. No one questioned the nature of his citizenship on these occasions.

3) The United States is encouraging Europeans to speak up on behalf of Star Wars and to lobby Congress in its favor. Have they the right to speak in favor but not against?

4) Star Wars, and all matters involved in nuclear war, affect the whole world. If the United States does something which might increase the possibilities of nuclear war, that will affect, and possibly destroy, every nation, not merely ourselves. In fact, if Star Wars should merely savage our economy that, too, will affect every nation. Must foreigners nevertheless cower in a corner and wait for possible destruction without daring to say a word?

5) Is this a general rule? Has no one the right to criticize, or even discuss, the policies of a nation unless he is a citizen of that nation? If so, by what right do Americans constantly berate the Soviet Union for *their* internal policies, and *their* military plans? None of us are Soviet citizens. For that matter, what gives Reagan the right to call the Soviet Union an "evil empire"? He is not a Soviet citizen.

I hope the newspaper misreported the event. I hope whoever made that crude and Neanderthal remark (if, indeed, it was made) did so only in the momentary heat of debate, and apologized afterward.

If not, then Arthur was greatly wronged and I regret that bitterly.

AFTERWORD: After this essay appeared, I received an aggrieved letter from Jerry Pournelle, complaining that I had no direct knowledge of the matter and that Arthur Clarke had been perfectly friendly throughout and had not been offended. However, I didn't back off. I quoted my source in the essay, and I was careful to make it clear that I had no personal knowledge of the affair and that the newspaper report might not be completely accurate. However, everything I said, on the assumption that the newspaper report was reasonably correct, I stand by and won't retract. As for Clarke not being offended, I know him to be, by *personal* knowledge, an amiable, pleasant fellow who is not easily offended. I am not quite as amiable, however, and *if* the incident took place as reported, then I am offended on his behalf.

SCIENCE
FICTION AND
SCIENCE ✦

29

Catastrophes

N MY ESSAY ENTITLED "CONTRO-
versy" (see Chapter 46), I listed a few examples of pseudoscientific nonsense
and included, among them, Velikovskianism. I was not surprised to get a letter
denouncing me for that. Here is one of the things the letter writer said:

"There is still a flailing out at a Velikovsky cult. I doubt if there is any
such group in existence . . . He could be let [sic] to rest in peace."

Alas, there is an active Velikovsky cult. If anyone doesn't believe that,
let him denounce it in print as I, on occasion, do, and then sit back and wait
for the letters.

And I am perfectly willing to allow Immanuel Velikovsky to rest in
peace. There remain, however, his ideas that are still alive and are upheld with
emotional fervor by a bunch of fringers (i.e., those who are to be found on the
scientific fringe) and which, as a rational scientist, I am compelled to fight.

I would be glad not to label those ideas "Velikovskianism" and thus
allow their originator to sink into peaceful oblivion, but his supporters use his
name freely in connection with those ideas, and I have no choice but to do the
same.

The letter writer also denounces what he calls "gradualism" but what is
more often called "uniformitarianism" by historians of science. Let me explain.

In the early 1800s there were two views of the history of the Earth. One
was upheld by a French scientist, Georges Cuvier. He studied fossils with great
skill and is the revered father of paleontology. However, he was also a fer-
vently religious Protestant and, while recognizing the great age the Earth had

to have, he could not abandon the opening chapters of Genesis. He suggested, therefore, that every once in a while the Earth was subjected to a vast Flood that wiped out life. There followed a new creation. The Bible, he maintained, dealt only with the most recent creation, while the fossils were remnants of earlier creations. In making this suggestion he lent his great (and deserved) prestige to the idea of "catastrophism," first advanced a half century earlier by a Swiss naturalist, Charles Bonnet.

On the other hand, a Scottish geologist, Charles Lyell, published a three-volume book between 1830 and 1833, in which he marshaled the evidence in the favor of a steady and *uniform* evolution of the Earth—a uniform laying down of sediments, of erosion of mountains, and so on—with no interruption by life-destroying catastrophes. In this book, he popularized the idea of uniformitarianism first advanced nearly half a century earlier by another Scottish geologist, James Hutton. It can be called "gradualism," if one wishes.

In the controversy that followed, Lyell won out. As the fossil record was studied more extensively and intensively, it became clear that at no time since life first came into being some 3.5 billion years ago did any catastrophe take place that wiped out all of life and made a new creation necessary.

My letter writer says, "Gradualism . . . is dead . . . A Reformation has converted the scientific world. Velikovsky could feel right at home."

The implication is that Velikovsky back in the 1950s introduced the idea of catastrophes again, and that although scientists denounced him, they have quietly accepted all sorts of catastrophes (my letter writer lists a few) and produced a Velikovskian world.

This, of course, is a laughable distortion that arises, I believe, out of ignorance rather than malevolence.

Extreme uniformitarianism is not true, and never was. The notion that no catastrophes at all exist cannot be maintained and never was maintained. Even Hutton knew of volcanic eruptions and of earthquakes. To be sure, since the time of Hutton and Lyell, we have learned of new catastrophic events they knew nothing about. Ice ages are catastrophes; large meteor strikes are catastrophes; novas and supernovas are catastrophes; but these were discovered and appreciated long before Velikovsky.

What's more, paleontologists have discovered periods of "great dyings," during which many species of organisms suddenly became extinct for no clear reason, but possibly in response to some catastrophe. The most dramatic such incident involves the disappearance of the dinosaurs (and many other forms of life) at the end of the Cretaceous, 65 million years ago. Nowadays, some paleontologists suggest that such great dyings take place regularly at 26-million-year intervals, and wonder if this might be caused by the periodic invasion of the distant cometary cloud by a hitherto unobserved dwarf star that is a companion of our Sun.

Someone once said that war consisted of long stretches of boredom interrupted by short intervals of stark terror. In the same way, the evolution of the Earth consists of long stretches of uniform development interrupted by brief catastrophes—where those catastrophes have never yet been large enough to wipe out all of life, so that evolution remains continuous, as Lyell maintained and Cuvier denied. Consequently, Lyell is still right and Cuvier still wrong.

Now, then, what Velikovsky did was not to argue catastrophism versus uniformitarianism on some general basis. He insisted on a *particular* catastrophe. He suggested that about 1500 B.C., a massive object was hurled out of Jupiter, passed near the Earth, produced all the plagues described in the Book of Exodus, rained manna on Earth to feed the fleeing Israelites, at one point stopped the rotation of the Earth when Joshua ordered the Sun to stand still and then started it again with the same rate as before. The object returned later to bring about certain miracles described in the Book of Isaiah and then settled down to a nearly circular orbit as the planet Venus. All this he based on vague legends, myths, and medieval wonder-tales.

Now, then, any reasonably educated scientist with a sense of humor would, in the 1950s, when Velikovsky first published his book, *Worlds in Collision,* have burst out laughing, and many did. They are *still* laughing. Scientists without a sense of humor, upon witnessing the manner in which the newspapers and magazines fell upon Velikovsky's views and treated them as "science," were outraged and are still outraged.

I was one of the laughers and wrote a review that hilariously ripped the book into shreds—whereupon the newspaper that had requested the review refused to publish it. (It was not Velikovsky who was censored, but the anti-Velikovskians, believe me.) And I laugh now, too. Velikovsky's ideas are, from top to bottom, a load of bat guano. He, himself, however, is an interesting writer and, apparently, a sincere and resolute man. I have nothing against him personally, only against his ideas.

Nothing that astronomers, geologists, and biologists have discovered, either before or since Velikovsky published his book, has in any way supported the specific catastrophe the man described. The discovery of *other* types of catastrophes at *other* times, and on physical evidence more sensible than ancient fiction, has nothing to do with Velikovskianism, does not support it, and does not create a world in which Velikovsky would "feel right at home."

There is one person whom Velikovskians are more annoyed with than they are with me and that is Carl Sagan. To be sure, my letter writer can't resist mentioning him, although mildly, and without any really hard words. My letter writer doesn't seem to be a bad sort of fellow. He's wrong, but we all manage to be wrong once in a while.

In the same issue in which my essay mentioning Velikovskianism appeared, there was also a "Viewpoint" article by Carl Sagan entitled "The Nuclear Winter."

That elicited a letter from a *different* reader altogether, a letter that was far less benign, and that was handwritten in a passion. I gathered the writer was furious at Carl and at all nuclear freeze people and, in fact, at anyone who had a bad word to say for nuclear war.

That saddens me. Are there people who feel it is unpatriotic to do anything that would make it difficult to fight a nuclear war? Are there people who feel that it is important to hurl nuclear destruction at the "evil empire" even if it means having nuclear destruction hurled at us? Are there people whose chests would swell with pride as they watch Earth go down to oblivion, feeling such destruction to be a small price to pay for the privilege of seeing an enemy destroyed, and delighting in being able to watch, with dying eyes, that destruction, plus the destruction of ourselves, our friends, and our allies, and perhaps most or all of the rest of life?

When Patrick Henry said, "Give me liberty, or give me death!" he was speaking of himself personally. Each man has the right to assert his own values for himself—but not for the whole world.

I know not what course others may take, but as for me, let the Earth, and life, and humanity remain and flourish, whatever happens to me.

◆

AFTERWORD: In writing these essays for *Asimov's,* I frequently have the urge to write about science. The trouble is that my monthly essay series in *The Magazine of Fantasy and Science Fiction* is about science and I want to keep the two essay series separate. For the *Asimov's* series, then, I try to deal only with those aspects of science that are of direct interest to science fiction readers. Even so, I've managed to include eleven of my *Asimov's* essays in the category of "science fiction and science."

Moonshine

WHEN I WAS VERY YOUNG, I read a number of stories and saw several motion pictures which featured some unfortunate individual who tended to turn into a wolf at the time of the full Moon.

The logic behind this troubled me, however. Why the full Moon? I had frequently seen the full Moon and been exposed to its light and I had felt no effect of any kind as a result. Was moonshine substantially different from sunshine or from artificial light?

For that matter, was the light of a full Moon different from the light of a Moon one day past the full, or one day before it? I could hardly tell the difference in the Moon's shape on those three days. How could a werewolf tell, therefore, and on an all-or-nothing basis, too? Shouldn't such a werewolf turn 95 percent wolf on the day before or after the full Moon? In fact, should he not turn half wolf on the night of the half Moon?

I could work out no satisfactory answers to such questions and the easiest way out was to decide that werewolves could not be affected by the Moon in the manner described. (As I grew older, I began to realize there were much more serious questions raised by this matter of human beings turning into wolves, and concluded that there could be no such things as werewolves.)

This business of attributing strange powers to moonshine continues, however. Every once in a while, for instance, I hear of reports concerning statistical studies that seem to show that drugs have pronouncedly different effects on the human body according to the phases of the Moon, that crimes of violence, homicide, and suicide are particularly numerous when the Moon is full, and so on and so on. This makes it seem that there may be something to old folk-beliefs concerning the importance of the Moon, such as the one that different plants ought to be sowed at particular phases of the Moon.

As a science fiction writer, I'm automatically attracted to such suggestions because of the plot suggestions to which they give rise, if nothing else; but, as a scientist, I must stop and consider—all the more so since I can't trust myself, in my s.f. writer aspect, to be objective.

First, I know very well that human beings have been aware of the changing shape of the Moon from prehistoric times. The first calendars were based on the Lunar cycle, and various religious, mathematical, and scientific concepts arose out of that cycle. The Moon was so incredibly important to the early thinking of humanity that it is only natural to suppose that all sorts of powers would have been attributed to the Moon that it may very likely fail to have in actual fact. (Thus, the connection between Moon and insanity is considered to be nonsense, but it is, nevertheless, enshrined in our word "lunacy.")

It is possible, therefore, that people are so predisposed to believe in Moon effects that in gathering statistics on the matter, they are unconsciously swayed in their data selection in such a way as to demonstrate what they already tend to believe; i.e., that human behavior varies with the phases of the Moon.

And yet suppose that, as more and more statistics were gathered, the results were to become irrefutable, and that it had to be admitted that the phases of the Moon had important effects on human behavior. How could that be explained?

One might conclude that moonshine has some powerful effect on human beings for some as yet unknown reason. That, however, although an attractive way out to those with a tendency to mysticism, is bad science. One does *not* fall back on the unknown until all possible known effects have been investigated and found wanting.

For instance, one obvious factor that changes with the phases of the Moon is the quantity of light that falls upon the landscape at night. In the preindustrial era, people who had to travel by night would prefer, if they could, to travel during the week of the full Moon so that there would be as much light as possible (assuming the absence of clouds). For similar reasons, when Astronomy Island (a group of amateur astronomers) carries through its annual summer expedition to Bermuda to observe the stars, they invariably choose the week of the new Moon so that the light of the stars won't be washed out in moonshine.

It is not that kind of behavior (voluntary and logical) we're interested in, however. What about the effect of the Moon on reaction to drugs or on psychopathology? Is there anything about the Moon's light that is different from that of the Sun? After all, moonshine is only reflected sunshine. To be sure, the light from the Moon is partly polarized, but so is scattered light from the daytime sky partly polarized.

One thing the Moon *does* affect is the tides. The pull of the Moon, exerted with greater intensity on the side of the Earth facing it than on the side opposite, produces two humps of water, and any given spot on Earth turns through these humps at half-day intervals. What's more, the humps of water grow higher or lower as the Moon's phases change. The phases change as the position of the Moon with respect to the Sun changes, and when the Sun is pulling in a direction parallel to that of the Moon (at full Moon or new Moon), the humps are highest. When the Sun is pulling in a direction at right angles to that of the Moon (at either half Moon), the humps are lowest.

It follows then that every half day there is a high-tide/low-tide cycle, and every two weeks a high-high-tide/low-high-tide cycle.

Can these tide cycles affect human beings? At first thought, one doesn't see how, but it is certain that they affect creatures who spend their lives at or near the seashore. The ebb and flow of the tide must be intimately involved with the rhythm of their lives. Thus, the time of highest tide may be the appropriate occasion to lay eggs, for instance. The behavior of such creatures therefore seems to be related to the phases of the Moon. That is not mysterious if you consider the Moon/tide/behavior connection. If, however, you leave out the intermediate stop and consider only a Moon/behavior connection, you change a rational view into a semimystical one.

But what connection can there be between worms and fish living at the edge of the sea, and human beings?

Surely there is an evolutionary connection. We may consider ourselves far removed from tidal creatures *now* but we are descended from organisms that, 400 million years ago, were probably living at the sea-land interface and were intimately affected by tidal rhythms.

Yes, but that was 400 million years ago. Can we argue that the tidal rhythms of those days would affect us now? It doesn't seem likely, but it is a conceivable possibility.

After all, we might argue it out thus—

We still have a few bones at the bottom end of our spine that represent all that is left of a tail that our ancestors haven't had for at least 20 million years. We have an appendix that is the remnant of an organ that hasn't been used by our ancestors for even longer. In the same way, whales and pythons have small bones that represent the hind legs their ancestors once had many millions of years ago; the young hoatzin bird has two claws on each wing that date back to the eons before birds developed full-fledged wings; the horse has thin bones that represent all that is left of two side hooves each leg once had but has no longer. In our own case, we (and other mammals), as embryos, even develop the beginnings of gills that quickly disappear, but that hark back to when our ancestors were sea creatures.

Such vestigial organs are well known and occur in almost all organisms (and represent extremely strong evidence in favor of biological evolution). Why should there not also be vestigial remnants of ancestral biochemical or psychological properties? In particular, why should we not retain some aspects of the old tidal rhythms?

Our complex minds might still sway rhythmically in the half-day and fourteen-day tidal cycles that affected our ancestors so many millions of years ago. This would be unusual and surprising but, nevertheless, rational and believable. To omit the tidal component of the chain of cause and effect, however, and to suppose that our behavior sways with the phases of the Moon is likely to send us on a mystical chase after nothing.

How can we demonstrate this tidal rhythm more effectively? Is there anything better than simply continuing to collect data and to correlate behavior with the Moon's phases?

It seems to me that if these rhythms affect such things as our response to drugs or our tendency to violence or depression, then the rhythms must affect our internal workings. There must be a fourteen-day rise and fall in hormone production, or hormone balance, or such a rise and fall in the activity of our immune system, or our cerebral drug receptors, or various aspects of our neurochemistry.

Such variations in our biochemistry would be much more persuasive, it seems to me, than the study of effects that are once or twice removed. We would then have more solid reasoning and less moonshine.

✦

AFTERWORD: After this essay appeared, I received some angry letters from women berating me for not mentioning the menstrual cycle. They seemed to think this showed a deep antifeminist prejudice in me. In every case, I answered by saying that I had never dreamed anyone would think there was a connection. As nearly as I can make out from my knowledge of women, the menstrual cycle is often irregular, sometimes extremely so. Even the average period is not exactly equal to the Lunar cycle, and it's certainly not the case that the onset of menstruation invariably comes at the full Moon or at any other phase. Rather, on any given week, regardless of the phase of the Moon, roughly one quarter of the women of the appropriate age are menstruating. Why, then, is the menstrual period nearly equal to the Lunar cycle? Might there not be such a thing as coincidence? (The menstrual periods of other primates are widely removed from the Lunar cycle, by the way.)

31

Household Robots

I N MY ESSAY "THE INFLUENCE OF Science Fiction" (see Chapter 1), I mentioned my influence on Joseph F. Engelberger, the president of Unimation, Inc., the most important company in the world today as far as the production, installation, and maintenance of robots is concerned. It is the nearest thing, so far, to the fictional U.S. Robots and Mechanical Men, Inc. of my positronic robot stories.

We are today, of course, only at the very beginning of the "age of robots," but already it is a lusty beginning. There are over seventy-five thousand industrial robots in Japan (more than in all the rest of the world combined) and additional robots are being added at the rate of twenty thousand a year. I suspect the rate itself will increase, and that other nations will be making efforts to follow after Japan vigorously in this respect.

It is important, however, to remember that the robots now in existence are by no means the positronic robots of my fiction. They are to my fictional robots rather as a slide rule is to a pocket computer.

The "industrial robots" are merely computerized levers; they are specialized arms controlled by computers. They are so specialized that they are fit only for the most limited tasks and have absolutely nothing in the way of "brains." (This is not surprising. Even among life-forms, extreme specialization obviates the need for intelligence, since the more constricted the capabilities, the less the need for judgement or any capacity for making shrewd decisions.)

This means there is no use talking about the Three Laws of Robotics in their connection.

In the summer of 1981, for instance, an industrial robot in Japan was malfunctioning, and it was necessary for some human being to make repairs. There was a chain fence around the robot that should have been opened before the repairman approached. The opening of that fence would have shut off all power to the robot and that was an externally applied First Law that prevented the robot from harming a human being. That First Law had to be applied by the human being; the robot did not possess it as an inherent part of its structure.

The human being failed to do this. He stepped over the fence, leaving the robot with potential for power. To be sure, he placed the robot on manual so that it wouldn't work unless it was turned on—but then he accidentally nudged the on switch.

The robot automatically got to work. The arm moved down to do what it was designed to do. It caught the employee, pinning him against a machine processing automobile gears. It continued its motion as though it were completing its task, and the employee was killed.

Remember that machinery of all sorts, even very simple machinery, has been killing human beings, by accident, all through history. Remember, too, that in this case, the fault was entirely that of the human being for not opening the fence and for nudging the switch.

Nevertheless, when the news was finally disclosed to the public some months later, newspapers everywhere featured headlines reading ROBOT KILLS MAN.

That gives us a false idea, of course. Somehow, one gets the impression of a vicious robot in ambush, trapping an unwary human being and then bursting out, with slavering jaws, and brutally murdering him.

You would be surprised how many reporters promptly phoned me, demanding an accounting of the reasons why the robot had violated First Law. I got the peculiar notion that they were blaming *me*. And yet it was rather flattering, too, I suppose.

The question is, though: will the time come when robots will be more than computerized levers? When they will look more like human beings? When they will be more nearly subject to the Three Laws? When, in fact, will they come closer to my fictional notions of four decades ago?

I think they inevitably will. I also think the time is not very far off.

As long as they are used in industry only, to be sure, specialization will remain a necessity. They will be items on the assembly line and that doesn't call for much brains even in human employees. (That is why humans, who *do* have brains, are stultified by such jobs, and why they should be reserved for robots.)

Suppose, though, we were considering robots in the household—not robot laborers on the assembly line, but robot servants in the home. In the home, needs are more generalized. You would want a robot to run the various appliances, wash the dishes, serve tea and cakes, take coats, run the vacuum cleaner, brew the coffee, fry the eggs, and so on. It would be ridiculous to have twenty different robots, each specialized into fingers that pushed buttons, or trays that carried teacups. What would be wanted would be a generalized robot that would do all the tasks, perhaps not with the precision of the true specialist—but each of them well enough.

And, as a matter of fact, the research department of Unimation, Inc.—Joseph Engelberger's company—is working on this very thing. A prototype exists, and it is possible that it will be perfected to the point where various models will be on sale for use in the home during the 1990s.

Inevitably, it seems to me, these models will be rather humanoid in shape and, with time, will grow steadily more humanoid. There are two reasons for this.

First, for a generalized robot to do a number of different tasks with adequate skill, it would be best if it was able to use human technology with reasonable ease. It would have to handle the various household appliances, do the dusting, cleaning, washing, arranging, stacking, opening, closing, and so on.

All these things have been designed for human working. Things about the house have been designed to be gripped by human hands, to be pushed by human fingers, to be encompassed within the human reach, to be usable according to the capacity of the human body to stretch and bend. For a robot to make full use of human technology within the home, the robot will have to have a shape that is at least roughly human, that will bend in the same places to the same degree—stretching, pinching, twisting, and so on. And the more the robots are perfected, the closer the duplication will have to be.

After all, to build a technology of totally different design to suit a nonhumanoid robot would be impractically expensive. Besides that, we would want a technology suitable for both because of the fail-safe characteristic. We would want a technology that humans can make use of in default of robots, and vice versa.

Second, a robot working on an assembly line need not interact with human beings, but a robot in the home *must* interact. And if it does do so, it would do so more effectively if it was humanoid in shape. As it gets "friendlier," that is, easier to use, it should get more humanoid in shape—particularly, once it is designed to accept spoken orders and to answer in its own voice.

There's a personal point I must mention in this connection.

Mr. Engelberger expects to have his prototype household robot sufficiently usable to be put to work in his own home by 1985, and it would then be sufficiently humanoid and friendly to deserve a name for itself. In fact, it has already been given a name. The name is Isaac, and it's no accident. It is so named in my honor.

He isn't even the first to do this. There is a four-foot, roughly humanoid robot that has been seen upon many appropriate occasions and, on two occasions, has shared a platform with me. There is even a photograph of me with the robot, with my head resting on its head in a friendly manner, which has been much circulated.

It is not a true robot, merely a device under remote radio control, but its name is Isac—again in my honor, despite the missing *a*. And what is the name of the firm that produces it? Isac Robotics.

In fiction, too, there have been a number of cases of stories written by writers other than myself which have referred to robots by some version of my first or second name.

The connection is unmistakable—and very flattering. Yet it does give rise to certain uneasy thoughts. Is there any possibility that "isaac" may become a generic term for household robots? People may some day be saying, "I bought a new isaac yesterday," or "Just on the day the boss comes to dinner my isaac goes out of order."

And my publishers haven't helped. In 1982, Doubleday published a complete collection of my robot stories. I called it *The Complete Robot Short Story Book,* but my publishers thought that was too long. They cut it in half and the book has come out with the following on the cover in large and conspicuous lettering: ISAAC ASIMOV THE COMPLETE ROBOT.

I'm afraid I'm sunk.

✦

AFTERWORD: It's now six years since the above essay was written and I stated that Joe Engelberger might have a working robot in his home by 1985. Here it is 1988 and, for all I know, he may have one there—but I haven't heard about it. Too bad.

32

The Sun and Moon

I NEVER LECTURE ON ANY ASTRO-
nomical subject without becoming aware of the fuzziness on the part of the
general public concerning the names of the various objects making up the
Universe.

I don't really blame them. Astronomy isn't taught below the college
level and very few people learn astronomy on their own. The vast majority,
therefore, get their knowledge of astronomical terminology from the newspapers, movies, or television, which, on the whole, are rich sources of misinfor-
mation.

Thus, whenever someone asks me a question that includes the phrase
"from another galaxy," I always counter with the question "What's a galaxy?"
Invariably, the original questioner looks puzzled and sometimes aggrieved, as
though only a cad and a bounder would ask that.

It's no disgrace to be unaware of such things if you are a member of the
general public, but it is no great credit, either. We, however, are not members
of the general public. As science fiction readers and writers, we should know
astronomical nomenclature.

Therefore, let's have a small discussion of it.

To the ancient Greeks, all the objects in the sky, every one of them
without exception, was a star *(aster* in Greek). The stars fell into several
categories, however. Most of them turned steadily about the sky while main-
taining their relative positions, just as though the sky were a turning solid
sphere (which is what the ancients thought it was, since they had nothing to

judge by but appearances) with the stars fixed to it like luminous nail-heads. These, therefore, were the "fixed stars."

Some heavenly objects, however, shifted position against the background of the fixed stars, and these were called "wandering stars" (or, in Greek, *aster planetes*, from which we get the English word "planet").

There were seven of these bodies known to the ancients: the Sun, the Moon, Mercury, Venus, Mars, Jupiter, and Saturn.

With the coming of the Copernican system, it became apparent that the Sun was the center about which five of the planets, Mercury, Venus, Mars, Jupiter, and Saturn, circled. It didn't make sense to label the Sun and the other bodies with the same name, since the Sun was huge, shining with its own light, and (as far as the early Copernicans could tell) fixed in space, while the other bodies were small, shone only by reflection, and moved about the Sun. The Sun, therefore, was no longer numbered among the planets.

It was recognized that the fixed stars were objects like the Sun, and that they appeared as mere points of light only because of their vast distance. There was no longer any need of an adjective to distinguish them from the planets. They became simply "stars," a term applied to any object in space that glowed by its own light over extended periods of time.

A question arises immediately. Can "suns" be used as a synonym for "stars"? It often is. In science fiction stories, an extraterrestrial might casually refer to "our sun" to distinguish it from the one that shines in Earth's sky. If a world circled a closely spaced double star and if we imagined intelligent beings on that world, they might fairly refer to "our suns."

That, however, introduces the possibility of confusion and, ideally, language exists to eliminate confusion. It is preferable to use the word "star" generically, for all glowing bodies including our Sun, and to consider each of them as having (at least potentially) a name of its own in addition. In that case, the name of our particular star could be "Sun."

That doesn't quite wash, however. We call it *"the* Sun" and you virtually never see it without the definite article. Proper names don't carry definite articles unless you mean to imply that they are in some way unique. Speaking of *"the* Sun" is a form of home-chauvinism that dates back to the time when it was thought that the Sun was in actual fact unique.

It would be nice if we could therefore give the Sun a particular name. If it had one, then we could refer to those glowing objects as either "stars" or "suns" indiscriminately. In old-fashioned science fiction stories, the Sun was sometimes referred to as Sol, its Latin name. Personally, I would prefer Helios, the Greek name.

Either, however, is a lost cause. No one is going to call the Sun anything but (in English) "the Sun." It's chauvinistic to do so, but until there are extraterrestrials to raise objections, we will continue to do so. In that case, then, for clarity's sake, we should not use "sun" for any other star, but either call them "stars" or use a specific name.

What if a star has, as its only name, something like HD 348876+ in some star catalogue? Well, if for some reason that very star must be used in a story, you can make up a name for it. Human beings have made up names for every conceivable feature they have come across, whether they are a part of the Earth, a part of the body, or a part or wholes of anything.

But back to the "wandering stars." Since five of these revolve about the Sun, it seemed natural to redefine "planet" as any nonluminous body that revolves about the Sun (or, by extension, about any star). Since, by Copernican notions, the Earth, too, revolved about the Sun, the Earth, too, became a planet.

This meant there were six planets: Mercury, Venus, Earth, Mars, Jupiter, and Saturn, listed in the order of distance from the Sun. (Other, still farther planets were eventually discovered.)

But what about the Moon? It revolved about the Sun, too, but only secondarily. It revolved about the Earth and accompanied the Earth on the latter's voyage about the Sun.

Strictly speaking, the Earth and Moon revolve about a common center of gravity and it is this center of gravity that follows a smooth ellipse about the Sun. The Earth, however, is eighty-one times as massive as the Moon and the center of gravity is less than five thousand kilometers from the center of the Earth. It's a reasonable approximation, therefore, to suppose the Moon to be moving about a relatively unmoving Earth.

Since the Moon revolves about the Earth, primarily, rather than directly about the Sun, it is no longer included in the list of planets.

In January 1610, Galileo discovered that there were four small objects circling Jupiter in very much the fashion that the Moon circled the Earth. The Moon, therefore, turned out not to be a unique case. At once, I imagine, people began to speak of "the moons of Jupiter" and they still do. In 1957, I published a book, *Lucky Starr and the Moons of Jupiter*.

That leaves room for confusion, however. If all these bodies are to be known as "moons," and each also has a proper name of its own, then *our* Moon ought to have a name of its own. It could be called Luna from the Latin, or Selene from the Greek.

However, it won't be. It's going to be called *"the* Moon," with Earthly chauvinism, and therefore the name ought not be used for any other object.

Shortly after Galileo discovered the bodies circling Jupiter, Johannes Kepler termed them "satellites," from a Latin expression meaning "attendants."

This is the proper general term. We can speak of "the satellites of Jupiter" or of any other planet, where a "satellite" is any nonluminous body circling a substantially larger nonluminous body. The Moon, in that sense, is Earth's satellite.

If you want to refer to the body about which a particular satellite turns without naming it, you can speak of "the planet that Ganymede revolves about" which is very clumsy. You can take advantage of English's tendency to become telegraphic by speaking of "Ganymede's planet." That would be completely confusing, however. Jupiter is a planet of the Sun; that's clear. To say it is the planet of Ganymede is to use "planet" in two precisely opposite ways.

It is better to speak of a satellite's "primary" (from the Latin for "first"). "Primary" is a perfectly general word, which can be used for the larger of any two bodies that circle each other. Jupiter is Ganymede's primary. The Sun is the Earth's primary. The more massive of a double star system (or the brighter, if we don't know the masses) is the primary of that system, and so on.

But there goes my allotted space. I'll continue this discussion in the next chapter.

33

The Solar System

IN THE PREVIOUS CHAPTER, I DIS-
cussed problems of terminology involving the Sun and Moon. Let's continue.

The Sun and all the bodies that circle it are referred to, en masse, as "the Solar system." This comes from the Latin word Sol for "Sun" and properly indicates the predominance of the Sun. The Sun contains well over 99 percent of the mass of the Solar system, so that to any objective observer, it would seem that the Solar system consists of the Sun and some inconsiderable debris. It is only our special position on one of the pieces of debris that focuses our attention on objects in the Solar system.

The term "Solar system" (or its equivalent in other languages) is comparatively modern. It came into use only after it was understood that the Sun was the center about which everything else in the system revolved.

Science fiction writers and readers, however, often deal with other systems consisting of a central star and its attendant bodies. What do we call them? The temptation is to speak of "other Solar systems"* but that is like having an Englishman speak of other nations as "other Englands." You would know what he meant but it could lend itself to misinterpretation.

Since "Solar system" is named for Sol, the star that centers it, we could speak, individually, of "the Sirian system," "the Capellan system," "the

* Lately, people have been speaking of "other galaxies" when they mean "other Solar systems," a kind of TV illiteracy that is analogous to saying "other continents" when you mean "other towns."

Denebian system," and so on. For a general term, the temptation would be to speak of "stellar systems," from the Latin *stella* meaning "star."

Unfortunately, "stellar system" is a term that can be applied to collections of bodies that include more than one star. A double star or a star cluster might be a stellar system. If we want to speak of one particular star and its attendant planets only, we would have to speak of a "planetary system."

By analogy, if we want to speak of a particular planet and its attendant satellites, we would speak of a "satellite system." (Strictly speaking, one might expect "satellitary system" but such an adjectival form is too clumsy and is never used.)

Our own planetary system, the Solar system, consists of more than the Sun, the planets, and the satellites.

Beginning in 1801, small bodies were discovered with orbits lying between those of Mars and Jupiter. William Herschel early suggested that these be termed "asteroids," from a Greek word meaning "starlike." He suggested this because, through the telescope, the asteroids remained points of light in appearance, like the stars, rather than expanding into visible orbs as the other planets did. (The reason for this was that the new bodies were so much smaller than the longer-known planets.)

The term "asteroid" made some people uncomfortable. After all, the asteroids were not starlike in any way except their appearance through a telescope. Other names were therefore substituted. Sometimes, they were called "planetoids," meaning "planetlike," but if you stop to think of it, that's unfair. The asteroids are nonluminous bodies circling the Sun, and that makes them planets and not merely planetlike.

But if their only difference, compared to other planets, is their small size, they might be called "minor planets." They might even be called "planetesimals," the "-esimal" suffix indicating small size by analogy with the term "infinitesimal."

These, however, are relative terms and we might imagine that an intelligent inhabitant of Jupiter would be only too prone to classify Earth as a minor planet, or even as a planetesimal. In addition, the word "planetesimal" is already in use for the small objects that coalesced to form the planets during the early stages of the formation of the Solar system.

We are therefore forced back to "asteroid" which is, and will probably remain, the most common term for very small planets. The region between Mars and Jupiter is commonly termed the "asteroid belt" since that is where most of the asteroids are found, although some are now known that approach the Sun more closely than Mercury does, and others that recede as far from the Sun as Uranus does.

If the only difference between a planet and an asteroid is the matter of size, what particular size shall we set up as the boundary? That's purely arbitrary, of course, but in our own planetary system, the smallest object generally accepted as a planet is Mercury, which has a diameter of about five thousand kilometers. The largest object generally accepted as an asteroid is Ceres, which has a diameter of about one thousand kilometers.

It would seem that, in general, we might therefore take one thousand kilometers as a nice round dividing point. Any object with a diameter of one thousand kilometers or less that circles a star is an asteroid; anything larger is a planet.

There are at least eight satellites (including the Moon) that have diameters of more than one thousand kilometers and that would be considered respectable planets if they circled the Sun directly. Still, they don't, so satellites they remain.

Very small satellites could be referred to as "satellitesimals" according to the dictionary but I have never seen or heard the term used.

To another subject. Every once in a while, if we watch the sky on a dark night, we will see a streak of light that will only last a few seconds. A small body has entered the atmosphere and air resistance has raised its temperature to the point of incandescence. In English, the streak of light is called a "shooting star."

The Greeks, however, did not consider the streak to be a star. They considered it, rightly, a phenomenon of Earth's atmosphere, rather than of the sky, and so it is called a "meteor" from Greek words meaning "the upper atmosphere." (The study of the atmospheric changes that produce our weather is called "meteorology" for this reason, and has nothing to do with meteors. The study of meteors is "meteoritics.")

The term "meteor" refers only to the streak of light, by the way, and not to the object that produces it. If part of the object survives its trip through the atmosphere, then a lump of rock or metal will strike Earth's surface. That lump of matter is *not* a meteor. It is a "meteorite," the "-ite" suffix being generally used by geologists for rocks and minerals.

What's more, if one encounters the body before it strikes the Earth's atmosphere, so that it is not glowing, it is not a meteor then, either. (Shades of all those science fiction stories, including some of mine, that have had space-ships demolished by meteors.) In space, the object is a "meteoroid," by analogy with "asteroid."

A meteoroid is actually a very small asteroid, and there is no real distinction between the two, except that of size. We might argue that any planetary object with a diameter greater than one kilometer is an asteroid, anything smaller is a meteoroid, but that is purely my own personal boundary line.

Very small meteoroids, the size of pieces of grit or less, could be called "micrometeoroids" or "meteoric dust."

What about the strangely shaped, fuzzy patches of light that appear in the skies now and then? To the Greeks, they were *aster kometes* ("hairy stars") and so we now call them "comets."

Strictly speaking, a comet is only the glowing object seen in our skies. The object is then close enough to the Sun for its substance to be vaporized in part. A haze is produced about it ("coma") and this is driven outward by the Solar wind to form its "tail."

Comets have elongated orbits and when they are in the outer Solar system, they are cold and perfectly solid since they are then far from the vaporizing action of Solar heat. At those times, comets are indistinguishable from small asteroids to the casual glance. The actual difference is entirely a matter of composition. The asteroids are made up of involatile material and do not vaporize even when they move into the inner Solar system. The comet is made up partly or nearly entirely of volatile material and will evaporate.

It is my idea that the cometary body in its cold, solid state ought to be called a "cometoid" in analogy to "asteroid," but I must admit I have never seen or heard anyone else use that term.

AFTERWORD: In the previous two essays I have mentioned briefly (and irrita-bly) the common misuse of the word "galaxy" to mean "some other place." I'll go into the matter in greater detail in the following essay.

Oh, and one more point. In the preceding essay, which appeared eight years ago, I mentioned Mercury as "the smallest object generally accepted as a planet" and gave its diameter as about five thousand kilometers. Since then, however, the diameter of distant Pluto has been determined to be about three thousand kilometers. It succeeds to the title of the smallest planet, then, and it is still considerably larger than Ceres, the largest asteroid.

34

What's a Galaxy?

THERE ARE SOME WORDS TO-
ward which science fiction readers take a proprietary attitude. One of them is
"galaxy." We were familiar with that word when no one else but professional
astronomers ever used it or understood it. We even named a magazine for it,
one which, in its time, was an important addition to the field.

I myself feel particularly associated with the word since in my Foundation trilogy I made the Galactic Empire a science fictional household word.

It irritates me dreadfully, therefore, that the word is commonly used in
"sci-fi" movies and television in a way that clearly shows that the perpetrators
haven't the faintest notion what a galaxy is and don't care either.

They routinely describe events as taking place "in another galaxy," or
extraterrestrials as coming "from another galaxy," when what they really
mean is "another planetary system."

There are 300 billion stars in the galaxy we live in and that gives us
sufficient scope, surely, for other intelligences and distant events without having to find them in "other galaxies" every single time.

To put it into familiar terms, we need only imagine a movie in which
every time some human stranger arrives at a gathering someone says, "And this
is Tony Smith, from another continent," when what they really mean is "And
this is Tony Smith, from out of town."

To be forever saying "from another continent," instead of "from out of
town" or "from a city out West," strongly indicates that the speaker doesn't
know the meaning of the word "continent."

So what is a galaxy?

The tale begins with the fact that ancient observers of the sky noticed a dim, foggy band that circled the heavens and divided it into two equal halves. It was not an atmospheric cloud of any kind, for it turned with the sky and was clearly part of it. (Don't bother looking for it if you live in the city. Between the city lights and the dusty atmosphere, you'll never see it.)

The ancient Egyptians, who depended on the Nile for their existence, imagined the foggy band to be a heavenly Nile that fed the gods. The ancient Greeks thought it was a jet of milk issuing from the breast of Hera, when she was suckling an infant-god.

Such notions were fair enough. The foggy band did have a faint milkiness to it and the Greeks called it the "milky circle." Naturally, they used their own Greek language to call it that, so that to them it was *galaxias kyklos*.

The Romans referred to it similarly (but in Latin, of course) as *via lactea*, which means "milky way," and we adopted the Roman name in translation.

The ancient Greek philosophers sought to give the Milky Way a nonmythological explanation. Some thought it was the raw material out of which the stars were made and represented a supply that was left over. Some thought it marked an ancient path of the Sun. Some suggested the Milky Way was of the same substance as comets (which was reasonable since both Milky Way and comets seemed to be composed of foggy luminousness).

It was left to the philosopher Democritus to advance the most incredible explanation. About 420 B.C., he suggested that the Milky Way was actually made up of a vast crowd of stars so faint as to be individually invisible. But then, Democritus had all sorts of weird notions. He also thought that all matter was made up of tiny atoms that were also individually invisible, so you can well imagine that no one paid much attention to *him*.

But then, twenty centuries later, Galileo pointed his telescope at the Milky Way and found out (son of a gun!) that it was made up of a vast crowd of stars so faint as to be individually invisible. (Democritus turned out to be right about the atoms, too.)

It was still possible to think of the Milky Way as a band of faint stars lying outside the bright stars scattered evenly over the sky and not really part of them—but this notion was put to rest by William Herschel in 1785. He counted the stars in statistically chosen small portions of the sky through his excellent telescope and found that the number in each small portion rose steadily as he approached the Milky Way.

He concluded that the stars were not spread uniformly through infinite space, or through finite space with the Milky Way encircling them. He held that they formed a finite conglomeration of definite shape—that of a grindstone (or a thick poker chip, for those of you who have never seen a grindstone). He thought we were near the center of the grindstone and when we looked in the direction of the long diameter, we saw so many stars that were so distant they melted into the Milky Way—which was thus itself part of the conglomeration.

The conglomeration was called the "Galaxy," from the Greek phrase for the Milky Way. That gave us two expressions, both referring to milk. "Milky Way," a direct translation from the Latin, referred to the visible band in the sky. "Galaxy," from the Greek for "milky circle," meant the conglomeration of stars that included that band in the sky, and all the other stars visible in the sky as well.

For a century, astronomers assumed that the Galaxy included all the stars there were, even though as early as 1755, the German philosopher Immanuel Kant suspected that certain small, foggy objects seen here and there in the skies were "island universes," each a very distant collection of very large numbers of stars.

All such small, foggy objects were called "nebulae," the Latin word for "clouds," which was, after all, what they appeared to be. The assumption was that they were patches of dust and vapor, as ordinary atmospheric clouds were.

There is an oval foggy patch in the constellation Andromeda, for instance, which came to be called the Andromeda Nebula; an irregular one in the sword of Orion, the Orion Nebula; and another irregular one in Taurus, called the Crab Nebula.

In 1796, when the French astronomer Pierre Simon de Laplace suggested that the Solar system developed out of a swirling mass of dust and vapor, he cited the Andromeda Nebula as something that looked like a developing planetary system, which is why his suggestion has always been known as the "nebular hypothesis."

The Irish astronomer William Parsons, Earl of Rosse, made a systematic study of those nebulae with a quixotically large telescope he built on his Irish estate, the phenomenally bad weather of which kept it from being used much. It was he who gave the Crab Nebula its name and, in 1845, he detected a nebula which had a distinctly spiral shape, so that it came to be called the Whirlpool Nebula. Within five years, fifteen such spirals were detected and a class of objects called "spiral nebulae" was recognized.

Were all these nebulae part of the Galaxy? Most astronomers thought so. In 1918, the American astronomer Harlow Shapley showed that the Galaxy was much larger than had been thought in the nineteenth century and that the Solar system was far off-center within it. The Galaxy was, in fact, one hundred thousand light-years across (and Shapley first thought it was even larger than that) and that made it seem more likely than ever that that was all there was.

Another American astronomer, Heber Doust Curtis, gathered evidence that upheld a contrary view. There were a surprisingly large number of "novae" (or "brightening stars") in the direction of the Andromeda Nebula and that could not possibly be unless the Andromeda Nebula was itself a vast collection of stars as Kant had once suspected.

There was a great debate between Shapley and Curtis in 1920 and Curtis won. At least, after the debate there was a steady shift to Curtis's side of the argument. Some nebulae, such as the Crab Nebula and the Orion Nebula, were established as "galactic nebulae"; that is, clouds of dust and gas that were definitely part of the Galaxy. Others, however, such as the Andromeda Nebula and the Whirlpool Nebula, lay far outside. A new class of nebulae was recognized, the "extragalactic nebulae."

Galactic nebulae were luminous when they contained stars within them. Extragalactic nebulae were luminous because they consisted of many stars, very many. It took very many stars to give them detectable luminosity at their enormous distances. In fact, they had to be galaxies like our own. Slowly and rather reluctantly, people began to speak of the Andromeda Galaxy and the Whirlpool Galaxy.

Our Galaxy is simply one of many, so what do we call this galaxy we live in? I'll consider that in the next essay.

35

Our Own Galaxy

IN THE PREVIOUS ESSAY, I TALKED of the evolution of the word "galaxy" and how it came to be used for those huge conglomerations of stars that are the most noticeable units of the Universe on a large scale. As far as we can tell, they are distributed more or less evenly through the Universe in all directions.

The number of galaxies we can detect in our telescopes is in the neighborhood of a billion. The total number of galaxies in the Universe may be something like a hundred billion.

What do we name these galaxies individually? In particular, what do we call the galaxy we live in?

To begin with, I am not particularly enamored of the term "galaxy" as covering a class of objects. The word derives from the Greek for "milky circle" and the galaxies are not milky ways. The Milky Way is the luminous band that circles our sky and that is how a galaxy looks from the *inside*, so there is only one Milky Way. To call all the other objects that resemble the one we live in "milky ways" or "galaxies" is unfortunate.

After all, we speak of "the Sun," but other objects of the same sort are "stars." We speak of "the Moon," but other objects of the same sort are "satellites." By analogy, we should speak of "the Galaxy" but call other objects of the same sort something else.

What else? My own choice would be "star-systems," which is what they are. Furthermore, it might be nice to attach a number to that general term to signify, logarithmically, the number of stars they contain. A giant galaxy containing 10 trillion stars (10^{13}) would be a star-system-13. Our own Galaxy would, in those terms, be a star-system-11. The Magellanic Clouds would be an example of a star-system-10. You could have dwarf galaxies as small as star-system-6.

The beauty of this nomenclature is that it doesn't make distinctions between conglomerations of different size. For instance, globular clusters are much smaller than the average galaxy and the only ones we have detected are clearly satellites of galaxies, revolving about the center of the galaxy with which they are associated. But then a small star that circles a much more massive one is nonetheless a star; and a small star-system that circles the center of another should be nonetheless a star-system. The largest globular clusters would be star-system-6, though most would be star-system-5 or star-system-4. The Pleiades would be star-system-3. For that matter a single star, such as the Sun, would be star-system-0.

The nomenclature could be used for galactic clusters. Our Local Group, made up of two dozen galaxies, is a star-system-12. Giant galactic clusters could be up to star-system-15, and the entire Universe would be, very possibly, a star-system-22.

If we were to adopt this nomenclature, that object in Andromeda would be the Andromeda-star-system-11.5 and the object we live in would be the Galaxy-star-system-11.

However, no one's going to adopt my suggested nomenclature, and we must work with what we have—"galaxies," as a general term. Some of the closer galaxies have common names that depend on their location or appearance. The Andromeda Galaxy is in the constellation Andromeda, and the Triangulum Galaxy is in the constellation Triangulum. There are also the Whirlpool Galaxy, the Sombrero Galaxy, and so on.

This is colorful, but not very useful, since we would soon run out of names. There are only 88 constellations and the vast majority of galaxies are so distant that their appearance is nothing more than a tiny smudge.

Can we use this system for the star-system we live in? We can give it pride of place and call it "*the* galaxy" or "*our* galaxy," as opposed to other galaxies, or capitalize it and call it "the Galaxy" as opposed to all other galaxies. However, you can't hear a capital letter, and it is inconvenient to be always stressing "the" or "our," and neither is a clear enough distinction.

Most often, the star-system we live in is referred to as the Milky Way Galaxy. This is tautological since we are saying the same thing twice, first in

English, then in Greek. Besides, it can be a source of confusion. The Milky Way is a distinct object in the sky and people who encounter the phrase casually may think that it is the Milky Way that is the Galaxy and that we, and the other individual stars in the sky that we see, are not part of it.

Why don't we call the star-system in which we live the Home Galaxy? It's the galaxy we live in, after all. We speak of "hometown" and "home country," so why not Home Galaxy?

For the most part, however, galaxies are not referred to by trivial names, but by numbers, since numbers are objects that cannot be exhausted and can be used for any conceivable number of galaxies. Even 100 billion galaxies can receive each an individual number without exhausting the supply. (In fact, the number of numbers over 100 billion is every bit as great as the number of numbers there are all together.)

The first to supply numbers was the French astronomer Charles Messier (1730–1817). He was a comet hunter by profession and considered it the acme of delight to be the first to detect a fuzzy object approaching the Earth and to announce a newly discovered comet. However, he was always coming across a fuzzy object that disappointed him by being a fixed feature of the sky— something that was always there.

In order to prevent other comet hunters from being fooled, he made a list, in 1784, of a little over a hundred such objects which should be ignored by serious cometeers. These objects are still sometimes referred to as Messier 1, Messier 2, and so on, or just M1, M2, and so on. Some of the objects on his list are clouds of gas. M1 is the Crab Nebula and M42 is the Orion Nebula. Some are globular clusters. M13 is the Great Hercules Cluster, for instance.

About a third of the objects on Messier's list turned out to be galaxies, when these objects were recognized as such a century and a half after Messier. Thus, M31 is the Andromeda Galaxy, M33 is the Triangulum Galaxy, and M51 is the Whirlpool Galaxy.

Can we use this system to name our own Galaxy? Why not? We could call the star-system we live in M0 and let it head the list.

Of course, Messier's list was far too short. As time went on, it was extended. The German-British astronomer William Herschel (1738–1822), who made his fame and fortune by discovering the planet Uranus in 1781, went on to study the sky as thoroughly as he could and, between 1786 and 1802, prepared no fewer than three listings of fuzzy objects (nebulae), which contained a total of 2,500 items, with the location of each carefully noted.

William's son, John Herschel (1792–1871), continued his father's work in this respect and, in 1864, published *The General Catalogue of Nebulae and Clusters* which contained 5,079 objects, with positions and descriptions. It speaks of the careful labor of the two Herschels that of these 5,079 objects, 4,630 (or 91 percent of the whole) were discovered by them.

Even this went rapidly out of date, and the work was continued by a Danish-British astronomer, Johann L. E. Dreyer (1852–1926). In 1878, he published a supplement to the *General Catalogue,* listing hundreds of new items. The Royal Astronomical Society suggested he do a complete overhaul of the *Catalogue.*

This he did, and in 1888 he published *The New General Catalogue of Nebulae* in which 7,840 nebulae were listed and numbered and described. In 1895, he prepared an *Index Catalogue* listing nebulae that were not mentioned in the earlier catalogue, and in 1910, he prepared a second *Index Catalogue.* The three catalogues together contained 13,226 entries and the vast majority of these proved, eventually, to be galaxies.

Other, more exhaustive listings have been made since but Dreyer's lists include all the nearer galaxies that are most often referred to. As a result, most of the galaxies mentioned in astronomy texts are identified by their NGC *(New General Catalogue)* or IC *(Index Catalogue)* numbers even today. Thus, the Andromeda Galaxy is not only M31, it is also NGC224, while NGC147, NGC185, NGC205, NGC221, NGC6822, and IC1613 are all dwarf members of the Local Group of galaxies, ranging in size from star-system-8.4 (700 million stars) to star-system-10 (10 billion stars).

The same reasoning that would make our Galaxy M0 would also make it NGC0, or IC0. However, one of these is enough, and M0 is the oldest.

Besides, I still prefer Home Galaxy as the name it should bear.

AFTERWORD: Needless to say, there is no sign of anyone showing any interest in this intelligent suggestion for the name of our Galaxy. I am in a continual state of amazement over the numerous intelligent suggestions I make that are ignored.

36

Star Wars!

AN ESSAY HAS BEEN WRITTEN by my good friend Poul Anderson (as decent and intelligent a person as I have ever met) entitled "Star Peace?" I want to present here a view that does not agree with Poul's in all respects.

In the first place, I'm not at all sure that, as Poul says, "no sane man" wants a nuclear war. I think that there are ideologues who would be delighted to fight a nuclear war they thought they could win. Two or three years ago, Ronald Reagan and Caspar Weinberger speculated on the possibility of a "limited" nuclear war, till wiser heads prevailed upon them not to talk about it.

I do agree with Poul that the policy of "mutual assured destruction," with its apt acronym of "MAD," is, indeed, mad. Poul mentions that it was introduced by Lyndon Johnson and Robert McNamara, with (perhaps) the implication it originated in the minds of (if you'll excuse my using a dirty word) liberals. Perhaps so, but I was alive at the time and I have a good memory and I don't remember conservatives howling against it. I don't remember any move on the part of the Republican right to limit the number of atom bombs we should build.

For myself, I must admit Johnson and McNamara were no heroes of mine. I put myself, in print and on the record, against their steady escalation of the Vietnam War from the very start (at a time when Poul was, in print and on the record, all for it). I was also against the nuclear arms race (on both sides) and it is just possible that Poul was all for our outpacing the Soviets in this, and, as a matter of fact, he seems annoyed in his article that, according to his figures, we *didn't* outpace them and, therefore, weren't MAD enough.

I can't argue the technology of Star Wars. I don't know enough. I can't even argue the expense of it. I don't know enough. However, I don't think anyone knows enough to argue such things at this point.

What I do know is that every large war-related project has always proved more difficult than expected, has always taken longer than expected, and has always been more expensive than expected. I see no reason to suppose that Star Wars will be a miraculous exception to this general rule.

Now the question in my mind is this: why are conservatives so gung ho on Star Wars?

The natural answer is that, being sane, they love peace. Yes, but why peace via Star Wars rather than through disarmament, let us say? Disarmament is "pie in the sky," to be sure, but so is Star Wars. We can't trust the Soviets to disarm honestly, but neither can we trust the Soviets not to try to build a Star Wars of their own and perhaps get there first and make themselves invulnerable to us at a time when we are not invulnerable to them.

Is it impossible the Soviets can match us? Ever since 1945, we have developed weapons system after weapons system, each one designed to make us "secure" at last. In each case, the Soviets persistently and resolutely matched us, so that both we and they are more insecure than ever.

And yet there *is* a difference between disarmament and Star Wars as far as assuring peace is concerned.

If there is mutual disarmament, even supposing that it can be brought about and that the Soviets and we both stick to it faithfully, where does it leave us? I will omit any consideration of what the lack of war jobs will do to either economy. Just consider that if we and the Soviets disarm, the Soviets will still be in existence and will still irritate us and behave in a manner that most of us will find horribly offensive.

But suppose we go the Star Wars route, and suppose we get there first. That is, after all, to be expected. We can certainly outspend the Soviets and we have good old "Yankee know-how" on our side.

Well then, supposing that, where are we? We will then be able to knock down most or all of their missiles if they attack, and then hand out a counter-blow that will destroy them, so that, being sane, the Soviets will not attack, and we will have peace. In fact, Poul points out that Reagan has twice suggested that we will share the technology with the Soviets, so that they can be invulnerable, too. Then there will be peace on both sides, a situation Poul calls "Star Peace," though he is honest enough to place a question mark after the phrase.

Now obviously we are not going to give the Soviets the technology while we are in the process of developing it, because the Soviets could not be trusted to give us any advances *they* have worked out, and to give them ours while not receiving theirs would be to make certain they will develop Star Wars first.

It is only *after* we have worked out a completed Star Wars and put it in place that we will give them the technology.

But will we? Will anyone who believes we will please raise his or her hand? If anyone did, which I doubt, listen—

The fact is we can't and we won't. Suppose we give them the technology and allow a Soviet Star Wars in space alongside ours. Now they can't fire missiles at us and we can't fire missiles at them. Both sides can still use submarines, however, and other tricks for setting off explosions without going into space. In addition, both we and the Soviets can make use of tanks and ordinary bombing planes and, in general, an improved nonnuclear technology. After all, both sides may have Star Wars, but neither side has disarmed.

In that case, how do we stop the Soviets from walking all over Western Europe? It's only our nuclear arsenal that we can count on to stop them. In short, a Star Wars on both sides means that we may be forced to fight a relatively conventional war with the Soviets and in such a war the odds will be on the Soviet side.

So why did President Reagan say we will give them the technology? I wouldn't dream of saying it's because he doesn't know what he's talking about. It is quite sufficient to remind you there are such things as "campaign promises."

Now, then, we have Star Wars and we *don't* give the technology to the Russians, and so they don't have it. We are invulnerable to a major nuclear strike and they are not. Isn't that perfect? We just tell them what we want them to do. "Throw out your Communist government," we will tell them, "and elect a good Republican one, allowing a few Democrats (not too many) in the opposition." If they don't do it, they know darn well we can clobber them with any number of missiles and they will have no way of retaliating.

So they surrender and that is peace indeed! Far better than disarmament, isn't it?

Is it possible, though, that this is a fairy tale I am handing you? Does it seem really likely that the Star Wars enthusiasts are thinking along warlike lines? Couldn't they really want peace? —Well, let's consider something else.

In the last couple of years, the notion of a "nuclear winter" has been advanced. Some scientists maintain that in case of even a moderate number of thermonuclear explosions, enough dust from impact, plus smoke from fire storms, will fill the stratosphere and cut off sunlight for a long enough period to destroy a major portion of Earth's plant life, so that animals (and proud humanity) will then perforce starve. If the exchange is bad enough, virtually all life may be wiped out.

The *possibility* is real enough. We all know the mushroom clouds that are produced by nuclear bombs. What do you suppose makes them up if not dust particles of all sizes? Single volcanic eruptions have introduced climatic changes, and in some cases the changes have been detectable worldwide.

I consider the nuclear winter debatable, of course, since we can only calculate the results, not observe them directly, but I feel the likelihood is too great to *dare* make a direct observation. ("Say, let's have a nuclear war and see if we wipe out all of humanity, or only half!")

Nevertheless, the very same people who are all for Star Wars object furiously to the very notion of a nuclear winter. In his article, Poul speaks very mildly concerning the nuclear winter but in an earlier letter to Shawna and myself (which I presume I may quote since he did not say it was confidential) he says of the nuclear winter that "the left liberal establishment is giving it a hard sell."

I think we might equally well say with respect to the nuclear winter that the right conservative establishment (which controls the government right now) is giving it a very hard negative sell.

Why?

Could it be because a nuclear winter makes a first strike forever impossible? What is the use of shooting off your arsenal to destroy an enemy if the result is a nuclear winter that does indeed destroy the enemy, *and* all the neutrals, *and* you yourself?

Imagine that we have a Star Wars in place and serve the Soviets with an ultimatum: behave yourselves or we destroy you!

The Soviets say, "We have no defense but you can't destroy us without destroying yourself, too. Shoot, then. We dare you."

And what do we do? Obviously, if we are sane, we don't shoot, and we are then forced perhaps to fight a semiconventional war that we may not be able to win. No wonder the Star Wars enthusiasts are furious over the mere suggestion of a nuclear winter.

If we are not sane, of course, we can issue a presidential proclamation to the effect that no such thing as a nuclear winter exists, and fire our arsenal. After all, if the nuclear winter *does* then swirl down upon us we can always say, "Oops!"

It seems clear to me, then, that there is only one way out of the impasse and that is careful disarmament to very low levels on all sides. Perhaps this can't be done, but if not, then I don't think civilization can long survive, and Star Wars can't and won't save us.

✦

AFTERWORD: The above essay was written three years ago. Since then, I have listened to a remarkable series of cheerful comments from government officials to the effect that amazingly successful tests are being formed, that great progress is being made not only on Star Wars proper but on various spin-offs. In short, everything is marvelous.

Far be it from me to be cynical about this, but I have an excellent memory and I lived through the Vietnam War from beginning to end and I remember that for ten years, we were beating the Vietnamese, and destroying them, and seeing the light at the end of the tunnel, and nailing their coonskins to the door, and so on, and so on. The government told us we were winning the war all through, until the very moment that we lost it.

I didn't believe them then, and I don't believe them now. I said, then, that the Vietnam War was stupid and that we had to get out as soon as possible. (A prowar friend asked me angrily, "How?" and I answered, "You didn't ask me how to get in, so don't ask me how to get out. If you were smart enough to get in without my help, be smart enough to get out without my help.") And I say now that Star Wars is the biggest rathole ever invented and it will swallow up our entire nation if we don't get out of it.

As for the nuclear winter, we don't have to argue that point. Nuclear war is suicide, even if there is no nuclear winter. Nuclear war is suicide even if Star Wars keeps *all* Soviet missiles from reaching us.

Since I wrote the above essay, the Chernobyl disaster took place. One *(one!!)* nuclear reactor had a near meltdown. The radioactive cloud that resulted blanked much of the Ukraine and Western Europe and could be detected even in the United States. Wheat fields, we are told, were contaminated; livestock in England had to be killed. In addition to the thirty-one Soviets who have already died, it is suspected that tens of thousands of people will eventually die of cancer because of the Chernobyl disaster. These tens of thousands will include people in the Soviet Union *and* in Western Europe.

That's *one* nuclear reactor deep in the Ukraine.

Now suppose that the United States, feeling safe behind its Star Wars defense, does a Rambo and bombards the Soviet Union with hundreds (thousands?) of nuclear bombs, wiping it out once and for all. Whether the nuclear winter that results is severe, or mild, or even nonexistent, what happens to the radioactive fallout? Even if you ignore the many millions of deaths inside the Soviet Union (as Rambo would say, they're only Russkies), what about the slow death of many millions of people in Western Europe and elsewhere? Is the fun of killing Russkies worth it?

My own feeling is that the Soviets who have lived through the Nazi invasion and know what war is like are scared stiff and would welcome some reasonable compromises that would lower the danger of nuclear war. It's we, who haven't felt a foreign invasion since 1814 and who feed ourselves on the mythology of Wayne and Stallone, who keep thinking of somehow mysteriously winning a modern, high-tech war.

I am very anxious that we get scared stiff, too, and begin to look for ways of attaining a rational disarmament and a reasonable form of world government.

The New York Times Laughs Again

SOMETIMES I WONDER WHAT the characteristics may be that qualify a person to write editorials for the New York *Times*. They don't necessarily have to be very demanding, of course, since the editorials in the *Times* (unlike those in this periodical) are unsigned, so that no one person ever has to stand behind his words.

My own feeling, though, is that when it comes to science and technology, New York *Times* editorial writers must be put through severe and thorough tests on scientific knowledge and foresight. If they fail, and fail handsomely with lots of room to spare, they are snapped up. If, on the other hand, they fail only narrowly and qualify otherwise (nice appearance, good command of language, ability to drink three martinis in rapid succession) they are asked to take a six-week crash course in science stupidity.

But to cases—

In 1903, the American astronomer Samuel Pierpont Langley made the last of three attempts to build a heavier-than-air flying machine that would work. For the purpose, he received a $50,000 grant from the American government, which was not blind to the possible military application of airplanes.

Langley just barely missed. His third attempt would have worked if he had had a slightly more powerful engine in it.

After the third attempt, however, the New York *Times* obtained an editor somewhere who wrote an editorial on the subject. Langley was castigated for wasting public funds foolishly because anyone with the brains of a

New York *Times* editorial writer could see that human beings would not fly for a thousand years.

Nine days after the editorial appeared (nine days!) the thousand years suddenly ran out when the Wright brothers flew their plane at Kitty Hawk. I don't suppose the New York *Times* ever apologized.

Another case! In the 1920s, Robert Hutchings Goddard was experimenting with small liquid-fueled rockets. He was doing so in Worcester, Massachusetts, and the neighbors complained. The rockets made a noise and might be dangerous. (They might be, at that.) Goddard therefore transferred the site of action to New Mexico with the help of a Guggenheim grant of $50,000.

The New York *Times* sped him on his way with one of its editorial specials. They found an editorial writer who claimed he had gone to high school and put him to work. The writer laughed heartily at Goddard, saying that of course his rockets couldn't work once out in space, for as every high school student knows, rockets have nothing to push against in the vacuum of space.

Admittedly, those high school students no brighter than a New York *Times* editorial writer knew that. Isaac Newton, however, and many high school students who had passed their tests, knew that rockets would work in outer space and, in fact, it was rockets at last that carried men to the Moon. I don't know if the New York *Times* ever apologized in this case either.

Which brings us to the present day.

It seems that a NASA advisory council has recommended a project that will have astronomers engage in spotting and tracking sizable objects in the vicinity of Earth, calculating their orbits and then keeping them in view, to determine if, when, and how those orbits might be perturbed and modified by the gravitational pull of various planets. Then, if one of them ever seemed to have moved into a possible collision course with Earth, a spacecraft armed with a hydrogen bomb could nudge it aside. What would be needed was an initial appropriation of $100 million.

The New York *Times* got to work at once. An editorial on the subject in a department called "Topics" was published on 17 February 1981.

The reason I noticed it was that, by coincidence, on the very day before, I had given a lively talk to a luncheon meeting of the Dutch Treat Club, a fine organization to which I belong, and had recommended just that sort of project.

I did not know that NASA was getting into the act at the time I made the talk but that didn't matter. I'd been at it a long time. I first suggested such a project in an article entitled "Big Game Hunting in Space" in the August 1959 issue of a magazine called *Space Age*.

The first sentence of the New York *Times* editorial reads, "Leave it to the space nuts to drive concern over environmental risks to new heights."

"Space nuts"? Who are the "space nuts"? They must be you and I, O Gentle Readers. Surely we recognize ourselves. It's we space nuts who, back in 1903, would probably have felt that man would fly in less than a thousand years. It's we space nuts who, back in 1929, would have known that rockets would work in a vacuum and who would have felt that human beings would reach the Moon somehow.

We didn't have the kind of chic expertise that kept the New York *Times* editorial writers laughing at silly things like that.

The editorial writer seemed to think the project had arisen out of the fact that there is an impression right now that an asteroid collision with Earth 65 million years ago killed off all the large animals on the planet, including the dinosaurs, and nearly sterilized it altogether.

The thought of being concerned about something that happened 65 million years ago inspired the editorial writer to happy heights of sarcasm. He writes, ". . . who . . . could possibly begrudge the space enthusiasts the paltry $100 million needed to check out the deflectability of an asteroid? Such knowledge may prove useful over the next 65 million years."

Well, sure! Any person with the brains of a New York *Times* editorial writer would know that if something happened 65 million years ago, it isn't going to happen again until 65 million years from now. After all, figure it out, the last time a world war started was forty-two years ago. Therefore, we know for sure there won't be another world war until forty-two years from now. That's 2023, so why worry about possible world wars *now*, for goodness' sake?

As a matter of fact, it was in this very century that two heavy collisions of outer space material with Earth took place. Fortunately for us, both—one in 1908 and one in 1947—struck uninhabited portions of Siberia.

Both, however, were city-busters, in the sense that if either one had happened to strike a good-sized city they would have snuffed out every life in it in minutes. What's more, if such a city-buster were to zero in *now* and strike a city in either the United States or the Soviet Union, the nation damaged might suspect a sneak nuclear strike and might well retaliate instantly under the impression that there was no time to waste checking the matter. And that would give us a thermonuclear war.

The NASA advisory council mentioned this possibility of starting a thermonuclear war and the New York *Times* editorial writer mentioned it, too. I suspect that the possibility of such a war made the proposal seem funnier than ever to him.

I must admit there's not much chance of this happening very soon. The chance, however, is not zero. A large meteor skimmed by Earth in 1974 and passed through the atmosphere. It missed Montana by just thirty-six miles straight up. A microscopic change in orbit and it would have gouged out a hole half a mile across—possibly in Helena.

But $100 million!

Come on, you space nuts! A hundred million dollars just to fight off the small off-chance of destroying a city and starting a thermonuclear war?

Perhaps we should put that sum into perspective. The nations of the world are spending $100 million on their war machines every two hours! A single modern bomber of the kind the United States keeps wondering about whether to build costs *over* $100 million. That's one plane, for goodness' sake.

If we can spend that much on one plane and are thinking of building a fleet of them—just on the off-chance that they may create plenty of mayhem and destruction—is it such a terrible crime to spend that much money on a project that might *prevent* mayhem and destruction?

From where we sit, you and I, in our science fictional worlds, we don't see things with the zero foresight of New York *Times* editorial writers. Perhaps it might help if they were to be encouraged to read a science fiction magazine such as mine in order that they might learn about the real world.

But I suspect they won't. I'm afraid they are too attached to their world in which human beings can't fly and rockets can't work and the Moon can't be reached and large meteorites never hit the Earth.

Too bad!

AFTERWORD: I feel a little guilty over the above essay. After all, the New York *Times* is my hometown newspaper and I read it every morning with avidity.

What's more, I agree with its editorials about 90 percent of the time. But I only feel a *little* guilty. Nothing excuses stupidity.

It might be argued, of course, that the editorial comment was only meant as a little lighthearted raillery, but lighthearted raillery that reveals stupidity is nothing to laugh at.

38

Faster than Light

IN THE NEXT ESSAY, I WILL DISCUSS
time travel as one phenomenon that is almost certainly impossible, even in
theory, and yet one that cannot be abandoned as a concomitant of even the
most serious science fiction stories. The plots it makes possible are too interesting and lend themselves too well to all sorts of investigations of the human
condition.

One other impossibility that equals it as a science fiction essential is
"superluminal" ("faster than light") travel. Without superluminal travel, science fiction writers are confined to the Solar system (plus, possibly, a few of
the very nearest stars) unless they are willing to involve themselves with
starships that travel for generations, or with longtime freezing, or with time
dilatation.

It is only routine superluminality that makes galactic empires, and such
things as interstellar warfare, really practical.

There is this difference between time travel and superluminal travel,
however. I imagine that most people are willing to think of time travel as
essentially fantasy, but to consider superluminal travel as fantasy seems to
annoy, and even enrage, a large fraction of the s.f. readership. *Why* isn't
superluminal travel possible? What is so magic about the speed of light?
Surely, if you keep accelerating long enough and hard enough, you are bound
to "break the light barrier."

People think this only because they judge from everyday experience. If
a force is applied to an object, it accelerates—that is, it moves faster in the

direction in which the force is applied. As long as the force continues to be applied, the object continues to move faster and faster. There is no sign (under ordinary conditions) that this situation will change—that there is a mysterious speed limit at which the object will suddenly stop accelerating, no matter what the force.

To be sure, as a force is applied to an object, physicists are quite certain that the momentum of that object increases indefinitely and comes ever closer to the infinite. The same can be said of an object's kinetic energy. The value of the momentum of a moving body is the product of its mass and its velocity (mv). The value of the kinetic energy of a moving body is the product of its mass and half the square of its velocity $(mv^2/2)$.

Since the commonsense notion is that the mass of a body (simplistically defined as the quantity of matter it contains) does not change with motion, it follows that momentum and kinetic energy must increase only because the velocity increases. And if momentum and kinetic energy increase indefinitely as a force continues to be applied, that can only mean that velocity must increase indefinitely. There seems no way out of that syllogism, so what is all this junk about the speed-of-light limit?

This "junk" started with Albert Einstein in 1905. It seemed to Einstein that the speed of light in a vacuum must always be measured at the same speed (just under 300,000 kilometers per second) no matter what the motion of the light source might be relative to the observer who was making the measurement. This seemed to follow from the Michelson-Morley experiment two decades earlier, but Einstein insisted he did not know of that experiment but came to his conclusion as a result of certain thought experiments that showed that any other behavior of light would result in paradoxes.

This constancy of the speed of light did not seem to make sense. Ordinary moving objects, such as a thrown ball, had speeds that depended in part on the motion of the person or object throwing the ball, and it certainly seemed this rule should apply to everything including light. Why should light have a special status?

But supposing Einstein's assumption is so. In that case, the whole Universe ought to be organized in such a way as to make it so and Einstein developed his "Special Theory of Relativity" to describe a Universe in which light behaved in this unusual fashion. In order for light so to behave, Einstein showed that mass ought to increase in quantity for a moving object. It should increase, in fact, according to a set relationship: $M = m / \sqrt{1 - v^2/c^2}$, where v is the speed of the object, c is the speed of light in the vacuum, m is the mass of the object when it is not moving ("rest mass"), and M is the mass of the object when it is moving at velocity v.

Up to the beginning of the twentieth century, no living thing and no human artifact managed to attain a speed of as much as 0.1 kilometers per second, or 1/3,000,000 the speed of light. Even now, when we add supersonic airplanes and interplanetary rockets to the list of human artifacts, 15 kilometers per second, or 1/20,000 the speed of light, is about the top speed we have obtained.

If we use Einstein's formula and imagine a 1-kilogram object speeding at 15 kilometers per second, its mass at that speed would be 1.0000000013 kilograms. It would have gained 1 1/3 micrograms, or a little over a billionth of its rest mass. It is doubtful whether such a gain in mass with motion could be measured with any degree of precision, or indeed if it could be directly measured at all—and this is in the case of a speeding rocket. Ordinary speeds here on Earth's surface would be far smaller than that of a rocket, and the gain in mass would be correspondingly smaller. No wonder it seemed to people, and even to scientists, that mass did not change with motion.

In fact, suppose we imagined an object moving past us at the enormous speed of 30,000 kilometers per second (a speed that nothing we have ever seen with the unaided eye has even begun to approach). Such a speed is 1/10 that of light and by Einstein's equation a 1-kilogram object moving at such a speed would have a mass (at that speed) of 1.005 kilograms. It would have increased in mass by only about 0.5 percent, and would be only 1 1/200 of its rest mass.

If we can imagine 30,000 kilometers per second, we can imagine still higher speeds. A 1-kilogram mass, moving at 60,000 kilometers per second, would have a mass of 1.021 kilograms. At 90,000 kilometers per second, it would have a mass of 1.048 kilograms; at 120,000 kilometers per second, it would have a mass of 1.091 kilograms; and at 150,000 kilometers per second, it would have a mass of 1.155 kilograms.

But 150,000 kilometers per second is half the speed of light. Yet even then, the gain in mass is only 15.5 percent. The moving mass is not quite 1 1/6 times the rest mass. This doesn't seem very serious. In fact, the mass of a moving object doesn't reach the figure of 2 times its rest mass until it is moving at a speed of 260,000 kilometers per second, or just about 7/8 the speed of light. Please note, however, that the mass has been increasing at a faster and faster rate as the speed increases.

The more mass an object has, the less it can be made to accelerate in response to a given force. A force applied to an object moving at 260,000 kilometers per second (and therefore with twice its rest mass) will produce only half the acceleration that that force would have produced if it had been applied to the same object when it was at rest. As an object speeds up under a constant force, its mass increases ever more rapidly and its speed increases ever more slowly. The mass increase predominates, so that momentum and kinetic energy continue to increase more rapidly even though speed increases more slowly.

By the time we reach a speed of 290,000 kilometers per second (97 percent of the speed of light), the mass of the moving body is 3.892 kilograms, almost four times the original mass. At 295,000 kilometers per second (98.3 percent of the speed of light—if that is taken at the slightly incorrect 300,000 kilometers per second figure), 5.52 kilograms; at 299,000 kilometers per second (99.7 percent of the speed of light), 12.22 kilograms; at 299,999 kilometers per second (99.9997 percent of the speed of light) 383.5 kilograms.

At the speed of light itself, if that could be reached, the mass would be infinite—as would be the momentum and the kinetic energy.

A faster speed is impossible because neither mass, momentum, nor kinetic energy can be more than infinite. Besides, at infinite mass, no force, however great, can produce any acceleration, however small, so the speed cannot increase. —So the speed of light is the limit that cannot be passed.

And yet all this depends upon the validity of Einstein's equation, which in turn depends upon a correct deduction from Einstein's basic assumption. What if the equation is wrong, or has been incorrectly deduced, or is based on a faulty assumption?

We would still be wondering about that, perhaps, were it not that a decade before Einstein advanced his theory, subatomic particles were discovered. These tiny objects can be observed to move at large fractions of the speed of light. Their mass can be measured with considerable precision, and it was found not only that their mass increased with speed, but *precisely* by the amount predicted by Einstein's equation.

That means that light hurries through the vacuum at the ultimate and absolute speed limit. Ways of evading that limit (tachyons, black holes, hyperspace) have been suggested, but all involve phenomena concerning which we can only speculate, and in favor of which there is no observational evidence *whatever.*

Nevertheless, superluminal travel cannot and will not be abandoned in science fiction. Certainly, *I* will never abandon it.

39

Time Travel

I HAVE OFTEN SAID, IN SPEAKING
and in writing, that the qualified science fiction writer avoids the scientifically
impossible. Yet I can't bring myself to make that rule an absolute one, because
there are some plot devices that offer such dramatic possibilities that we are
forced to overlook the utter implausibilities that are involved. The most glar-
ing example of this is time travel.

There are infinite tortuosities one can bring to plot development if only
you allow your characters to move along the time axis, and I, for one, can't
resist them, so that I have written a number of time-travel stories, including
one novel, *The End of Eternity*.

You can get away with a kind of diluted time-travel story, if you have
your character move in the direction we all move—from present to future—
and suspend the usual consciousness that accompanies the move by having him
(please understand that, for conciseness, I am using "him" as a shorthand
symbol for "him or her") sleep away a long period of time, as Rip Van
Winkle did, or, better, having him frozen for an indefinite period at liquid
nitrogen temperatures. Better still, you might make use of relativistic notions
and have your character move into the future by having his subjective time
slowed through motion at speeds close to that of light, or motion through an
enormously intense gravitational field.

These are plausible devices that do not do damage to the structure of the
Universe, but they are one-way motions, with no return possible. I did it in
Pebble in the Sky although I made use of an unknown (and unspecified) natural

law involving nuclear fission. This was a weakness in the plot, but I got past it in the first couple of pages and never brought it up again so I hoped no one would notice it. (Alas, many did.)

The same device can be used to make repeated jumps, always into the future, or to bring someone from the past into the present.

Once you have a device which sends someone into the future, however, it is asking too much of writer nature not to use some device—such as a blow on the head—to send a person into the past. (Mark Twain does it in *A Connecticut Yankee in King Arthur's Court.*) For that, there is some scientific justification at the subatomic level, where individual particles are involved and entropy considerations are absent. For ordinary objects, where entropy *is* involved, there is none.

But all one-shot changes in either direction are only devices to start the story, which then usually proceeds in a completely time-bound fashion. That's not the true, or pure, time-travel story. In true time travel, the characters can move, at will, back and forth in time. Nor is it fair if this is done through supernatural intervention as in Charles Dickens' *A Christmas Carol.* It must be done by an artificial device under the control of a human being.

The first true time-travel story was H. G. Wells' *The Time Machine,* published in 1895. Wells, who was probably the best science fiction writer of all time,* carefully explained the rationale behind it. It requires four measurements to locate an object: the object is somewhere on the north-south axis, somewhere on the east-west axis, somewhere on the up-down axis, and somewhere on the past-future axis. The object exists not only in a certain point of three-dimensional space but at a certain instant of time. A merely three-dimensional object is as much a mathematical abstraction as is a two-dimensional plane, or a one-dimensional line, or a zero-dimensional point. Suppose you considered the Great Wall of China as existing for zero time and therefore consisting of three dimensions only. It would then not exist at all and you could walk through its supposed position at any time.

Since duration is a dimension like height, width, and thickness, and since we can travel at will north and south, east and west, and (if only by jumping) up and down, why shouldn't we also travel yesterward and tomorrowward as soon as we work out a device for the purpose?

That was 1895, remember, and Wells' analysis at that time had some

* If others, since, seem to have reached greater heights, it is only because they stand on Wells' shoulders.

shadow of justification. But then, in 1905, came Einstein's special theory of relativity, and it became clear that time is a dimension but it is *not* like the three spatial dimensions, and it can't be treated as though it were.

And yet Wells' argument was so winning and the plots it made possible so enticing that science fiction writers generally just ignore Einstein and follow Wells. (I do so myself in *The End of Eternity*.)

The dead giveaway that true time travel is flatly impossible arises from the well-known paradoxes it entails. The classic example is "What if you go back into the past and kill your grandfather when he was still a little boy?" In that case, you see, the murderer was never born, so who killed the little boy?

But you don't need anything so drastic. What if you go back and change any of the many small items that made it possible for your father and mother to meet, or to fall in love after they met, or to marry after they fell in love? Suppose you merely interface with *the* crucial moment of sex and have it happen the next evening, or perhaps just 5 minutes later than it did, so that another sperm fertilizes the ovum rather than the one that should have. That, too, would mean the person committing the act would never come into existence, so who would commit the act?

In fact, to go into the past and do *anything* would change a great deal of what followed, perhaps everything that followed. So complex and hopeless are the paradoxes that follow, so wholesale is the annihilation of any reasonable concept of causality, that the easiest way out of the irrational chaos that results is to suppose that true time travel is, and forever will be, impossible.

However, any discussion of this gets so philosophical that I lose patience and would rather consider something simpler.

Suppose you get into a time machine and travel 24 hours into the future. The assumption is that you are traveling only in the time dimension, and that the three spatial dimensions are unchanged. However, as is perfectly obvious, Earth is moving through the three dimensions in a very complex way. The point on the surface on which the time machine is located is moving about the Earth's axis. The Earth is moving about the center of gravity of the Earth-Moon system, and also about the center of gravity of the Earth-Sun system, is accompanying the Sun in its motion about the center of the Galaxy, and the Galaxy in its undefined motion relative to the center of gravity of the Local Group and to the center of gravity of the Universe as a whole if there is one.

You might, of course, say that the time machine partakes of the motion of the Earth, and wherever Earth goes, the time machine goes, too. Suppose, though, we consider the Earth's motion (with the Solar system generally) around the galactic center. Its speed relative to that center is estimated to be about 220 kilometers per second. If the time machine travels 24 hours into the future in 1 second, it travels 220 kilometers $\times$ 86,400 (the number of seconds in a day), or 19,008,000 kilometers in 1 second. That's over 63 times the speed of light. If we don't want to break the speed-of-light limit, then we must take not less than 23 minutes to travel 1 day forward (or backward) in time.

What's more, I suspect that considerations of acceleration would have to be involved. The time machine would have to accelerate to light speed and then decelerate from it, and perhaps the human body could only stand so much acceleration in the time direction. Considering that the human body has never in all its evolution accelerated at all in the time direction, the amount of acceleration it ought to be able to endure might be very little indeed, so that the time machine would have to take considerably more than an hour to make a 1-day journey—say, at a guess, 12 hours.

That would mean we could only gain half a day per day, at most, in traveling through time. Spending 10 years to go 20 years into the future would not be in the least palatable. (Can a time machine carry a life-support system of that order of magnitude?)

And, on top of that, I don't see that having to chase after the Earth would fail to cost the usual amount of energy just because we're doing it by way of the time dimension. Without calculating the energy, I am positive time travel is insuperably difficult, quite apart from the theoretical considerations that make it totally impossible. So let's eliminate it from serious consideration.

But not from science fiction! Time-travel stories are too much fun for them to be eliminated merely out of mundane considerations of impracticability, or even impossibility.

AFTERWORD: It is, of course, possible to retort that time travel and faster-than-light travel (the subject of the previous essay) might become possible if we learn more about the Universe. "After all," I have heard people say, "we don't know everything, do we?"

That's true, we don't know everything, but we do know that it is unlikely in the extreme that we will learn something new about relativity, quanta, or thermodynamics that will make time travel or faster-than-light travel (or certain other things, such as antigravity) possible. So extreme, in fact, that it would be much safer to bet that the Earth will stop rotating tonight and that there will be no Sunrise tomorrow morning. *Much* safer.

SCIENCE
FICTION AND
FANTASY ✦

40

Fantasy

SOME READERS HAVE BEEN OBjecting to a few stories we have published as being "fantasy." We printed one or two of these letters and promptly (and predictably) got a rash of letters objecting to the objection and urging us to include fantasy, if we wished.

This is part of the difference between what I might term the "exclusivists" and "inclusivists" among ourselves. Exclusivists are those people who have firm definitions of what science fiction is and who resent the inclusion of any story that doesn't meet that definition. They would, in other words, exclude the marginal stories. Once you know that, you automatically know what an inclusivist is, don't you? Inclusivists either lack a firm definition, or have one but aren't wedded to it. Either way, they would include all sorts of things.

I, myself, am an exclusivist in my capacity as a writer and, to a certain extent, as a reader. The science fiction I write is generally "hard," deals with science and scientists, and eschews undue violence, unnecessary vulgarity, and unpleasant themes. There is no philosophical reason for that; it merely happens to fit my way of thought. And, as a reader, I tend to enjoy the kind of science fiction I write, and to give but brief attention to other kinds.

As editor and editorial directors, however, Shawna and I are inclusivists, and we must be. We can't rely on all readers having our tastes exactly, and if we insisted on catering only to those who did, we would narrow the basis of support of the magazine to less than might suffice to support it. Rather than pleasing *x* people 100 percent of the time, it would be safer to please 10*x* people 90 percent of the time.

Therefore, if we were to come across a good and thought-provoking story that might be considered a fantasy by the exclusivists, we would be strongly tempted to publish it—especially if we were short on good, thought-provoking "straight" science fiction.

(At this point, I might point out—and not for the first time—that we are at the mercy of authors and of circumstance in designing the makeup of the magazine. Readers sometimes seem to have the notion that we are, for some mysterious reason of our own, deliberately filling the magazine with novelettes and skimping on the short stories, or having too many downbeat stories in one particular issue, or too many first-person stories. The trouble is that if we have a several-month stretch in which very few lighthearted—or third-person—or very brief—stories reach us that are good, we can't avoid running short on them. We can't print bad stories just because we need one that's funny, or short, or whatever. This also goes for readers who berate us at times for not including stories by so-and-so in the magazine. We would love to include such stories, but the author in question has to send them to us first. *Please* keep that in mind.)

But back to fantasy. "Fantasy" is from the Greek *phantasia*, which refers to the faculty of imagination. The word is sometimes spelled "phantasy" in homage to Greek, but I find that foolish. (In fact, I find the Greek *ph* foolish altogether and think it would be delightful if we spoke of "fotografs" and "filosofy," as the Italians do.) A contracted form of "fantasy," with a similar meaning, is "fancy."

In a very broad sense, all fiction (and a great deal of nonfiction) is fantasy, in that it is drawn from the imagination. We in our group, however, give the word a special meaning. It is not the plot of a story that makes it a fantasy, however imaginative that plot might be. It is the background against which the plot is played out that counts.

The plot of *Nicholas Nickleby,* for instance, is entirely imaginative. The characters and events existed entirely in Charles Dickens' imagination but the background is the England of the 1830s exactly as it was (allowing for a bit of amiable, and in some cases, unamiable satire). This is "realistic fiction." (We can even use the term where the background is made artificially pretty. Surely, the cowboys of real life must have been pretty dirty and smelly, but you'd never think it to look at Gene Autry or Randolph Scott.)

If, on the other hand, the background does not describe any actual background as it is (or once was) then we have "imaginative fiction." Science fiction and fantasy are each an example of imaginative fiction.

If the nonexistent background is one that might conceivably exist someday, given appropriate changes in the level of science and technology, or given certain assumptions that do not conflict with science and technology as we know it today, then we have science fiction.

If the nonexistent background cannot ever exist no matter what *reasonable* changes or assumptions we postulate, then it is fantasy.

To give specific examples, the Foundation series is science fiction, and *The Lord of the Rings* is fantasy. To be more general about it, spaceships and robots are science fiction, while elves and magic are fantasy.

But there are all kinds of fantasy. There is "heroic fantasy" in which the characters are larger than life. In this case, the outsize nature of the characters may be so enormous as to verge on the grotesque, as in the case of Superman or the other superheroes; or the characters may be so human in many ways that we find ourselves accepting them as real, as in the case of the elves and hobbits of Tolkien's masterpiece. The so-called "sword and sorcery" tales, of which Robert E. Howard's Conan saga is the progenitor, is a subdivision of this.

There is "legendary fantasy," which deliberately mimics the mythmaking activities of an earlier age. We can have modern retellings of the Trojan War, or the voyage of the Argonauts, or the saga of the Ring of the Nibelungen, or of King Arthur and his Knights of the Round Table. A marvelous recent example of this last is Marion Zimmer Bradley's *The Mists of Avalon.*

There is "children's fantasy" of which the well-known "fairy tales" are the best example, though these were definitely adult folk tales to begin with. Modern examples can stretch from the inspired madness of Lewis Carroll's *Alice in Wonderland* to the realism of Hugh Lofting's Dr. Dolittle tales (so realistic we almost forget that animals which talk and think in human fashion are actually fantasy).

There is "horror fantasy" in which tales of ghosts and malign beings such as devils and ghouls and monsters are used to thrill and frighten us. The motion pictures are rich in this type, from the inspired greatness of *King Kong* and *Frankenstein* to the good-natured foolishness of *Godzilla.*

And there is "satirical fantasy," such as the marvelous tales of John Collier (did you ever read "The Devil, George, and Rosie"?)—and this, frankly, is my favorite type of fantasy.

There may be other types, and numerous subdivisions of each; in fact, you may have a different system of classification altogether. However, the salient facts are that fantasy is a very broad and heterogeneous field of literature, and that every variety can vary in quality from the very good to the very bad. In every case, the very good will tempt us. After all, fantasy, like science fiction, is imaginative literature and there are times when this cousinship can excuse our being inclusivistic.

In fact, it doesn't take much to switch from fantasy to science fiction, and it can be done easily enough if you are a skilled practitioner. I, myself, rarely write fantasy; but when I do, once in a while, I tend to write what I can only think of as Collier-influenced material.

I began writing my George and Azazel stories as unabashed fantasies, and my reason for wanting to do them was because the satirical element made possible elaborate overwriting and straight-faced slapstick. My science fiction is chemically free of such things, and I'm human enough to want to indulge now and then.

I sold two specimens to a competing magazine and the beauteous Shawna objected.

"But they're fantasies," I said, "and we almost never do fantasies."

Shawna said, "Well, then, make them science fiction."

And I did. Azazel is no longer the demon he was at the start; he is now an extraterrestrial creature. Earlier I had assumed he was brought to Earth and into George's control by means of some magical spell—but I had never described it. I still don't, but you are free to suppose that he is pulled through a space warp.

What he does is no longer outright magic. I manage to describe it in terms of rationalistic (if imaginary) science. The result is science fiction, even if not of a very "hard" nature.

Now some of you may find George and Azazel stories too nearly "fantasy" for your tastes, but I will continue to write them and hope that Shawna will buy one or two of them now and then, because I love them. And someday, when I have written enough of them, I will collect them into a book.

AFTERWORD: At this moment, I have enough George and Azazel for a book, and my good-natured publisher, Doubleday, will soon publish it.

41

Wish Fulfillment

IT SEEMS TO ME THAT MOST FANtasy is born of wish fulfillment, and that should be a strong component in its perennial popularity.

After all, the Universe is *not* what we want it to be and from childhood on we desperately wish that were not so.

Wouldn't it be wonderful if you were so good-looking that members of the opposite sex would swoon with desire for you? Wouldn't it be great if you were so strong or so skillful at the martial arts that no one would dare cross you, especially that rotten bully down the street? Wouldn't it be marvelous if you could fly by just flapping your hands slightly, or could be invisible if you wanted to be, or could have anything you wanted just by snapping your fingers? Go ahead, make up your own list.

It's not only fantasy that feeds your desires. Modern advertisement offers you wish fulfillment in huge quantities and makes millions as a result. Let a woman but use a particular brand of toothpaste and that handsome fellow, who had earlier been indifferent, becomes instantly enamored. Just place a drop of this ointment on your skin and eternal youth is yours. Just wear a certain brand of jeans and unlimited sex will come your way.

Popular songs tell you that wishing will make it so.

You might think that all this is just food for the childish in us, but there are people who find support for wish fulfillment in science, too. "What man can imagine," they intone solemnly, "man can do." And the history of technology offers us many examples.

It has been a millennia-long dream of humanity to fly, and look here—
we can fly. We can fly faster and longer than birds. We have built contraptions
that can carry hundreds of people through the stratosphere at supersonic
speeds. How's that for wish fulfillment?

And we have television, and electric lighting at the touch of a button,
and elevators to take us to the top of a tall building, and automobiles that are
more convenient than any set of seven-league boots, and anesthetics that do
away with pain, and magic potions called "antibiotics" that cure disease, and so
on, and so on, and so on. Ask any primitive storyteller to imagine a wish and
it is very likely we can point to something in modern technology that would
correspond.

Just the same, while science is important as a device that can guide the
way to astonishing things made possible, it is even more important as a way of
setting *limits*. It marks the impossible.

Sure you can fly by taking advantage of the laws of aerodynamics and
by expending sufficient energy, but that's not the way *I* want to fly. *I* want to
fly by having my body lift into the air, and move this way and that, quickly
or slowly, *without any expenditure of energy on my part*. I want effortless flying
without machinery. I can imagine that without any trouble, but I can't do it,
and I suspect it will be forever impossible for anyone to do it. The implacabil-
ity of the law of conservation of energy and the unlikelihood of being able to
monkey with the gravitational interaction stand in the way.

What started me thinking in this direction was the premiere of the new
"Twilight Zone" series on television. It opened with two half-hour dramas.
The first was a dramatic version of Harlan Ellison's "Shatterday." (I once
heard Harlan read the story to an assembled audience. He is an absolutely
terrific reader, and I sometimes wonder why he never thought of trying to
break into the movies as a character actor.)

The second, however, is what I want to talk about. It was called *A Little
Peace and Quiet* and dealt with a nice woman who had four totally impossible
and noisy children, a thickheaded, noisy husband, and a noisy dog. Unfortunately, she found it impossible to impose any sort of order on them. My own
idea, as I watched, was a simple and direct one. Kill them all.

However, our heroine found a locket in a box in her backyard. She put
it on and then, when driven to distraction by her horrible family, she
screamed, "Shut up. Just shut up," and they were all quiet. In fact, they were

more than quiet; they all froze. Everything froze, and it became quite apparent that the woman's locket was a device that, at will, could stop time.

Nor was it a local phenomenon, for as the drama proceeded, and she had other opportunities to make use of her new ability, it became perfectly clear that it stopped time for the whole Earth and, very likely, for the whole Universe.

What's more, she could start it again any time by saying, "Start talking."

That amounted to several wish fulfillments at once. She was, of course, invisible to anyone else while time was stopped. She could do anything she wanted, such as lifting something out of another woman's shopping cart, or taking sexual liberties with a very handsome young man who was frozen and helpless. (She didn't, but it was made perfectly clear that she had the impulse to.)

As fantasy, it was fascinating. As science, alas, it was impossible.

Let's say you could stop time. Is there any way of doing that? Certainly. Travel at the speed of light and the rate of progress in time is zero—but only for you, not for the rest of the Universe.

The question is, how do you stop time for the rest of the Universe and not for you?

Well, suppose you could travel at infinite speed. In that case you could dash from point A to point B to point C, doing anything you wanted to do and it would all happen in zero time. The rest of the world would seem to you to be frozen.

But how can you travel at infinite speed? The speed of light is the ultimate limit, and after you have traveled back and forth for 186,000 miles or so, one second will have passed in the Universe generally. In other words, people wouldn't be frozen, they would simply be moving very, very slowly. (The importance between zero time flow and very slow time flow is crucial in connection with the denouement, but naturally I won't tell you what that was.)

You might suppose that very slow movement under ordinary circumstances would do. Ordinarily, the heroine would accomplish whatever she wanted after moving about for a total of far less than 186,000 miles, or even, perhaps, for less than 1 mile. But, to move at the speed of light, or near it, would require enormous mountains of energy and, as near as could be made out, our heroine's gift for motion in a frozen world entailed no effort whatever.

Or let's look at it in another way. The world is frozen and the heroine can move freely, without energy expenditure, and we are going to accept that. But how frozen is frozen?

If time has stopped, then everything is permanently locked into space and can't move. Yet the heroine is able to lift objects, drag human beings from one place to another, and so on. Even if some unexplained magic can keep her moving freely in a zero-flow-of-time situation, how can other things be made to move? They are, in effect, being made to move at infinite speed, requiring infinite energy.

In short, logic would seem to imply that even if time could be stopped and even if our heroine could move freely despite that, she should at least be limited to the point of being unable to manipulate other objects.

Consider something else. In the story, it seemed that only objects you saw were frozen. But what of air molecules, for instance? If time stopped so that you and I seemed to be frozen in space to someone who was free of its effects, the molecules in the air ought also to be stopped. If our heroine tried to move she would have to shove air molecules out of the way, which would mean inflicting infinite speed upon them and expending infinite energy. In short, she couldn't move—she, too, would be frozen in the spot.

Hey, that might be a good idea. Just imagine a story in which someone stopped time and found that not only the Universe was frozen but he (or she) was held permanently prisoner by the matter around him even to the extent where he could not say, "Start talking," and end it. Presumably, for the purpose of the story, he would retain consciousness and since time had stopped, he would be immortal. Imagine being imprisoned forever and *knowing* it.

Except—would our hero be conscious? Unless we are willing to make consciousness a totally mystical phenomenon, it has to depend on the movement of atoms and electrons in the brain.

But the movement couldn't take place if time were stopped, or if it did take place, it would represent infinite speed and, therefore, infinite temperature, and our protagonist would be instantaneously turned into plasma.

But don't get me wrong. I'm not a spoilsport. I *enjoyed* the drama, and though I might have muttered to my dear wife, Janet, "All this is impossible," I didn't let that interfere with my enjoyment. It's just important not to mistake fantasy for science, that's all.

♦

AFTERWORD: It might seem stupid of me to analyze a frothy fantasy and spoil my enjoyment of it just because I am such a scientific stick-in-the-mud. Well, don't think it for a moment. I am perfectly capable of enjoying even the most silly fantasy and although something in my brain keeps ticking off impossibilities, I can easily ignore it. It's called "suspension of disbelief" and I'm extremely good at it.

42

Sword and Sorcery

I DON'T REPRESENT MYSELF AS AN expert on the history of science fiction and its various sister fields and cousin fields, but I suspect I won't be far wrong if I say that the contemporary sword-and-sorcery tale owes its existence to the imagination of Robert Howard and to his invention of the Conan stories in the 1930s.

Part of the success of this type of story lies in the fascination of the bulging muscles and incredible strength and fortitude of the hero. I imagine that almost any male would at least occasionally wish he had biceps as hard as chrome steel and could wield a fifty-pound sword as though it were a bamboo cane and could use it to cleave vile caitiffs to the chine. Imagine single-handedly putting fifty assailants to flight with a sword in one hand and a fainting damsel in the other?

Oddly enough, I shudder at such things. I have lived so thoroughly effete a life, and am such a failure at suspending *some* kinds of disbelief, that I remain too conscious of what a hero must smell like after having performed such feats and I've never read of one of them using a deodorant even once. It seems to me that the Conans of the world must rescue maidens from fates worse than death only to subject them to other fates worse than death.

Of course, maidens might like that sort of thing, and so might damsels —but I don't really know. I've never put them to that particular test.

Heroes date back much farther than Conan, you may be sure. They are as old as literature, and the most consistently popular ones are notable for their muscles and not much else. As Anna Russell says of Siegfried, who is the hero of Richard Wagner's *Der Ring des Nibelungen,* such heroes are "very brave, very strong, very handsome, and very, *very* stupid."

You can find such heroes in almost every culture. The Sumerians had Gilgamesh, the Greeks had Heracles, the Hebrews had Samson, the Persians had Rustam, the Irish had Cuchulain, and so on. Each one of them would get into all kinds of trouble since any child could deceive and entrap them, and they then had to depend on their superhuman strength, and nothing else, to get out of the trouble.

It took the ancient Greeks to come up with something better. In *The Iliad,* the hero is Achilles, another killing machine. In *The Odyssey,* however, the hero is Odysseus, who is an efficient enough fighter (he wouldn't have been allowed in any self-respecting epic, otherwise) but, in addition, he had BRAINS.

There is a tale that is not told in *The Iliad,* but is referred to in *The Odyssey* and is elaborated by poets after Homer, to the effect that after the death of Achilles, there was a question as to which of the Greek heroes deserved to take over Achilles' glorious god-manufactured armor. One of the claimants was Ajax, who was second only to Achilles in strength and was very likely the least intelligent of the heroes, and the other was Odysseus. It was a case of brawn versus brain.

In Ovid's *The Metamorphoses,* the story is told particularly well. Ajax stands up to state his case to the assembled Greeks and tells of the long, harsh battles in which he was a staunch bulwark, in which his mighty arm fended off the Trojans, and of the time he singly defended the ships at a low point in the war.

When I read this for the first time, I was impressed. Ajax convinced me. I didn't see how it was possible for Odysseus, a fighter of lesser strength, to maintain his claim to the armor. But then, the wise Odysseus arose and totally demolished Ajax's arguments. It was not simple strength, not the mere clash of sword and shield that was deciding the war, but strategy—policy—thought. I cheered Odysseus and so did the Greeks, and he got the armor. Poor Ajax went mad with frustration and killed himself.

There is a touching passage in *The Odyssey* that serves as a postscript. Odysseus visits the underworld and sees relatives and friends who had passed away, including his mother and Achilles. Ajax is there, too, and Odysseus approaches the dead hero with friendly words, but Ajax moves away silently. Even after death, he cannot forgive.

In other cultures, too, there is the occasional tale of brute strength defeated. One of the great story plots is that of David and Goliath, the little man defeating the giant by clever choice of weapons. Reynard the Fox defeats the threatening wolves, bears, and lions in the medieval animal tales, and so does Br'er Rabbit in the black legends.

In this battle of brains and brawn, however, the audience is never quite at ease with the victory of brains. The uncomplicated Lancelots and Rolands are cheered to the echo, but clever victors are often met with a certain reserve and suspicion. In many post-Homeric legends, Odysseus is represented as an unprincipled schemer and physical coward. The cleverness of the fox and rabbit is usually represented as based on lies and dishonesty.

In legends, the clever character is often envisaged as someone smart enough to control aspects of the Universe through his superior knowledge and wisdom. He is a magician or sorcerer. There are occasionally magicians who are on the side of right and who serve the physical hero, as Merlin serves King Arthur. Sometimes, they even *are* the hero as Vainamoinen is, for instance, in the Finnish legends.

Very often, though, the magician is the villain, who threatens the hero with sneaky enchantments, who fights from behind the protective wall of his powers. Our poor hero, who fights in the open with simple and honest thwacks of his sword, must somehow reach and destroy the cowardly, unethical magician.

Clearly, the readers are expected to feel that it is noble and admirable for the hero to pit his own superhuman strength against the lesser physiques of his enemies, and also to feel that there is something perfidious about a magician pitting his own superhuman intelligence against the lesser wit of his enemies.

This double standard is very evident in sword and sorcery, in which the Sword-hero (brawn) is pitted against the Sorcery-villain (brain), with brawn winning every time. The convention is, furthermore, that brawn is always on the side of goodness and niceness (a proposition which, in real life, is very dubious). This is similar to the convention in Westerns, in which all disputes are decided by which character can draw his gun the fastest and shoot the straightest. It is then understood that the clean and virtuous White-hat is always fastest and straightest, a proposition which must surely be a variety of wishful thinking impossible to justify in any realistic fashion.

Science fiction, in its early days, often fell into this cliché of smart-is-wicked. Think of all the mad scientists who populated the stories published during the first decade of the science fiction magazines, to say nothing of the comic strips and movies ever since. Think of all the Flash Gordons who have pitted their mighty thews, and their stupidity, against the evil intelligence of the Mings—and won.

I don't say that I don't enjoy this, too. I particularly like it when it is leavened with a sense of humor as in the case of the television miniseries *Wizards and Warriors*. However, the fact is that in the history of the large mammalian predators, humanity came out as sovereign by virtue of brain over brawn, and heroic fantasy would reverse the decision and give the victory to the lions and elephants. (If you disapprove of what human beings are doing to the Earth—as I do—you may wish the lions and elephants *had* won, but I'm not saying that brains are good, merely that they are victors.)

Present-day science fiction has, as one of the characteristics that differentiate it from other forms of fiction, a tendency toward the deification of reason. Scientists are sometimes heroes, and intelligence is very frequently the weapon that must be used, even by those who are not scientists, to solve the problems posed. In my own stories, I almost never make use of violence, and even when I do, it is never the means whereby the crisis is resolved. In my stories, it is a case of reason against reason, with the superior brain winning. (And sometimes it is not completely clear that the superior brain represents the cause of right and good, for I have the uneasy feeling that right does not always triumph—or is even always clearly definable.)

The definition of "good science fiction" ought to include, then, the tendency to have problems solved by the use of brains—the human specialty —rather than by the use of stupid strength.

Not all heroic fantasy takes the reverse stand. In Tolkien's *The Lord of the Rings* intelligence is exalted. Nevertheless, I consider the typical sword-and-sorcery tale to be anti–science fiction—to be the very opposite of science fiction. It is for that reason that you are not likely to find anything of the sort published in my magazine, unless it is particularly exceptional in its characteristics.

AFTERWORD: Everything has its exceptions. I am sure that the average person favors brawn over brains (or Sylvester Stallone would be a poor man today) and yet how do we account, then, for one of the most popular (if not *the* most popular) of all fictional characters—Sherlock Holmes?

43

Fairy Tales

WHAT ARE FAIRY TALES? The easiest definition is, of course, that they are tales about fairies, where a fairy is a kind of imaginary being possessing many supernatural powers.

We most commonly picture fairies, in these degenerate times of ours, as being cute little beings with butterfly wings, whose chief amusement is nestling in flowers. That, however, is a foolish narrowing of the notion. Properly, fairies are *any* imaginary beings possessing many supernatural powers. Some are large and grotesque.

Therefore, stories dealing with witches, wizards, giants, ogres, jinn, afrits, baba-yagas, and many of the other creatures of legend may fairly be considered to be fairy tales. Since the powers of such "fairies" include the granting of wishes, the casting of spells, the conversion of men into other creatures or vice versa, fairy tales are obviously a kind of fantasy, and some might even consider them one of the strands that went into the making of modern science fiction.

Because many fairy tales have unknown authors and were transmitted in oral form for many generations before they were written down by students of such things, and because, as a result, they lack polished literary form, they have been called "folk tales." But then some of our most beloved fairy tales have been written by known authors in comparatively modern times (for instance, "Cinderella" and "The Ugly Duckling"), so I think we had better stick to "fairy tales."

Fairy tales have always been considered suitable reading for youngsters. Adults who have forgotten them, or who have never read them in the first place, seem to think of them as charming little stories full of sweetness and light. After all, don't they all end "And they all lived happily ever after"? So we all say, "Oh, my, wouldn't it be great if our lives were just like a fairy tale."

And we sing songs that include lines such as "Fairy tales can come true / It can happen to you—"

That's all nonsense, of course, for, you see, not all "fairies" are benevolent. Some are mischievous, some are spiteful, and some are downright wicked, so that some of the fairy tales are rough going.

This all hit home once, about a quarter of a century ago, when I was even younger than I am now. At that time, I had two young children and I was wondering what I ought to do with them, so I attended some sort of parents/teachers meeting at the local school. At that meeting, a woman rose and said, "Is there some way we can keep children from reading the awful science fiction things they put out these days? They're so frightening. Why can't they read the delightful fairy tales that *we* read when we were young?"

Of course, I wasn't as well known in those days as I am now, so I'm sure she didn't mean it as a personal blow at me, but I reacted very promptly just the same, as you can well imagine.

I got up as though someone had shoved a long pin up through the seat of my chair and began to recite some of the plots of those delightful fairy tales.

How about "Snow White"? She's a nice little girl, whose mother had died and whose father has married a beautiful woman as a second wife. The new stepmother doesn't like Snow White, and the more good and beautiful the girl comes to be, the more her stepmother doesn't like her. So Stepmother orders an underling to take Snow White into the woods and *kill* her and, just as a little added attraction, she orders him to cut out her heart (after she is dead, I hope, though the stepmother doesn't specify) and bring it back to her as evidence.

Talk about child abuse!

The wicked stepmother theme is a common one in fairy tales. Cinderella had one also, and two wicked stepsisters to boot, and she was mistreated by them all constantly—ill fed, ill dressed, ill housed—and forced to watch those who abused her swimming in cream while she slaved away for them.

Sure both stories end happily but how many children are scarred forever by these horribly sadistic passages? How many women, innocent and good, who marry a man with children and are prepared to love and care for those children are met with undying suspicion and hostility from those children because of the delightful fairy tales they've read?

There are wicked uncles, too. "The Babes in the Wood" is a short, all-time favorite. They are driven into the woods by their wicked uncle and starve to death there. Of course, the robins cover them with leaves, if you want to consider *that* a happy ending.

Wicked uncles were so popularized by fairy tales that they are to be found in formal literature. They make excellent villains in Robert Louis Stevenson's *Kidnapped,* and in Dickens' *Nicholas Nickleby.* If you have read fairy tales and are young, I wonder if you don't view some perfectly pleasant uncle of yours with careful wariness.

Or how about "Little Red Riding Hood" in which an innocent little girl *and* her grandmother are swallowed by a wolf? Permanently, too, because if you've ever watched a wolf eat a little girl, you know that she gets torn apart. So don't believe that bit about the hunters coming and cutting open the wolf in order to allow the kid *and* her grandmother to jump out alive. That was made up afterward by people who had watched kids going into convulsions after reading that delightful fairy tale in its original form.

My favorite, though, is "Hansel and Gretel." Here are two perfectly charming little children who have the misfortune to have a father who is a poor woodcutter. There happens to be a famine and they run out of food. What happens? The children's mother *(not* their stepmother, but their very own mother) suggests they be taken deep into the woods and left there. In that way, there will be two fewer mouths to feed. Fortunately, they find their way back, to the disappointment and chagrin of their mother. Consequently, when famine strikes again, the mother is right on the ball with her insistence that a second attempt be made to get rid of those little pests. This time the device is successful.

Can you imagine how much confidence this instills in any child reading the story? Thereafter, he keeps a sharp eye on the refrigerator and the pantry to see if the food is running short, for he knows who's going to be taken out to the garbage dump and left there in case the family runs short.

But that's not the worst. In the forest, Hansel and Gretel come across a gingerbread house owned by a witch, who promptly imprisons Hansel and starts fattening him up for a feast, with him as main course. Cannibalism—just in case the kid reader didn't get enough kicks out of abandonment and starvation. Of course, it ends happily because the kids get away from the witch (killing her by burning her in an oven, of course) and come home to their loving father. Their mother (hurray, hurray) has died.

Can you imagine mothers wanting their children to read stuff such as this, instead of good, wholesome science fiction? Why if we printed stories à la Grimm (grim, indeed) in our magazine, we'd be harried out of town by hordes of indignant citizenry.

Think of that when next you feel moved to complain about the "violence" in some of our stories. Why, they're mother's milk compared to the stuff you expect your eight-year-olds to read.

Of course, fairy tales reflect the times in which they were told. Those were hard times. Poor woodcutters were *really* poor and there was no welfare roll they could get onto. Famines were *really* famines. What's more, mothers frequently died in childbirth, and fathers had to marry again to have someone take care of the youngster. Naturally, the new wife promptly had children of her own (or had them already by an earlier husband) and any woman would favor her own children over some stranger. And fathers did die young and leave their property to an infant child and appoint a brother the guardian of both child and property. Naturally, the brother, knowing that once the child grew up and took over the property in his own right, he himself would be out on his ear, was tempted to prevent that dire possibility from coming to pass.

Nowadays, with children less likely to be orphaned before they have reached the age of self-care, those plots are passé and seem needlessly sadistic. They were realistic in their own times, however.

Nevertheless, if some of the problems of the past have been ameliorated, others have cropped up. Parents are less likely to die while their children are infants—but are more likely to get divorced. If wicked uncles are passé, wicked landlords are not. If wolves don't roam the suburbs much anymore, drug pushers do.

Some define "science fiction" as "today's fairy tales." If so, you have to expect them to deal with the realistic dangers of today, but we *will* try to keep them from falling into the depths of depravity of yesterday's fairy tales.

44

Magic

ARTHUR CLARKE, IN ONE OF his notable oft-quoted comments, said that technology, sufficiently advanced, was indistinguishable from magic.

That's clear enough. If a medieval peasant, or even a reasonably educated medieval merchant, were presented with the sight of a superjet streaking through the sky, or with a working television set, or with a pocket computer, he would be quite convinced that he was witnessing sorcery of the most potent sort. He might also be pretty certain that the sorcery was the devil's work. Consequently, if a person from the present (his future) were to go back in time with a pocket computer, for instance, and demonstrate its workings, the result might well be exorcism, and perhaps even the torture chamber.

The question in my mind, though, is whether the proposition can be reversed. Is magic necessarily indistinguishable from sufficiently advanced technology? If so, you see, all the tricks of the trade of fantasy could be transferred to science fiction. After all, you don't have to describe the advanced technology in detail (if you could, you would build a working model, patent it, and become very rich, perhaps).

For instance, as a child, I found "Ali Baba and the Forty Thieves" fascinating. Imagine coming up to a blank mountain wall, saying, "Open sesame!," having the wall split in two, and having the halves move apart to reveal the entrance to a cave. Now that's magic!

My wonder and bemusement at such a thing continued undiminished even after I had grown accustomed to approaching doors and having them open automatically at my approach. That wasn't magic; that was just a photo-cell and therefore no cause for wonder at all (even though I would agree that a medieval merchant, presented with such an automatically opening door, would surely consider it magic).

Perhaps it is the "Open sesame!" that is the real wonder of it. After all, a door that opens at the mere approach of anyone at any time shows no discretion. If there is a code word that only you know, then you control the door; you have *power*.

But then, it is easy to imagine a computer which will only allow the door to open at some appropriate code word punched onto its keyboard. Indeed, the time may well come when such a computer may be designed to respond to the spoken command. In that case, it is inevitable that some jokester will have the computer open the door at the command "Open sesame!"

We might go even further and outdo the story. After all, in the tale, the door opens to anyone's command of "Open sesame!" and because Ali Baba overhears it, he gains entrance to the cave and grows rich. A computer may be designed to respond only to the typical sound pattern of a particular voice and then only you may open the door, even if the whole world besides knows the code word.

Next, how about Snow White's stepmother, the wicked Queen, who asks her mirror who is the fairest of them all and has the mirror assure her that she is? Well, we don't have talking mirrors, but we do have talking television screens, and the medieval merchant would see no distinction.

Some day, when it will become routine to have conversations under conditions of closed-circuit television, a fair young maid can phone her boyfriend and say, sentimentally, "Who is the fairest in the land?" and heaven help the boyfriend if his image in the mirror doesn't say, "You are the fairest in the land."

A third example that I always found impressive as a child is that of the giant who finds he must chase the hero who has gotten away with one or more of said giant's ill-gotten treasures. The giant promptly puts on his "seven-league boots" and is off on a chase. No matter how great a lead our young hero has, we may be sure he will be quickly overtaken.

Now what are seven-league boots? It is usually explained that the giant can traverse 7 leagues (21 miles) at every stride. The stories never explain how long it takes him to make one stride, but children always assume (at least I did) that the giant makes as many strides per minute as a man ordinarily does.

The stride of a walking man is about 1 yard. That is, when a foot moves from its rear position to its fore position in ordinary walking, it moves through a distance of a yard. In the same time, the much huger stride of the giant moves through 21 miles or 36,960 yards.

A man walking in an unhurried manner travels at a speed of 3 miles per hour. The giant walking in an unhurried manner travels at 36,960 times this speed or 110,880 miles an hour. This is indeed fast—much faster than I had imagined as a child, or (I am sure) than the tale spinner who first spoke of seven-league boots imagined.

Someone equipped with seven-league boots can travel from New York to Los Angeles in 1.6 minutes, and can go around the world in 13.5 minutes.

That is astonishing even as an example of high technology. It is faster than any present-day airplane and is even faster than the rocket ships carrying our astronauts to the Moon.

In fact, so unexpectedly fast are seven-league boots that they defeat their own purpose. Any giant moving 21 miles at a stride, with strides coming as frequently as in an ordinary man's ordinary walk, would be traveling with a speed some 4.4 times escape velocity. In short, he would, at his first stride, launch himself through the atmosphere, and, in a few more strides, find himself in outer space.

And yet there is nothing to keep us from developing seven-league boot capacity. After all, that enormously speedy giant is still moving at only 1/6,250 the speed of light.

I think I have shown then that magic can be indistinguishable from sufficiently advanced technology, but is that *always* so?

Obviously not, for it is common enough in tales of magic and sorcery to have people able to make themselves invisible, for instance; or to change a man into a frog and vice versa; or to be made capable of understanding the language of animals (and to then find that a horse can discourse as sensibly as Socrates). It is questionable whether such things are within the reasonable purview of technology, though with sufficient ingenuity I know that a science fiction writer can think of a way of making such things sound technologically plausible.

However, consider that bit of magic that appeals to childhood most of all. There is no question in my mind that *the* most wonderful of all objects is

Aladdin's lamp. —Tell the truth, now! Haven't you ever dreamed of owning it?

Imagine having a jinn under your absolute control; one who answers, "I hear and obey," to all requests, however unreasonable; one who can supply you with uncounted trays of jewels at the snap of a finger; one who can build you an elaborate and luxurious palace overnight and have it come ready-filled with beautiful and compliant damsels.

Ah! That's what I call *living*.

And I think that we have now put our finger on the vital difference between magic and however high technology. Presented with something so strange we cannot comprehend how it's done, whether by some technological advance or some actually working magic, we have only to ask one question: "What are the limits within which the ability to do this must work?"

Magic need have no limits; technology must have.

Thus, the jinn of the lamp can build a palace overnight, or even in an instant, and it wouldn't occur to the reader to ask, "But what was the source of the energy required to perform this task?" The jinn of the lamp could travel to Jupiter to obtain the rare egg of the dyk-dyk bird and be back in twenty seconds and no one would dream of pointing out that lo! he has traveled far faster than the speed of light.

I suspect that no technology, however advanced, will ever defy the law of conservation of energy, or of momentum, or of angular momentum, or of electric charge. I suspect that no technology, however advanced, will defy the laws of thermodynamics, or James Clerk Maxwell's equations, or the indeterminacy principle, or the tenets of relativity and quantum theory.

I say that I "suspect" this because I am perfectly ready to admit that we don't yet know all there is to know about the Universe, that there may turn out to be special conditions, of which we as yet know nothing, in which any or all of these limits can be bent or broken.

However, even if these limits are demolished, other limits, more basic and more unbreakable, will replace them. *Some* limit there will remain, as seems absolutely unavoidable to me.

Magic, however, is unlimited; that is its essence. When a science fiction writer presents a tale of magic that must abide by rules and respect limits (as L. Sprague de Camp does in his wonderful *The Incomplete Enchanter*) then it is no longer magic; it is merely an exotic technology.

♦

AFTERWORD: Now that I'm reading all these essays one after the other, I can see that the one above is very much Chapters 38 and 39 viewed from the other side. Those were science looking at magic, and this is magic looking at science. As a matter of fact, Chapter 41 is magic looking at science also. However, they are not complete overlaps, and it seems to me that they make a rather important point in four different ways.

SCIENCE
FICTION
MAGAZINES ✦

45

Opinion

I RECEIVED A LETTER THE OTHER week, written by someone who took exception to one of my essays (the one you'll find as Chapter 65), claiming it was not a proper subject for an editorial and questioning whether I knew what an editorial was.

That set me to thinking. I call these particular essays "editorials" but what is an editorial? I think I know, but what if I'm wrong? The letter writer had not been kind enough to tell me the answer, so that I was left to my own poor devices. Well, suppose I was asked to write a dictionary definition. What would I write?

Obviously, one way of settling the matter is to look up what is already written in some reputable dictionary, but I didn't want to do that right away. First, I wanted to figure out for myself what *I* thought an editorial was.

Since I have a simple mind, my first attempted definition was "Editorial: that which I write when I write an editorial for *Asimov's.*"

Aha, nice and circular as a definition, and not even original. John Campbell once defined science fiction as "the kind of story bought by a science fiction editor." Damon Knight (I believe) went even further and said, "Science fiction is what I point to when I say, 'This is science fiction.' "

So I accepted my circular definition and took another step. What do I write when I write an editorial for *Asimov's?* I write on all sorts of things, but in every case, I express my opinions about whatever it is I am writing about. Obviously, then, I think that the definition should read: "Editorial: an essay expressing the opinion of an editor on some subject he believes is, or should be, of interest to his readers."

I then looked up the definition of editorial in The American Heritage Dictionary of the English Language and it says, "An article in a publication expressing the opinion of its editors or publishers." Webster's New International Dictionary of the English Language (second edition) says, in part, "An article published as an expression of the views of the editor." The Random House Dictionary of the English Language says, "An article in a newspaper or other periodical presenting the opinion of the publisher, editor, or editors."

I am sure that you see we are all in substantial agreement, but I think my definition is clearly the best because it mentions "some subject . . . of interest to his readers." That shows I'm not just writing arbitrarily on any subject at all, but (like the noble person I am) that I have the readers' interests at heart at all times.

To be sure, I don't pretend to divine omniscience and there's no way I can *know* what is of interest to all the readers, or even a majority of the readers, or even just a substantial minority of the readers. So I have my definition speak of a subject the editor "believes" to be of interest. Nor do I insist that the subject "is" of interest, but merely that, as an alternative, it "should be" of interest.

You'll notice that with those precautions I end up quite able to write about any subject I choose and to defend my definition-right to do so. And to prove that, I will now proceed to talk about the first thing that enters my head—

When I had written *The Caves of Steel* and *The Naked Sun* back in the 1950s (see my essay presented as Chapter 59), I had written the first about a planet (Earth) in which human beings far outnumbered robots, and the second about a planet (Solaria) in which robots far outnumbered human beings. I promised a third novel about a planet (Aurora) in which human beings and robots struck a reasonable balance.

I tried to write it and failed. One of the reasons (I now realize in retrospect) was that I had a thoroughly humanoid robot as one of my protagonists in the two books, and if I was to deal with a world in which human beings and robots struck a reasonable balance and where at least some robots were thoroughly humanoid, then I was going to have to deal with the possibility of sexual relations between humans and robots—and I didn't feel up to it.

When I finally returned to the task after a lapse of twenty-five years, I realized I *still* had to deal with that possibility, but now things had changed. First, my writing skills had, in my opinion, improved; second, there was a more permissive attitude as far as dealing with sex in literature was concerned; and, third, I had gained courage as a result of the success of *Foundation's Edge.*

I therefore wrote *The Robots of Dawn* in which sex between robots and human beings (and other kinds of sex, too) is dealt with in straightforward fashion.

I held, however, to my principles. The sex was not clinical, it was not exploitative, it was not thrown in for the sake of sensation or prurience. It was essential to the plot, and it was dealt with only to the point where it was necessary to do so.

I wasn't certain what the results would be. Would people be annoyed with me for dealing with sex at all when, ordinarily, I write (as a charming young nun once noted in an essay she had written on my books) "with decorum," and refuse to buy my books? Or would they be annoyed with me for *still* writing with decorum even about sex and turn me down angrily for being insufficiently exciting?

Actually, they did neither. I am glad to say that *The Robots of Dawn* proved to be my second bestseller and it may possibly do nearly as well as *Foundation's Edge.* What's more, the letters I have so far received from readers have been uniformly favorable.

But *why* did there have to be such sex?

Consider— If you have a robot that is roughly as intelligent as a human being, and who looks exactly like a human being (either male or female) and has all the functioning parts of a human being, surely your knowledge of how obsessed and inventive human beings are about sex will lead you to the conclusion that there *will* be sex between human beings and robots, and that you will have to deal with the consequences. If there isn't, your novel will be ignoring so obvious and important a part of life that you will be laughed at. There would be no way the book could be taken seriously.

Ah, but mightn't I have avoided the unpleasant necessity of dealing with such a subject by simply not having thoroughly humanoid robots? No, because all my robot short stories dealt, in one way or another, with the antagonism of human beings for robots, and when I wrote *The Caves of Steel* I had to take up the problem of what would happen to this antagonism if the robot was just about indistinguishable from a human being.

One thing inevitably led to another, you see, and any writer worth anything at all must follow where his art leads. (I'm sorry if that sounds pretentious.)

But then, suppose a writer is dealing with another kind of nonhuman approximation to the human. What if a nonhuman animal can be made, in some way, close to human in intelligence? What if this animal is sufficiently creative to carry on an intelligent conversation and even to write a story that is publishable? And what if this animal approximates the human in appearance?

You see that the situation is not terribly different from that of a humanoid robot.

I took the easy way out by making a robot so human and so good-looking and so noble and good that love and sex seem to follow almost naturally.

But if the humanity is only approximate and the appearance is definitely subhuman and the character still has much of the animal in it, what then? The situation is a lot harder to deal with.

Suppose you are a male teacher of such a female animal. The teacher-pupil relationship is a close one and sex can rear its inconvenient head. Abelard and Heloise are a classic example of this and there have been others both before and after. Can that relationship cross the gulf of species?

To be more specific, can a male human being who teaches an intelligent female orangutan fall in love with her? And if so, what happens? It isn't a story that I could write, but it isn't so different in concept from *The Robots of Dawn*.

Leigh Kennedy wrote such a story. It was entitled "Her Furry Face" and it appeared in the Mid–December 1983 issue of *Asimov's*.

It was not a pleasant story, and it received flak from a number of readers, but it was our editorial opinion that it was an honest story and an important one, dealing with a legitimate science fictional problem. The higher apes are being taught sign language and they might end up seeming intelligent in some primitive human sense. If we could just go a little further somehow—

Well, bestiality *does* exist, and with animals that are not even vaguely human in intelligence.

So think about it. Not pruriently, but just as a possible complication involved in ethological advance. Isn't that what good science fiction is supposed to do? Make you think?

♦

AFTERWORD: I didn't write these essays with any thought of making them fit into neat categories, but when I prepared this collection, it seemed that placing the essays in categories would make them more palatable. Inevitably, I would hit a few for which I couldn't quite decide the proper place. The above essay, for instance, doesn't fit conveniently, but I finally put it in the "Science Fiction Magazines" group because I did consider the problem of editorials in it.

Incidentally, though a few essays in this group might apply to magazines generally, as, for instance, Chapters 47 and 51, the truth is that primarily they deal with *Asimov's.* I think that this doesn't surprise you.

46

Controversy

PRIMARILY, THIS MAGAZINE IS A VE-
hicle for entertainment. What we hope to do is to give pleasure to as many
people as possible and to earn an honest dollar as a result. We do not want to
do harm; we do not want to displease.

It is, however, impossible to express opinions of any sort, impossible to
approve or disapprove of anything, without running into strong objections on
the part of some readers. I suppose we might try to avoid this by retreating
into utter blandness, but not only do we refuse to do that under any conditions, we are convinced that even if we did do this, that would not save us.

So while we don't seek controversy, we don't intend to go out of our
way to avoid it, either. What's more, I shall not hesitate to speak my mind in
these essays on subjects where it seems to me to be appropriate that I do so.
(This magazine is not my private soapbox, I assure you, and I try not to treat
it as such.)

In the July 1983 issue, for instance, we ran the essay "Great Moments in
Pseudoscience" by Martin Gardner, in which he did what he has been doing
with unwearying skill for most of his life—knocking the stuffing out of
pseudoscientific crackpottery.

As it happens, there are a great many people who find themselves attracted to one or another of the fields of pseudoscience—far more than there
are people who are totally resistant to such nonsense. A certain number of the
pseudoscientiphiles are articulate and intelligent, and a certain number of these

read the magazine. Some of these pseudoscientiphilic readers responded to the article angrily.

Well, we expect that (and so does Martin) but there were some characterizations of Martin himself that were ludicrously wide of the point. I know Martin well and, of the handful of people I am acquainted with who are totally and uncompromisingly rational, he is the most honest and open-minded. He is the only one, to my knowledge, who, in publishing articles, will go to the trouble of publishing letters that attempt to refute his points, and answering them politely and without venom. I assure you that there is nothing venomous in his constitution.

Some readers seem to think that because John W. Campbell, Jr., was (without question) the greatest editor in science fiction's history, and exerted more influence on the field than anyone else has, that there is something criminal in criticisms of him appearing in a science fiction magazine.

I knew John Campbell well, too, and no one, but *no one*, has more greatly benefited from his constant, generous help than I have, something I have attested to over and over again in my writings. Nevertheless, to say that in some ways Campbell was a good and kind man, a giant in the field of imagination and ideas, a genius in the art of editing, is not necessarily to say that he was perfect in all respects. (We all revere George Washington, but are we really expected to believe that he never told a lie, just because of a completely fictional tale about a cherry tree?)

The fact is that Campbell had a penchant for accepting pseudoscientific claims uncritically. At one time or another, he boosted UFOs, the Dean drive, dianetics, the Hieronymus machine, and psi powers. He had kind words for magic, too. He felt (he said to me often) that science was too narrow and that by discussing these beyond-the-fringe areas, he was helping to force it to investigate areas that might well turn out to be important.

Well, perhaps. That is, after all, the usual rationalization of those who find themselves in the difficult position of yearning for both pseudoscience and respectability. (My intellectual life is an easy one since I yearn for neither.)

However, I spent endless hours discussing these things with Campbell, and it always seemed to me that he wasn't interested in just needling science. He *believed*. And the trouble was that he was charismatic enough to make *others* believe, others who didn't know as much as he himself did and who were much more likely to go off the deep end into even more extreme foolishness.

Those he convinced of the value of pseudoscience and of the wickedness of scientific orthodoxy then convinced others, and this helped spawn the UFOmaniacs, Velikovskians, Von Dänikenites, Scientologists, pyramid-power freaks, psychic surgery nuts, and others who plague us today. He was not the sole originator, to be sure, and the pseudoscientiphiles would be here today in ample numbers even without him, but he *helped* and in that respect, he did harm to the cause of science.

Nor is it valid to say that it is cowardly to attack Campbell now that he is dead and cannot defend himself. In the first place, the act of death does not convert a person into a plaster saint, or alter truth, and in the second place, there are many who are presently alive and vocal who will gladly defend Campbell, perhaps more loudly and vehemently than Campbell himself would have done.

Finally, Martin argued against Campbell's views when Campbell was alive, and I, for one, denounced those views to Campbell's face on many an occasion. (It did not end our friendship, however. I was too aware of what he had done for me, and, for his part, he was always tolerant of criticism—one of his very many good points, and something I have tried to learn from him, though not always very successfully, alas.)

As for criticisms of him appearing in a science fiction magazine (and in *my* science fiction magazine), that is *exactly* the place for them to appear. If some outsider, some non-s.f. person, were to deal with Campbell's questionable views in some periodical of general circulation, you can bet that the writer would use those views as a stick with which to beat science fiction. Campbell's pseudoscience would be presented as the inevitable consequence of his interest in science fiction and there would be plenty of indication that science fiction is *part* of pseudoscience and that its readers form the mainstay of pseudoscientiphilism. In fact, I must say that Campbell has harmed not only science, but science fiction itself, in the views he espoused, because he made it possible for outsiders to sneer at and deride science fiction in this way.

Then, too, an outsider who held up Campbell's views to ridicule would not know of the many, many ways in which Campbell was great and good and kind. He would present *only* Campbell's flaws and weaknesses.

This is not so here. Martin and I know very well that good science fiction is not to be judged by Campbell's flaws, and that neither is Campbell himself to be judged by them—or, at least, entirely by them.

But let's get beyond John Campbell. Is it possible that "orthodox" science is close-minded and bigoted and refuses to investigate things that it has already decided, on emotional grounds perhaps, to be nonexistent?

Of course not! Individual scientists may be close-minded and bigoted, because individual scientists are human. Individual scientists are no more "science" than an individual science fiction reader is "science fiction."

Science is a system of investigation that can be turned on anything. The results of such investigations have uncovered evidence that fails to lend any support whatever to propositions that perhaps no one believes (that stones fall upward) or to propositions that perhaps millions believe (that ghosts exist). In fact, evidence has been uncovered that argues against some propositions in a seemingly conclusive manner (that the Earth is flat).

Now, then, an individual scientist has a finite lifetime and in that lifetime he usually wishes to investigate areas that offer the promise of some success so that he may pique his own interest and sate his own curiosity and (being human) so that he may possibly receive honors and respect.

It follows that he is *not* anxious to investigate reports of stones falling upward or of ghosts or of flat-Earth arguments or anything else that falls under the heading of "pseudoscience." They are pseudoscience precisely because, even when couched in scientific language, they deal with phenomena that have almost no chance of existing, so that it seems unreasonable to ask a scientist to waste his life on it.

There are many pseudoscientiphiles who demand that scientists investigate one or another variety of nonsense. Why doesn't such a pseudoscientiphile go to the trouble and difficulty of learning to be a scientist and of then investigating his belief himself with the necessary professional skills? If he finds out nothing, he will at least have had a life in which he followed his personal interests; if he finds out something, he may win scientific immortality.

If he simply stands on the sidelines and yells for someone else to do the work and take the risk, he is worth nothing.

AFTERWORD: John W. Campbell, Jr., has been a problem to me for the thirty-three years before his death. He did so much for me and meant so much to me (see my autobiography) and yet, at the same time, I disagreed so profoundly with his philosophy of life. I could never love him as much as I wanted to, or speak to him as harshly as I wished to. The above essay is my attempt to articulate, at last, exactly how I feel about him.

47

Magazine Covers

I N APRIL 1926, THE FIRST ISSUE OF the first all–science fiction magazine came out. It was *Amazing Stories,* Volume 1, Number 1.

The most characteristic aspect of the cover of that magazine, at least to me, was the lettering of the name. It began with a gigantic A in the upper left of the magazine (which was 8½ by 11 inches in size). Naturally, the remaining letters couldn't be that large; there wasn't room. They tailed off smaller and smaller therefore. The entire effect was that of an onrushing (or, perhaps, leave-taking) comet or rocket ship.

Why was it designed in that fashion? Well, I wasn't there when it was decided upon, but I can guess.

In those days (as in these) there were many magazines competing for reader attention and they were presented in the racks in bewildering plenty. There wasn't room enough to present them all full-face, so they were usually overlapped in both horizontal rows and vertical columns. Perhaps only the upper half of the leftmost quarter of the magazine was exposed.

Something characteristic of a magazine therefore had to be located in the upper left for easy recognition. Or, if the magazine was unknown, something obtrusive had to be there to stir reader curiosity. In the case of *Amazing Stories,* it was that giant A. I'm sure many youngsters, surveying the rack, were impelled by curiosity to lift up that particular magazine to see what the A signified.

It must have helped, for *Amazing Stories* did well enough to stay in business for over half a century—to this present day, in fact.

The very success of that technique established the up-and-right curve of the title as the thing to do for science fiction magazines. A surprising number of them later adopted this decreasing curve, usually in less exaggerated form. (There is no point in copying too closely, for it is necessary to establish some distinctiveness for the sake of reader recognition.)

When *Astounding Stories* first appeared, "astounding" tailed off. So did "marvel," "startling," "planet," and others in the case of magazines with those words included in the title.

There is more to a magazine cover than the name, of course. One also needs an illustration.

The function of a cover illustration is twofold. It must first attract the attention of the potential reader and it must, secondly, give that reader an instant understanding of the nature of the contents.

To attract attention, the illustration must be in harsh primary colors with the figures possessing sharp edges. Furthermore, it must depict a scene of dramatic interest.

To establish the nature of the contents, a detective story cover would show a man with a gun; a Western story cover would show a man with a horse; a love story cover would show a man with a woman. These serve as labels, instantly recognizable, and changing somewhat from month to month so that the reader will know when a new issue has appeared and can tell at once that it is something he has not yet read.

In science fiction, the cover illustration must show something that is not yet so—that is in some way futuristic—if the nature of the contents is to be described. One surefire way is to include futuristic machinery—spaceships, robots, or ray guns. Another is to show extraterrestrial beings, particularly if they can be shown threatening beautiful Earthwomen with a vague hint of sexual molestation. (Extraterrestrial creatures were so often portrayed with large eyes that the expression "bug-eyed monsters," abbreviated to "BEMs," became almost a generic term for such covers.)

Naturally, although the covers fulfilled their function of attracting readers and advertising the nature of the magazine's contents, they were also embarrassing. To people who were ignorant of science fiction or contemptuous of it, the covers were "cheap" and their all too easy recognizability made the reader the instant prey of disapproving parents or teachers. In those prehistoric days, science fiction readers learned to keep the covers hidden. Some even tore them off.

With the years, however, respectability grew and the intense need for signaling faded. Reader demand for less embarrassing covers also grew. What's more, the term "science fiction" was invented in 1930 and that became well enough known to serve as the necessary advertisement all by itself.

In March 1938, *Astounding Stories* became *Astounding Science Fiction*, thanks to John W. Campbell, Jr., the new editor of the magazine. Other magazines adopted "science fiction" as part of the title. In March 1939, a magazine entitled simply *Science Fiction* was born.

With *Astounding Science Fiction* leading the way, covers became more sedate. *Astounding* adopted unadorned horizontal lettering for itself and emphasized the "science fiction" at the expense of the "astounding." Cover illustrations cooled down and became more realistic and less cartoonish. For a while *The Magazine of Fantasy and Science Fiction* had no cover illustration at all—merely a list of story titles.

Needless to say, older fans (among whom I number myself despite the fact that I am as yet only in my late youth—though verging, I must admit, on early middle age) harked back to those early, disreputable days of science fiction with nostalgia. Ah, those big block letterings, and, oh, those bug-eyed monsters.

Came the day when I had to choose among various suggested styles for the cover lettering of *Isaac Asimov's Science Fiction Magazine*. One of them had the "Isaac" tailing off and the "Asimov's" under it also tailing off, so that the upper left had the big IA. I selected it at once, and I knew exactly why I selected it. It brought back the joys of my adolescent fanhood.

Naturally, I couldn't trust my own judgment in such matters, knowing, as I did, the influence behind it, so I asked Janet to choose, without telling her my choice. She chose the one I did. I next phoned George and told him what had happened and it turned out that, quite independently, he and Joel had both fixed on that same one. There was no argument, and the title-that-tailed-off returned to science fiction.

The illustration on that first issue was a photograph of your own unhumble servant. I was uneasy at that. After all, though it is possible that my wife and daughter (to say nothing of an occasional dazzled young fan of the female persuasion) may think I am beautiful, I can scarcely make myself believe that is a generally held view. I was therefore not at all sure that my face, muttonchops and all, would sell magazines. Nevertheless, since my personal name was part of the magazine name, it seemed useful to make the association as clear as possible at the start. (I was going to say "as plain as possible" but that would elicit all sorts of wise-guy remarks, I know.)

When I found that my face was also going to appear on later issues, I objected. I said that science fiction fans were too articulate a bunch to let that go without witticisms of all kinds—and I was right. After three issues, Joel decided it would be wise to make me less prominent. The cover was devoted to more traditional scenes of science fiction interest and my face was placed, in miniature, within the *o* of "Asimov's."

My face stayed, one way or another, for the next thirty-four issues. To be sure, it was absent from the *o* in the July-August 1978 issue but in that issue I was present on the cover itself as part of the action.

Beginning with the July 1980 issue, the size of the lettering was decreased in order to make the cover seem less cluttered and the size of my photograph was decreased, too, almost to the point of unrecognizability—something that some readers objected to. (I think that perhaps it made it too hard to score a bull's-eye when playing darts.)

By the time we had reached our fifth year, *Isaac Asimov's Science Fiction Magazine* had certainly won the battle for recognition. We were an established part of the science fiction scene and the impulse arose to redesign the cover to make it, on the whole, quieter and more attractive.

This was done (beginning with the 13 April 1981 issue) in several ways. First, the name was made less obtrusive. After all, *Isaac Asimov's Science Fiction Magazine* is very long for a title and the one essential word is "Asimov's." In the science fiction world there is only one Asimov and it is now firmly associated with the magazine. The new title design is therefore almost entirely "Asimov's." Everything else is still there, but in small and unobtrusive print. And no photograph; I had finally disappeared.

There is a white area that now rims the cover illustration like a frame, and "Asimov's" is in that white area, leaving the illustration much cleaner and uncluttered than it was before. The illustration is less directly illustrative and more symbolic.

It takes some getting used to (all changes do); but I like the new look. Once the readers grew accustomed to it, I'll bet they do, too.

◆

AFTERWORD: The above essay was written seven years ago. The type style of the cover has continued to change. The "Asimov's" remains prominent, but it has become easier to read. The "Isaac" and the words "science fiction" have become larger and more prominent. The word "magazine" disappeared with the July 1986 issue. The search for perfection continues, I suppose. Or perhaps the art designer thinks that a periodic change sharpens readers' interests. Maybe it does.

48

Unreasonable!

LIFE IS UNREASONABLE IN SO many different ways—and there isn't much anyone can do about it.

I, at least, have a soapbox and can relieve my pent-up frustrations by talking about it and giving examples, which is good, and will, I hope, contribute to my remaining young and healthy for an extended period.

What got me thinking about this was a letter mailed to *Asimov's* some time ago. The writer was in a state of fury over the fact that our policy was to ask the enclosure of a stamped self-addressed envelope before we complied with certain requests.

"If I am not worth the investment of a 20-cent stamp," he wrote, angrily, "then the hell with you!"

I instantly put a sheet of paper into my typewriter in order to answer him and give him the elementary explanation that would probably calm him down, but his unreasonableness extended to a failure to include a return address. I must therefore make the explanation here.

Were our correspondent the only one to request a mailing, he would, of course, be worth 20 cents to us—even perhaps a dollar or two. He is not, however, the only one, and I am truly astonished that this does not occur to him. We get many requests every day, and if we complied, the cost in stationery and postage would be substantial. The salaried time spent in typing up addresses would be equally substantial.

To ask each person who would like to get something from us to invest money and time which, on an individual basis, *is* insignificant is reasonable. To ask us to invest large amounts of money and time in order to show our regard for each individual reader is unreasonable (even though the regard does exist). To fail to see this is even more unreasonable.

This is not to say we don't sympathize with the strong feelings our readers have on many issues, even when we are fairly helpless to do anything about it.

The trouble is, of course, that this magazine (and most magazines) are not vast moneymaking concerns. We must operate on a strict budget and must economize where and when we can reasonably do so. We are not overwhelmed with delight by the nature of some of the personals that appear in the last few pages, but we receive payment for that, and if we gave up that payment, the price of the magazine would have to go up, and if enough of you rebelled against the increased price we would have to shut down. If we could find alternate advertising revenue, we would, but this is a hard world, and we can only sigh when idealistic readers complain about the personals. Surely it is unreasonable to ask us to risk suicide.

The price of the magazine does go up occasionally even so, but it is unreasonable to suppose that we do this out of greed for the reader's money. We are at the mercy of the costs of paper, printing, postage, and other things, which go up more or less steadily. We live in an inflation-ridden world, and to expect the magazine to keep its price fixed under such conditions is unreasonable.

We would like to send off subscription issues in wrappers rather than with unsightly address labels, but that, too, introduces a cost that we would have to pass on to subscribers, who would be unlikely to be overjoyed.

We would like to arrange to have the address labels come off easily so that the reader can remove it as soon as he receives the magazine, but such a label is bound to come off once in a while *before* the reader gets the magazine, and off the copy will go to the dead-letter office, and in will come the irate mail over missed issues.

We would like to put the address label on the back cover instead of the front cover for aesthetic reasons, but the post-office employees tend to look at the front, and those who advertise on the back won't see the humor of having part of their message covered up and, on the whole, we are in no position to antagonize either the Postal Service or the advertisers.

We would very much like to please everyone with our editorial policies, but it can't be done. Every time there is a change in the nature of the cover, for instance, the disapproving letters come in. These changes are often merely experimental, and sometimes when we decide, on mature consideration, that the change does not represent an improvement and we change back to the situation as it was before—the disapproving letters again come in.

I am rather pleased and gratified that so many letters have arrived, over the months, mourning the loss of my cheerful and smiling face in the letter *o* of "Asimov's," but I know very well that if we allowed ourselves to be lured into putting my mug back on the cover, at *least* as many letters would arrive groaning over the visual pollution it would produce.

I might argue that readers' letters in these respects are unreasonable, but, then, to expect the world to be reasonable is itself unreasonable, and we will simply continue to do our best. If the time comes that we can wrap our subscription copies, we will. If we can ever lower prices, believe me we will. Most of all, we will continue to keep editorial policies we feel have proven successful, and to change them when we feel that may be an improvement. And we will depend on the readers, as a whole, being pleased with the results.

What's more, we will continue to welcome all your comments, views, and complaints, reasonable or not, since we can never be sure, in advance, just what is reasonable and what not.

Nor do I wish to leave you with the impression that unreasonableness is confined to readers' letters.

Literary reviewers are sometimes unreasonable to the point of madness (ask any writer). For instance, my dear wife, Janet, and I put together an anthology of humorous science fiction—including stories, verse, and cartoons —which Janet carefully arranged in an attractive manner. The publisher, Houghton Mifflin, spared no expense in producing an attractive package, and the title, if you are curious, is *Laughing Space*. We were very pleased with the result, and so were most of the reviewers.

Yet one or two reviewers scowled darkly and complained that in this anthology of humor, we had unaccountably included humorous items. Why did we not include the mordant, bitter, and savage writings of so-and-so and so-and-so?

The proper and reasonable answer, of course, is that the anthology is ours, prepared in accordance with our tastes, and that we included what we thought of as humorous. Savage, bitter, and mordant writings are not what we think of as funny, though we cheerfully admit they are savage, bitter, and mordant. —But then, it is not unheard-of for reviewers to berate a writer for writing a book according to his own taste, and not the book the *reviewer* would have written, if the reviewer were only capable of writing. It would be unreasonable to expect anything else from some reviewers.

I have my own unreasonabilities, too.

I can never quite understand the difficulty that people have in appreciating the peculiar problems of a prolific writer. I write as much as I do, not because I rub Aladdin's lamp, but because I have a seventy-hour workweek and stick to it.

Yet every once in a while, someone asks me to do something for them and says, as a way of showing how insignificant the request is, "It will only take an hour of your time." —And I become unreasonably furious.

The person speaking to me means no harm. He (or she) honestly thinks an hour isn't much, and yet it is all I can do to remain polite.

The other day someone phoned me to say he was writing an article on cities of the future and could I favor him with "a few moments" during which I would describe to him my views on cities of the future, their size, their economies, their social structure, and their functions. I suppressed my unreasonable fury and said, as gently as I might, "I think that would take more than a few moments," and asked him to call me another time, when I would have more leisure.

I hope he doesn't call, but I expect he will.

I occasionally get enraged over the fact that when someone asks for "a few moments" or for "just an hour of your time" in order that they might profit from the exchange, they never offer to pay me for the time I lose from my own work—time I can ill afford to lose. Yet it is unreasonable of me to be surprised at that, so I try hard not to be.

AFTERWORD: Whenever I write an essay such as the above, trying to educate the world into being reasonable, I think cynically that no one will even notice. But they do! They do! People who would ordinarily ask for an hour of my time (for no payment) without preamble are now likely to say, "I know from reading your essays that you are a very busy man and don't have an hour to spare." —Then they go on and ask for it, anyway.

49

Slush!

IT SEEMS THAT A NUMBER OF readers are annoyed at receiving unadorned rejection slips—the sending of which is a time-honored tradition of the publishing business. I sympathize with them, for, living legend though I now am, there was a time when I was victimized by these things, too. So we've printed a few letters and I've given my usual brief, flip answers.

The letters we've printed are thoughtful and reasonably polite, but one letter we received was from someone who was far too angry to be polite, let alone logical, so let me use it as a springboard to discuss this matter of rejection slips in detail. It won't be the first time. I have already written an essay entitled "Rejection Slips" (see *Asimov on Science Fiction*), but perhaps I didn't express myself with sufficient clarity. Let me try again.

The letter that moved me to write this editorial opens, "Shawna:" It breathes fury at once. It is customary, after all, even in the angriest of letters, to begin with "Dear Shawna," but this the writer clearly could not bring himself to do.

He then goes on to the meat of it. He says, "The 'slush' you spit at in your comment (Sept., '84)—" At this point I stopped and got my copy of the September issue. Shawna spat? That's not like her at all. I know hardly anyone as respectable and well behaved as she is. I looked up her comment and here it is, in full: "In the days when we used the checklist system, we had some 8 people reading the 'slush'. We now have one—me. I'm also quite uncertain as to how much help a preprinted, general comment is to any specific writer or story. I do try to put short notes on the rejection slips of stories which show some promise."

Where is the spitting? It is a quiet and eminently reasonable statement. It may be that our letter writer feels the quotation marks about the word "slush" is derogatory, but that is merely Shawna's careful writing style. She felt the word to be a slang expression and many people put slang words and phrases into quotes.

Actually, "slush" is not slang. I looked it up in that great reference work of the American language, Webster's second edition. Under "slush," it gives, as the fourth definition: "Confused and emotional, but unsubstantial, talk or writing; gush; drivel."

Since many (but not all) of beginners' attempts at writing which find their unsolicited way to an editor's office are indeed slush, in that sense of the word, editors took to speaking of unsolicited manuscripts as representing "the slush pile" or, eventually, simply as "slush." It is now the common way of referring to said unsolicited manuscripts and does not necessarily have a pejorative meaning. One could just as easily speak of "over-the-transom manuscripts" or "under-the-door manuscripts" and sometimes one does. It is, however, easier to say "slush."

If slush were universally bad, then it would be so simple for an editor simply to send it back without reading it. That, however, would mean that when all the established writers died, the magazine would have to close up shop. Besides, all the established writers were once represented in the slush themselves. I certainly was.

No, poor Shawna must wade through the slush pile meticulously and hopefully, in search of the occasional gem, or near gem, that shows up. The reason she's "poor," however, is that it's a tedious and thankless task. It is a tedious one, because the vast majority of manuscripts are not publishable and show little or no promise; what can one do but return them? As for checking off "spelling atrocious" or "dumb plot," what good would that do even if Shawna could bring herself to make such cruel remarks? The writer would be just as furious at getting such a comment as at getting none. *More* furious.

And that's why the task is a thankless one. Writers who feel cheated at not getting a comment probably feel they are 95 percent of the way there and just need a little help to go the rest of the way. Believe me, that's not so. If you were 95 percent there, we would take the story like a shot. But suppose you only think you're 95 percent of the way there, and are only 2 percent of the way there because you used paper and not birch bark? What do we do?

In my younger days, I would occasionally accede to a beginner's request that I read a manuscript and give a detailed critique. I would read the manuscript and send it back with a list of the flaws. Never once, *never once*, did I get a letter of thanks in return. It dawned on me that they didn't want a list of the flaws; they wanted to be told they were wonderful. So I stopped and I've never done it again.

Besides, as I told one writer in the letter column, it is not an editor's job to teach writing. Shawna doesn't have the time to undertake such duties and she isn't paid enough to do that job in addition to her own. There are people who will undertake to look at a beginner's manuscript and come up with a critique, but they charge considerably more than most beginners can afford. (It comes as a nasty shock to some people that payment is expected for such work. There are some people who certainly seem to be quite certain that I, for instance, ought to be glad to do it for nothing.)

Back to the letter. The writer goes on to say that the slush "is, for the most part, sent to you by people who buy your magazine."

Well, of course. All the people who try to make it in Hollywood are moviegoers. All the people who try to make it as athletes go to athletic meets. The role of faithful onlooker, however, is insufficient, in itself, to earn you success. If we were to accept stories from our readers just because they *were* our readers, our other readers would object loudly and vociferously.

Look, this may sound awful, but we would take a good story from someone who never read this magazine, and reject a bad story from our most loyal reader. That's what we are in business for—to accept good stories and reject bad ones.

If I were in Shawna's place and my dear Janet were to send me a story I thought was a bad one, I would reject it—even though I might dread going home at the end of the day. And in my role as editor of anthologies, I have accepted a story from a writer whom I disliked so much that I was dreadfully sorry it was a good story. But it was, and I took it.

The letter writer has worked out what the trouble is. His final paragraph is heavily sarcastic: "But cheer up, Shawna—Isaac's egotism is showing on you and in no time at all you will have alienated your subscribers to the point that they will not only stop sending you their 'slush', they will have also stopped buying your magazine." And to prove his point, he (or possibly she, come to think of it) bravely signs himself (or herself) "A Former Subscriber." No other name, no address.

Well, I won't argue over my own egotism. Anyone who wants to believe me a monster of vanity and conceit is welcome to do so. However, Shawna is a sweet and rather retiring individual, who has no conceit about her.

Anyway, let me summarize. Our readers can be divided into two classes—

1) A vast majority—who read the magazine more or less faithfully, who like it with varying degrees of intensity, and who never submit anything for publication. They couldn't care less about our rejection policy as long as (whatever it is) it manages to get them good stories to read, and that is what we try to bring to them—to the best of our judgement.

2) A small minority who submit stories, and these can, in turn, be divided into three classes:

2a) A small minority of the minority who show definite promise and whom Shawna tries to work with by means of helpful comments and encouragement and who might well sell us a story after a while—sometimes after a short while.

2b) Most of the minority, who do not show much promise but who accept rejections—even unadorned rejection slips—quietly and either keep on trying or give up. I suspect a great many of them keep on trying.

2c) A small minority of the minority who take rejection with such anger that they march away in a huff. There's nothing we can do with these except to say "Good-bye" and wish them luck in another and better world, for with that attitude they're not likely to have it in this cruel and miserable one.

Actually, my main concern and sympathy is with class 2b. What do we do with those who don't show particular promise, but who plug away at it?

There's hope for them. Once in a while, our judgement that there is no particular promise in a particular writer may be wrong. And once in a while, simply by trying and trying, a writer can develop enough skills to begin to show promise. It has happened.

Therefore, we are always ready to receive and to read slush; and when we send an unadorned rejection slip, we are *not* inviting a writer to stop submitting. Please submit to us again and again. Eventually, we might possibly see something we like. If you stop submitting, we will *never* see anything we like.

And, please, don't get mad. Believe me, Shawna is doing her best—and I am, too.

50

Book Reviews

HAVE NEVER MADE ANY SECRET of the fact that I dislike the concept of reviews and the profession of reviewing. It is a purely emotional reaction because, for reasons that are all too easy to work out, I strongly dislike having anyone criticize my stuff adversely.

I don't think I'm alone in this. From my close observation of writers (almost all my friends are writers) I've determined that they fall into two groups: (1) those who bleed copiously and visibly at any bad review, and (2) those who bleed copiously and secretly at any bad review.

I'm class 1. Most of my friends aim at class 2 and don't quite make it and aren't quite aware that they don't make it.

Unfortunately, there's no way in which one can get back at a reviewer. I have sometimes had the urge to do some fancy horsewhipping in the form of a mordant letter designed to flay the reptilian hide off the submoron involved, but, except in my very early days, I have always resisted. This is not out of idealism but out of the bitter knowledge that the writer always loses in such a confrontation.

Instead, then, I take to muttering derogatory comments about reviewing and reviewers in general.

But I'm in a bad spot here. *Asimov's* (which is the apple of my eye) not only has a regular book review column, but has other items, less regularly included, that review one or another of the facets of the science fiction field. If I really despise reviewing so, why is it I allow reviewing in the magazine?

Because I *don't* really despise reviewing and reviewers. That is an emotional reaction that I recognized as emotional and therefore discount. I am a rational man, I like to think, and in any disagreement between my emotions and my rationality, I should hope it is rationality that wins out every time.

Now let's get down to cases.

A publisher to whom I was beholden asked me to read a book by an important writer and to give them a quote that could be used on the cover. I tried to beg off but had to admit that I hadn't read the book and they insisted that I at least read it and give it a chance.

So I did. I *tried* to read it—and the gears locked tight long before I finished. It seemed to me so unsuccessful a book that there was no way in which I could give it the quote that was wanted. I felt awful but I had to call the publisher and beg off.

Now, then, assuming my judgement was correct, should that book be reviewed? Why say unkind things about it?

In the case of an ordinary bad book, one might wonder. At the most, it might only be necessary to say, "This is a bad book because . . ." with a few unemotional sentences added. You don't crack a peanut with a sledgehammer.

An unsatisfactory book written by an important writer, however, requires a detailed review to explain *why* it seems to have gone wrong and *where* and *how*. This is not so much to warn off readers, who will probably have bought the book in great numbers, anyway, by the time the review comes out. It is because even a flawed book by a good writer can be an important educational experience.

Its failure can be used as a way of sharpening the general taste for the literary good. It will educate (properly reviewed) not only the reader, but the writer as well, the veteran as well as the neophyte.

And yet despite the value of such a review, I could not, in a million years, review the book myself.

There are emotional objections. How can I say unkind things about someone else when I detest having someone say unkind things about me? If I can't take it, I have no right to dish it out. Then, too, how can I review a book by a friend (or, possibly, a rival) and be sure of being objective?

If that isn't enough, there are technical objections. Even if everyone were to grant that I am a whiz at writing science fiction, that does *not* necessarily mean that I'm a whiz at understanding what makes science fiction good and bad. Even when I feel a story to be bad I don't necessarily have the ability to point out just where and how and why the badness exists.

So we have Baird Searles reviewing books for us. He has the talent for saying what needs to be said and I am grateful that he has.

Now consider what a reviewer must do, if he is to be good at his job.

1) A reviewer must read the book carefully—every word of it, if possible, even if it seems to be very bad. This is an extraordinarily difficult job. It is the mark of an unsuccessful book that it is hard to read, that it is clumsy, wearying, uninteresting, dull, monotonous, insulting to the intelligence, predictable, repetitious, infelicitous—any or all of these things. When you and I read a book of this sort, we stop reading. A competent reviewer mustn't. He must stick to it to give the book an utterly fair shake.

2) A reviewer must read with attention, marking passages perhaps, taking notes perhaps, so that he won't have to work from memory alone in writing his review, so that he won't make factual errors or unreasonable criticisms.

3) A reviewer must read with detachment and not allow his judgement of the book to be twisted by his judgement of the writer. He may know a writer to be an irritating boor and yet realize the writer's book may be great. He may know a writer to be a saint and yet realize the writer's book may be awful. He must concentrate on the book and only on the book.

4) A reviewer must not only be a person of literary judgement, but he must have a wide knowledge of the field so that he can judge a book in comparison with other books by the author, with books by other authors of similar experience or similar intent, and with the field in general.

5) A reviewer must be a competent writer himself, for the most literarily penetrating review ever written loses its point if it, itself, is so badly written that any reader grows bored, irritated, or confused.

6) Finally—and this is the point where even the cleverest reviewer (perhaps *especially* the cleverest reviewer) can come a cropper—the review must not be a showcase for the reviewer himself. The purpose of the review is not to demonstrate the superior erudition of the reviewer or to make it seem that the reviewer, if he but took the trouble, could write the book better than the author did. (Why the devil doesn't he do it, then?) Nor must it seem to be a hatchet job in which the reviewer is carrying out some private vengeance. (This may not be so, you understand, but it mustn't even *seem* to be so.)

These are not easy conditions to meet and the fact is that though there are many reviewers, there are not many good reviewers.

And why not? Probably all reviewers will gladly accept Sturgeon's Law (that 90 percent of everything is crud) with respect to the books they review —and it holds just as solidly for the reviews they write.

And is there anything a good book reviewer must receive from the editor for all that is expected of him? Certainly! In a word, independence.

When an editor hires a book reviewer, he doesn't (or shouldn't) buy a scribbler who has agreed to put the boss's opinions into words. No, it is the book reviewer *and his opinions* that have been hired. The book reviews in this magazine do not necessarily express the opinions of George, Shawna, or myself, although they might. In fact, George, Shawna, and myself do not necessarily agree among ourselves as to the worth of a particular piece of writing.

But it is the reviewer's opinions you want, not ours, and it is his you will get. He is the professional in this respect.

Baird Searles, in my opinion, is one of the good reviewers, and we are glad we have him, and we hope he stays with us a long time. He does not ask us for our views before he writes his column, and if (inconceivably) he asked us, we wouldn't tell him.

And it's because reviewers can be like Baird Searles that we have a review column.

✦

AFTERWORD: Just to show you how stupid I can be, in the first version of this essay, I actually named the book and author I was talking about. Very gently, George had to teach me the facts of life. "We would certainly want to get a story from the author some day, Isaac," he said. "Do you think we will if we publish this essay as written?" So I made a few alterations. I like to think of myself as an honest, plainspoken individual, but *unnecessary* honesty can verge on stupidity, and who needs that?

51

Integrity

NEARLY EIGHT YEARS AGO, I wrote an essay entitled "Book Reviews" (see Chapter 50). I thought I had disposed of the subject on that occasion and I didn't think I would have occasion to write about it again.

However, unexpected things can happen, and in this case a kind of minicrisis has arisen. Mind you, not to *Asimov's,* but it has arisen in another magazine, and the same sort of thing *might* arise here. It is a matter that I would think about even if I knew for certain that we were immune to the problem, but since we aren't, thought is even more essential. Fortunately, I like thinking.

What happens, for instance, if a book review gives offense? Naturally, we try to take what measures we can, given what native intelligence and decency we have, to avoid that as much as possible. Thus, we naturally try to retain a reviewer who is thoroughly professional and capable.

Our man on books, for instance, is Baird Searles. We have had him on the job from the very beginning and he has (so far) produced no crises for us. What's more, he has written what have always seemed to us to be perfectly reasonable and useful reviews.

Naturally, we don't ask Baird to do the impossible. Suppose, for instance, he decided to review one of my books. Nothing he did would seem satisfactory. If he honestly liked it, and said so, the readers would not be impressed. They might assume that Baird was simply trying to stay in good with the "boss." Or, if he honestly disliked it, and said so, the reaction might be "Wow! Can you imagine what he would say if he weren't pulling his punches?"

In other words, Baird would be bound to be misinterpreted whatever he did in such a case, and neither he nor I could afford that. It is not only important to *have* integrity, but to be *seen* to have integrity.

The result is, then, that Baird does *not* review my books, or those of anyone connected with the magazine. He mentions the existence of such books and lets it go at that. That's nothing unusual. I believe this sort of thing is done in other magazines or newspapers that publish book reviews.

But suppose Baird were to write a review of someone else's book and it proved offensive.

To whom? —Well, to begin with, to *us:* to Sheila, or to Gardner, or to me.

Why? Simply because he was praising a book one or more of us thought was terrible? Or panning a book we thought was great?

In that case, tough on us. We have no right to object. Baird works for the magazine for the purpose of expressing *his* opinions of a book, not ours.

The same would be true if the author of the book objected to the nature of a review. We'd be sorry, indeed; we don't want to make anyone unhappy if we can avoid it; but we're paying for Baird's opinion, not the author's.

But what if the review were legitimately offensive? For instance, suppose it contains errors that make it look as though the book has not been read carefully. Suppose the author is accused of being ignorant of the fact that Mars is smaller than Earth, when actually he has mentioned the matter in two different places. Or suppose, on the basis of the views of one of the characters in the book, the reviewer accuses the author of being a racist. That would be wrong, too, for we review the *book* and not the author, and we understand that the views of the characters in a book do not necessarily reflect those of the author. In either case, an apology is due and (after consulting with the reviewer) one would be offered. The review might even be altered if the author sees the content before it is published.

Fortunately, Baird has *never* gotten us into this kind of trouble.

But suppose the review is simply an unfavorable review and has nothing in it that requires an apology. And suppose an author says, "Look, if you give me another bad review like that, I'm not going to submit any more stories to you."

If he's an important writer, that's not something we would like to hear, but, on the other hand, it's something that's extremely unlikely to happen. In fact, I've never known it to happen. Professional writers, however much they may dislike unfavorable reviews, accept them as a fact of life, and are resigned to them.

But there's another kind of pressure, harder to avoid.

What if a *publisher* takes offense at a perfectly unexceptional review that has only the demerit of being unfavorable? And what if that publisher advertises regularly in the magazine? And what if he says, "If you give me bad reviews like that, I'm pulling my advertisements out of the magazine"? And what if his ads are an important source of revenue for the magazine?

No, it hasn't happened to us yet, but it has happened to another magazine, and it might happen to us. And, if it does, what do we do?

There are several alternatives, of course. We might cave in, for instance, and pull the review. We might then go to the book reviewer and say, "Listen, go easy on any books put out by this publisher. We need his money."

This instantly vitiates the book review column and if the book reviewer has professional integrity, he will quit his job at once. In fact, if pressure were put on an editor by the business officials of a magazine to issue such orders to the book reviewer, the editor, himself, might resign on the spot.

What's more, it wouldn't be so easy to find a new book reviewer who would be willing to cut his opinions to suit an advertising publisher, or a new editor who would be willing to pressure a book reviewer to do so. And if replacements were found who were willing to do this sort of thing, I'm sure they would be too sleazy in character to do their jobs well.

So, really, that can't be done.

Well, perhaps, you can weaken the cave-in. You can say to the book reviewer, "Listen, be good-natured in general. Say nice things about everyone." You would still be asking him to lie, though.

Or perhaps you might say, "I don't want you to lie, but just don't review books you don't like. Review only the ones you like."

In that case, you would have an unbearably bland column. I knew a book reviewer once who praised everyone he reviewed. I used to love to have him review me, but I found, after a while, that I didn't particularly value his reviews of me, or of anyone else either. There is no delight in the praise of a particular book if all books get pretty much the same praise.

Besides, the advertiser would get restive. He wouldn't be content to have his books ignored; he'd want them *reviewed*—and *favorably*.

The next alternative might be simply to drop the book review column. If we do that, however, we are depriving the reader of a valuable service. It is difficult, these days, to read all the s.f. books that are published. It is therefore extremely useful to have a person with a trusted judgement estimating the worth of various books and giving you some clue as to which to investigate, with possible purchase in mind.

And even dropping a column would be a cave-in. Any cave-in at all would sharpen the bloodlust of the advertiser and urge him to get after the next magazine.

Well then, what do we do if we can't cave in? —We might try reasoning with the advertiser. We would point out that the magazine can't be expected to compromise its integrity; that removing the advertisement would hurt the advertiser as well as the magazine; that if word got out as to *why* the advertiser removed his advertising (and word would surely get out, somehow) that would be very bad publicity for the advertiser. Any favorable reviews he got for his books, thereafter, would be tainted in the minds of the readers. The magazine, on the other hand, would be admired for its integrity.

But what if the advertiser won't listen to reason and puts matters into ultimatum form? "Either I get favorable reviews or I pull out."

It seems to me that there is, in that case, only one thing to do. We say, "Good-bye, sir."

And what do we then do about the lost advertising income? Davis Publications is a strong and honest firm, but it is not exactly Time-Life Books or *The Reader's Digest*. It can't afford to support forever a magazine that doesn't pay its own way.

Well, we'd try to replace the lost advertising—or, if necessary, we'd try to get along without the revenue by various economies—or, if all else failed, we'd go under.

It is not written in the stars that *Asimov's* must endure forever.

It *is* written in the stars, however, that *Asimov's* must maintain its integrity.

AFTERWORD: It pleased me that the editors of two other important science fiction magazines praised this essay and thanked me for writing it.

Incidentally, in the Afterword to my essay "Book Reviews" (Chapter 50) I said that I had rewritten the essay to avoid offending an author. I merely refrained from mentioning his name and that of his book; I did not abate one word of my opinions. And since I am not a professional book reviewer and have no talent in that direction, it is suitable that I not mention names.

SCIENCE
FICTION
AND I ✦

52

Nostalgia

IT IS WELL KNOWN THAT, WITH age, there comes an increasing tendency toward nostalgia, a tedious recalling of the days of youth, when hair was thick and dark and the blood ran hot. It is puzzling, however, that I am showing such a tendency, since no touch of age has yet fallen upon me. It must be my excellent memory that accounts for it in my case.

Thus, most of you callow youths out there are unaware that there is a science fiction organization known as First Fandom, but I know it well and think of it fondly. To qualify for membership in this august organization (the members of which sometimes refer to themselves as "the dinosaurs of science fiction") one must have been active in fandom *before* 1938. This year is, of course, an important dividing line since it is the year that John Campbell began his effective control over *Astounding Science Fiction* (now *Analog*). In other words, First Fandom is pre-Campbell fandom.

There came a time when I was invited to enter. I replied sadly that although I had been a science fiction reader prior to 1938, I was never active in fandom and therefore didn't qualify.

That did not satisfy the aged stalwarts of the organization. They turned to their old magazines, removed them from their sealed, nitrogen-filled cases, adjusted their reading glasses, and behold—they found a letter of mine in a 1935 issue of *Astounding* in which I demanded smooth edges and expressed pleasure and displeasure over various stories. That qualified me, and I have been a member ever since.

At every World Science Fiction Convention, there is a meeting of First Fandom, and I, of course, attend (if I am at the convention). At one such convention, perhaps nine years ago, it struck me that my fellow members, in sharp contrast to me, were well stricken in years, that they hobbled about, peered uncertainly at each other, cupped their hands behind their ears, spoke in quavering voices, and gummed thoughtfully at their gruel during meals.

I couldn't help but think that the time might come when (but no, I can't put the thought into words).

I said, "Gentlemen, listen. Why not extend the year of eligibility? Let's make the requirement that of having been an active fan before *1939*, this year. Next year, we'll make it 1940; then 1941 and so on. In that way, we will have a steady influx of callow youths into the organization—and in ever greater numbers as fandom increased with the years."

You wouldn't believe the sensation I caused. As one man, all the members tottered to their feet, and, leaning heavily on their canes, they shook their withered fists at me.

"Never," they quavered. "Never! It will be 1938 forever!"

"But," said I, "in the inevitable course of nature, we will one by one go to that great Convention in the Sky and then what will happen?"

Whereupon Lester del Rey, the dinosauriest of them all, said, "None of us will ever go to that great convention in the sky," and there it stands. I'm sure they're wrong, but I can't convince them.

Still, even though it is now over half a century since 1938, First Fandom remains active. They have taken to giving elaborate awards for excellence in past years.

At the 1982 World Convention in Chicago, for instance, they gave *me* an award. I wasn't there because I don't like to make long trips and Chicago is too far for me. However, Shawna attended and very kindly picked up the award for me and handed it to me when she returned to New York.

Here is what the award says: "Isaac Asimov has been voted by the members of First Fandom the author of third most outstanding medium length science fiction story of 1946, 'Evidence.' "

Well, third best is better than fourth best, right?

I remember "Evidence." It was the only story I managed to write during my not very long stay in the Army. At one time, I got a sympathetic librarian to lock me in the base library during a lunch period when it was supposed to be closed, and I used the library typewriter to do seven pages of the story. That was one time I felt like a civilian.

"Evidence" was also the first story I ever sold to the movies. Not an option, you understand. I sold it outright; and I mean *outright*. Orson Welles bought it. It was 1947 and I knew nothing about the economics of the writing game. (To tell you the truth, I don't know much about it even now.) Consequently, when Welles offered me $250 for the radio, movie, and television rights, I took the money and ran. Unfortunately, I didn't realize that you should set a time limit on these things. Welles still owns it.

And just to make it worse, he never made a movie out of it—not to this day. So when I sold *I, Robot* to the movies, I had to except "Evidence." That was not mine to sell.

Another thing about "Evidence" if I may be allowed a small digression. (Well, who's going to stop me?)

Martin H. Greenberg is, currently, the outstanding anthologist in science fiction, and some of his anthologies, I am very pleased to be able to say, he does with me. Together, for instance, we are doing a series of best-of-the-year short-story anthologies, starting with 1939. The most recently published of the series is Volume 8, which contains the best stories of the year 1946.

Marty sent me a batch of stories for that year when the volume was in preparation and I read through them to see if there were anything I would veto. After we settled on the twelve best between us, he said, "And for the thirteenth, I suggest we do 'Evidence.'"

I said, "There's no need to feel you have to include a story of mine, Marty."

He said, "I want to. I think it belongs."

So I let myself be argued into it.

Well, the volume was reviewed in *Publishers Weekly* and the review began: "There are 13 stories here, all of high quality." It then went on to refer to nine of them specifically, and of the four not mentioned, one was "Evidence," which makes it seem that as far as the reviewer was concerned, my story was tenth best at the very most.

Okay, I'll settle for third best.

The reviewer says, "Arthur C. Clarke is represented by his first three stories, each of which is now considered a classic."

That brings me to another piece of nostalgia. Bob Heinlein, Arthur

Clarke, and I (not necessarily in that order) are considered "the Big Three" and have been so considered for some forty years.

It gets boring, I suppose, though not to the three of us. Once, when Arthur and I were at the del Reys' apartment, we called Bob in California, just so we could have a three-way talk. I said (because I worry about these things), "You know, fellows, it must be getting awfully tiresome for the other writers, waiting for one of us to make room so someone else can be elected to the Big Three. It's rather unfair of us to insist on longevity and hog the limelight for decade after decade." And the other two said, simultaneously, "Who cares about the other writers?"

Well, *I'm* not going to volunteer to make room. Arthur is three years older than I, and Bob is thirteen years older, so I intend to hang on as long as I can.

Besides, they didn't have to work for it as I did. The instant Bob began to publish stories, everyone at once took it for granted that he was the best s.f. writer around. Even I did.

As for Arthur— Didn't Marty and I include his first three stories in the best of the year, and didn't the *PW* reviewer say each of them is now considered a classic?

And I? I worked along for two years, getting about a dozen stories printed, and did no more than edge into the Big Two Hundred. In fact, as I look back into it, I can't tell you when I became one of the Big Three. One day, there was no such thing and the next day, there was and I'd been a member for ten years.

Don't get the idea I don't enjoy it. It's a great thing. Once you're a member of the Big Three, it seems to be permanent. In the last quarter century, I've done comparatively little fiction yet no one threatens to review the matter of my eligibility. Arthur announced his retirement back in 1977, I think, and his position in the Big Three didn't even show a tremor.

I decided that this business of the Big Three could be very handy. When I finished *Foundation's Edge* I thought, in a secret corner of my mind: It's bound to win awards. Who's going to vote against one of the Big Three?

Ha, ha! Bob, who I thought was safely out of the race because everyone said that *The Number of the Beast* was going to be his final novel, decided to put out *Friday*. And Arthur came out of retirement very suddenly to do *2010*. That meant that 1982 was the only year in which each of the Big Three published a novel.

It should make the Nebula and Hugo awards rather exciting, and I'm practicing my good-sport concession speech, if I can ungrit my teeth long enough to deliver it.

◆

AFTERWORD: There is not an atom of a tendency toward cheap triumph in my soul, so I'll just mention, as a mere cold-blooded fact, that when the Hugo Awards were handed out, it was *Foundation's Edge* that got it. I had beaten Bob and Arthur. But so what?

(Heh-heh-heh-heh-heh . . . . . .)

53

Susan Calvin

I HAVE, ON OCCASION, FAILED TO make a prediction I might very easily have made. The reverse, however, is also true. Let me describe a prediction I made with perfect accuracy, when it was just about impossible I should have done so.

How did I manage to do that? Easily! The prediction was not a prediction. A does not predict B when A is the *cause* of B.

But I am being unnecessarily mysterious. Let me start at the beginning.

On 24 December 1940, I began my third robot story. It was going to be about a telepathic robot, and the plot I had worked out simply demanded a woman as a major character. I was not quite twenty-one and my experience with women was virtually nil (at that time). It occurred to me that, since I needed a woman scientist, I might use as my model Professor Mary Caldwell, who served as the guidance counselor for us graduate students.

There was no student who needed more counseling than I, you can be sure, and, for a wonder, Professor Caldwell was thoroughly sympathetic and pro-Asimov. There weren't many professors who were, in those days, because I was considered peculiar (largely because I *was* peculiar). Naturally, I was very pro-Caldwell.

I wasn't a good enough writer to draw a word portrait of Professor Caldwell, but I used her name and called my scientist Susan Caldwell. John Campbell bought the story for *Astounding* and then my heart misgave me. What if Professor Caldwell resented my use of her name? I could not afford to offend the one friend I had on the faculty.

In an agony of fear, I called Miss Tarrant, Campbell's woman Friday, and asked her to change the word Caldwell wherever it appeared in the story. "To what?" she asked, clearly appalled at having to do that.

Quickly I thought of a change that would be minimal. "Calvin," I said. In that way, Susan Calvin appeared—a woman who worked in a man's world, showing them neither fear nor favor, and proving herself to be the best of them all. And this was a quarter century before the contemporary surge of feminism. The story, "Liar!," appeared in the May 1941 issue of *Astounding*.

More than one critic has felt that Susan epitomized the dour work-centered ethic of traditional Protestantism and that she was deliberately named for the great Reformer John Calvin. Nuts! I told you how the name came into being. It had nothing whatever to do with old John. Such an idea never entered my head for a moment.

By 1950, I had nine robot stories that I was proud of, and five contained Susan Calvin. In that year, I collected them into a book, *I, Robot*, which is still in print today in both hard- and softcover editions.

In order to have the nine stories of the book hang together (after all, I had written them separately and without much regard for their self-consistency as a group) I made minor adjustments here and there—particularly in "Liar!," as it happened—and added a small frame based on Susan Calvin's life.

The second paragraph of the introduction read: "Susan Calvin had been born in the year 1982 . . . which made her seventy-five now."

Since I don't endlessly read and reread my own books (whatever you may think) and since it has been decades, actually, since I looked at *I, Robot*, the fateful year arrived without my giving it any thought at all.

On 5 April 1982, however, Christopher A. Nelson of Western Australia took typewriter in hand and composed a letter to *Asimov's*. With quite obvious delight, he included a clipping from the 1 April 1982 issue of *The West Australian*, his local paper. (And I trust the fact that it was April Fools' Day had nothing to do with the item he encircled in red crayon.)

The item is a birth notice and this is what it says, in full:

"CALVIN: To Elizabeth and Jeremy a daughter Susan born 30-3-82. Sincere thanks to Dr. Asimov from all who have long awaited this event."

In other words, in 1982—on 30 March 1982, to be exact—Susan Calvin was born, exactly as I had predicted in 1950, over three decades before.

To be sure, I had given no clear indication that dear Susan was of Australian birth, but neither did I rule it out. I did state in the introduction to

I, Robot that "She obtained her bachelor's degree at Columbia in 2003 . . ." but that is no positive indication that she was born in the United States. After all, I obtained *my* bachelor's degree at Columbia and *I* was not born in the United States.

Mind you, in the introduction, I had said that U.S. Robots and Mechanical Men, Inc. was also founded in 1982. The closest to that is Unimation, Inc., Mr. Engelberger's firm, which was founded over thirty years ago (thanks to the influence of *I, Robot),* but it has only become prominent in the last few years, so that's close, too.

I did not really think when I wrote the robot stories that they would come within the time frame I had set up but they may. It certainly seems much more likely that they will do so nowadays than it seemed back in the 1940s.

Might not Susan Calvin of Western Australia, the real Susan Calvin, come to the United States sometime during her childhood or adolescence? Stranger things have happened. Her parents would surely have told her of the significance of her name and she might, conceivably, go to Columbia and get her bachelor's degree in 2003, and she might find it impossible not to do what everyone would expect her to do, so that she would begin graduate work in robotics.

With every step she would take to move in the footsteps of the fictional Susan Calvin, it would be easier to continue in that direction and harder somehow to step out of it. I wouldn't be surprised, in fact, if some robotics firm would deliberately change its name to U.S. Robots and Mechanical Men, Inc. in order that they might hire her as a robopsychologist. After all, since I have that firm dominating the entire field in my stories, they might have some atavistic superstitious feeling that this move would bring them enormous success.

If I live to be a hundred, I might witness this and find myself considered the most remarkable prophet in the modern world, except that, as I told you at the start, it would not be a prophecy. I did not *predict* that a real Susan Calvin would be born in 1982; my statement was the direct cause of it. And it would be the cause of anything else that seemed to follow the course of events in *I, Robot.*

All this is not trivial, by the way, for this is merely an example of how a prophecy can "come true" by causing that which it prophesied.

In the Gospel of St. Matthew, for instance, the writer, in recounting the story of the circumstances surrounding the birth and infancy of Jesus, pauses periodically to quote a passage from the Old Testament and point out how a prophecy has been fulfilled. The incidents in Matthew are, however, supported by no other document. The only other place where the birth of Jesus is described is in the Gospel of St. Luke, and there the story is different in every detail.

If we insist that both Gospels were written under divine inspiration, then there's no point in arguing the matter and we must just put our imagination and ingenuity to work and figure out how to make the two tales consistent with each other.

If, on the other hand, we are hopelessly unspiritual and assume that both writers were recounting pious legends, then we might wonder if Matthew might not have chosen those legends that fit the verses he quoted—or even shaded legends to make them fit better. We'll never know, of course, but if that was done, then this phenomenon of prophecies that were not prophecies has had an enormous influence on the world.

Yet I imagine we can't always dismiss prophetic inspiration in a totally cavalier fashion. Things might turn up that are undoubtedly coincidental, and yet a little shivery, too.

In his letter, Mr. Nelson has a final paragraph, which reads:

"Note to Dr. Asimov: Further investigations on my part found Elizabeth's maiden name to be Caldwell. Surprised?"

Yes, I am. If the real Susan Calvin adopts her mother's maiden name as her own middle name (something women occasionally do these days), she would be Susan Caldwell Calvin.

Of course, I did tell the story in my autobiography, and Mr. Nelson clearly knows it, or he wouldn't make a point of telling me Elizabeth's maiden name. The question is, though, did Jeremy and Elizabeth Calvin know the tale and was that a further factor in having them name their daughter Susan? Or was it just an astonishing coincidence?

I wonder.

AFTERWORD: After this essay was published, I began to feel deflated. The more I thought of it, the more significant it began to seem that the birth announcement had appeared in a paper dated 1 April. Had I fallen for an April Fool joke? Maybe I had, but I have no evidence for it, so I'll let the essay stand.

54

Not an Expert

I SUPPOSE THAT IT IS ONLY REASON-
able that people take it for granted that I am an expert on science fiction. I
have written so much science fiction over so many years that it would seem I
must be, especially since I have a magazine named for me.

That was the idea behind a recent invitation that I take part in the
television series "Sunrise Semester." A series of programs was being given on
computers and I was asked to do one of them on the subject of computers in
science fiction.

There was an agonizing pause while I cranked myself up to the pitch of
making the admission. "I'm sorry," I said, "but I'm not really an expert on the
subject and can't discuss it intelligently."

That was followed by another and clearly incredulous pause on the part
of the young man who was doing the inviting. So I said hastily, and with
some embarrassment, "I can discuss computers in *my* science fiction. I know
about *that.*"

His face cleared and he said, "Oh, well, that will be all right. Sure, we
can discuss *your* science fiction."

And I was greatly relieved.

But you may be as puzzled as he was. How does it come about that I am
not an expert on the subject generally? I'll explain.

There was a time, eons ago, when not much science fiction was being
published and when I had nothing better to do with my time than read science
fiction every chance I got. Of course, I had to do my schoolwork and I had to

work in the family candy store, but that was something to get through as quickly as possible and *then* it was science fiction time.

I read every issue of every magazine as it appeared. There were so few magazines and I was such a fast reader that I not only had time to read *all* the science fiction being published, but I also had time to catalogue it.

I used three-by-five cards on which I listed each story, with author, issue of magazine, rating (zero to ten), and comments. I kept them carefully alphabetized, and made separate listings of stories under the heading of authors' names, with additional listings of stories in categories eight, nine, and ten.

In those days, I *was* an expert and could freely have discussed any aspect of science fiction writing and story content.

But then I began to write myself, and suddenly a great big portion of my time came to be given over to that. Even when I wasn't actually sitting at my typewriter, I was brooding over plots and story development. I found, to my surprise, I was falling behind. I was reading less carefully and abandoning stories if they didn't grab me from the start. (In the old days, I would painstakingly finish even the worst turkey, because I had to be able to rate them, didn't I?)

I put the matter to John Campbell, my great mentor in those days.

"Gee, Mr. Campbell," I said, "I don't read all the science fiction stories these days."

"What of it?" he asked.

"I'm worried that I won't know all the plots and developments being used and that I might unwittingly repeat some of them, not realizing they had been used."

"That's silly, Asimov," he said. "You just concentrate on writing *your* stories *your* way, and then, even if you duplicate an element in someone else's plot, no one will particularly notice."

I took heart at that and continued to devote inordinate time to my writing. Just the same, I still managed, well into the 1950s, to read most of the science fiction that appeared.

Then two more developments took place.

First, the 1950s saw an enormous boom in science fiction. For a while, there were literally dozens of science fiction magazines on the newsstands and, in addition, hardcover science fiction books began to appear. It became literally impossible to read all of science fiction, unless you devoted 100 percent of your time to it and read quickly—and perhaps not even then.

I did not even make the effort. Quite the reverse, in fact. In the midfifties I suddenly took to writing nonfiction in ever greater quantity and variety —which meant that more and more of my reading time had to be devoted to those fields in which I was now writing.

The result is that, since 1960 or so, I have been able to read only a small portion of the science fiction that has been published, and I have been falling steadily further and further behind. So it has come about that I am no longer an expert in the field of s.f.

This, however, is not a situation unique to myself. No one, these days, can keep up with the field, or would even think of trying to do so, unless it was his job—unless he was a full-time science fiction critic, collector, or anthologist.

Could *you* do it if you have a job, or other interests?

For instance, suppose you aspire to be a science fiction writer, as I did in the late 1930s. That means that you, as I once did, would have to spend considerable time swatting away at writing, as I once did. How, in that case, would you keep abreast of the field in what time remains?

You couldn't—and you wouldn't.

And yet (you must be thinking) surely you will *have* to. One rule in learning how to write is to read the works of professionals and experts. Their stories are your school and they are your teachers. You *must* read science fiction.

Of course you must. But you don't have to read *everything*, especially since you can't. You must read selectively.

How do you select? Well, science fiction is not a smooth, undifferentiated, and homogenized field. There are, for example, novels on the one hand, and short stories on the other.

If you're a beginner, trying to break in, it makes sense to tackle the shorter pieces. For a given investment in time, you can write a dozen short stories for each novel, try a dozen different ways of approaching a story, a dozen different moods, a dozen different sorts of plot, and so on. There will be time enough for the huge time investment represented by a novel when you have more nearly mastered your craft.

Therefore, it makes sense to spend your possibly limited time reading short stories rather heavily. (I wouldn't forbid your reading a good novel now and then—but you've a serious course of study to undertake, and don't forget that.)

Where do you find short stories? —In anthologies and in magazines. Both have their advantages. The anthologists select the best, presumably, and give you a concentrated handful of classics. On the other hand, the mere fact that the anthologized stories have been proved and tested means that they are anywhere from ten to forty years old and do not necessarily represent the present forefront of science fictional thinking.

In magazines, you may be more likely to come across clinkers (in your opinion at least, if not in the editor's) but on the other hand, it is in the magazines where the experimentation is being done and where you can see what editors are buying *now*.

Does that mean I am making a pitch for *Asimov's?* Yes, I am. If you've read this magazine at all, you will have noticed that we hang loose; that we're informal and friendly; that we rather enjoy being a home for talented beginners. We have taken on people such as Barry Longyear, Somtow Sucharitkul, and Sharon Webb, and helped them move along the road to blockbusterdom.

That doesn't mean that we don't welcome distinguished graybeards such as Fred Pohl, Avram Davidson, Robert Silverberg, and Brian Aldiss, also.

Therefore, if you are a serious science fiction reader, and (especially) if you are an aspiring science fiction writer, this magazine that you are holding is something you should be reading. You can use us. —And I don't pretend that I am being utterly altruistic in this. *We* can use *you*.

—One more word before I go. You may not like every story in every issue. This is not because George and Shawna are erratic and unreliable. It is because they search for variety. In the first place, readers' tastes vary, and in the second, science fiction writing has grown and elaborated, and different subdisciplines ought to be represented, where possible.

For the aspiring writer this is particularly useful. The kind of stories you like are the kind of stories you should be trying to write. You should therefore value the variety, because it enables you, by example, to learn where your own talents may best lie. But don't decide too quickly. What you dislike at first taste may become delightful as familiarity grows.

So good reading. —And good writing.

55

Violence and Incompetence

J ERRY POURNELLE, IN AN IN-
terview, once said, "Isaac Asimov has an asinine motto, 'Violence is the last refuge of the incompetent.'"

I presume it does sound asinine to some people.

A young man once said to me rather belligerently, "Dr. Asimov, if violence is the last refuge of the incompetent, why is there so much violence in the world?"

"Alas, young man," I said, "it is because there are so many incompetents in the world."

You see, violence is such an easy solution, especially if you're big and burly and have a gun, and your opponent is, and has, none of these things. You just beat him up and, possibly, kill him, and there's an end to your opponent.

Suppose, though, it's not a human being you're trying to kill, but an *idea*. If you're truly competent, you can beat an idea with another, possibly better, idea. If you're not competent, you may be forced into violence out of sheer frustration, and, as is true with anything an incompetent does, it often doesn't work.

Jesus of Nazareth had ideas that were obnoxious to those in power and so they took care of him with apparent permanence. They crucified him. I don't think anyone will maintain that that was a competent way of eradicating his ideas.

Christianity took over the Empire, not because it defeated the pagans in war or slaughtered them from ambush—indeed, violence was in the other direction. It won out because its ideas were better suited to its times than those of the pagans.

In later centuries, when Christianity tried to nail down its victory by violence against "heretics," it sometimes achieved its aims, but (in my view) inefficiently, and it very often did not achieve them at all. A hundred years of savage warfare between Catholics and Protestants wiped out neither; a thousand years of savage warfare between Christians and Muslims wiped out neither.

Let me repeat: violence exists, and it is an easy way of seeming to solve a problem. It is, however, an inefficient way, and frequently one that does not work. Anyone who can't think of anything better and insists on using violence is incompetent—even if he is as "successful" as Alexander the Great was.

After all, Alexander's empire did not survive his death. That the Roman Empire existed as long as it did was not the result of its successful wars, but the result of its development of a successful system of government. The Roman law, not the Roman legion, was the true secret of Roman competence. And when the laws lost their grip, the legions couldn't save the Empire.

I believe the rule works in literature as well.

Stories that are full of violence can be very popular, just as violence itself is, but I suspect they lack staying power. The nonviolent mystery, featuring a rational, nonviolent detective, appears passé now, yet the Sherlock Holmes stories first appeared a century ago and are still popular. Will the same be said of the evanescent reams of "tough guy" detectives? What will the score be a century hence? I'll not be there to check, but I have no fears. My bet is on the Holmeses, the Poirots, the Wolfes, and the little gray cells over the nameless shamuses and their big black guns.

I have used my motto concerning violence in my own stories. They are generally nonviolent and the resolutions are almost always achieved through the force of a "better idea."

I have written four mystery novels, and in each of the four there is but one murder. In three of them, that one murder takes place before the story begins. In the fourth, it takes place offstage. My mystery short stories rarely involve any form of violence.

And the same goes for my science fiction stories. The result is that I stay in print, and I am popular with publishers. I am playing for the long run (not deliberately, I must admit, but just because I hate violence, and it has worked out that way), and if this be asininity, I am satisfied with it.

That brings me to the Foundation trilogy which is, by all odds, my most successful work of fiction, and which (together with my new novel, *Foundation's Edge,* and any subsequent sequels I may live long enough to do) will, I am quite certain, be selling long after I have passed on to the big word processor in the sky.

It is in the Foundation trilogy that one of the characters, Salvor Hardin, says, "Violence is the last refuge of the incompetent," and the entire series of stories is designed to demonstrate that fact. (I did not do this deliberately, to be sure, since I write too quickly to do anything deliberately, but I do follow my instincts, and I think those are sound.)

This, in fact, is the true significance of the trilogy and the reason for its staying power.

People have given it credit for at least two inventions. I have been told, for instance, that, in the trilogy, I invented the "all-human galaxy" as opposed to the delightfully diverse life-forms that people the galaxies invented by E. E. Smith and John W. Campbell.

I have also been told that I invented the "historical novel of the future." The trilogy may not be the first to demonstrate the concept, but it is the first to develop it in detail.

Both inventions, however cute they may be, nevertheless cannot possibly (to my way of thinking) represent the real significance of the stories.

The real significance lies in the careful working out of the theme concerning violence and incompetence. I have one crisis worked out by the application of the idea of balance of power; another by the idea of the power of religion over the state; still another by the force of economic domination. The Mule loses out, not because someone else, who is quicker on the mental trigger, can shoot him down, but because of his own desire for unforced love.

In those cases where violence does take place (and there are indeed wars and deaths in the trilogy) these things never decide anything. The resolution takes place despite the violence and even in a direction against the violence.

Mind you, I do not for one moment think that my readers, as they turn the pages, say to themselves, "Gee, how cleverly Asimov is demonstrating his antiviolence thesis." I'm almost sure they never give that a thought at all, any more than I did, consciously, when writing the trilogy.

However, the thesis sinks in, unconsciously, for those people who have a tendency to thought and competence—a classification that tends to include the generality of my readers—and this thesis gives them pleasure. In many cases, they reread the trilogy several times (at least, so they tell me) and it can't be for the surprise endings, which are never a surprise after the first time. They can only reread it for renewed satisfaction in the presented view of humanity. All this pleases me so much.

I might, if I could bring myself to do so, add reams of violence to my stories, or sex, or various other forms of sensationalism. I'm sure that no one is going to say I lack the literary expertise to do so, if it were my determination to do so. And if I did, there is at least a chance I might gather more readers, make the bestseller lists, or achieve big movie sales.

But I want *my* readers, the minority of competents, who would like to see the world proceed on a rational course, without war and violence. We may lose, of course—but we may win. And that is as much as we can expect, for in a world in which violence now means nuclear weapons, germ warfare, smart missiles, and laser beams, those who view violence as a solution *must* lose.

✦

AFTERWORD: Among the science fiction writers, Jerry Pournelle is perhaps the leading exponent of Reagan's Star Wars program (see Chapter 36). When we last met, at a Nebula Awards banquet in 1985, he said, "Why are you so against defending ourselves against nuclear assault?"

I said, "Because I don't think Star Wars will work as a defense and it will delude us into a dangerous feeling of false assurance."

Whereupon Jerry rattled off the names of those scientists who supported Star Wars and said, "Do you doubt their technological competence?"

"Not at all," said I sweetly. "It's their sanity I doubt."

I don't suppose Jerry is often shocked into silence, but he was that time.

Violence and Incompetence

56

Family Matters

SOMETIMES I WONDER HOW I would have felt, when I was eighteen and trying to sell a science fiction story for the first time, if I could somehow have foreseen that the day would come when I would have my "own" magazine, with my name in the title.

I wouldn't have believed it, of course. In my most megalomaniac moments, I couldn't have pictured such a thing. Yet here it is, and though it may seem like a dream of Paradise, it has its problems.

Among the problems is my wife, Janet Jeppson. —No, it's not the problem you might think. She's a sweetheart and I'm deeply in love with her.

You see, she's a science fiction fan and has been one for years. That's not surprising as I probably wouldn't have met her in the first place if she weren't. We first met at a science fiction convention (as you will see if you read the second volume of my autobiography—*In Joy Still Felt*—published by Doubleday in April 1980).

Like many science fiction fans, Janet has been trying to write science fiction. She has had the ambition to write since grade school and, I suspect, would by now have succeeded in that ambition and have become an established writer, had she not allowed herself to be diverted into medical school and all that followed.

She is, by profession, a physician, a psychiatrist, a psychoanalyst, and, on top of that, director of training at the William Alanson White Institute of Psychiatry, Psychoanalysis and Psychology in New York City.

All that didn't leave her with much spare time for stroking the typewriter.

What spare time she had, however, she used in that direction. By the time I met her she had various novels, short stories, and essays written. Of these, she had sold a mystery story and had nearly sold a few other items.

Getting to know me served as an encouragement for her to continue to write, for anyone watching me gets the idea that writing is easy. (And so it is, if you have the talent and temperament for it to begin with, and then go on to accumulate several decades of unremitting hard work and experience.)

She worked furiously at a science fiction novel, therefore, writing in her spare time, revising, tearing up and starting over, and going through all the agonies inseparable from the task. Occasionally, she would ask me to look at the manuscript and give her some sage advice.

Steadfastly, I refused. She was not pleased with the refusal and it produced the only appreciable strain in our relationship over the years. But I held fast to my position, which was that if I as much as looked at the manuscript and changed a single word, she would, if she ever sold the story, always feel that it was my changed word that had done it.

"You must stand on your own feet, Janet," I said. "If the novel is sold, you must be certain that I had nothing to do with it, and that you did it all."

She found it difficult to accept that, but she came to realize the validity of that point of view.

When the time came for submitting the novel, knowing me finally helped. Various editors knew her because they knew me and that meant that in some cases (not in all) they gave it a fast reading instead of making her wait months.

In some cases, that just meant a fast rejection. Ben Bova, one of our very best friends, read the manuscript with a view to possible serialization in *Analog* and rejected it, albeit with kind words. But then he has, in his time, rejected stories of mine, too. That sort of thing makes us feel sad and disappointed, but it doesn't affect friendship, and shouldn't.

Eventually, Houghton Mifflin considered the novel and thought it might have possibilities. The editor, Austin Olney, asked for extensive revisions, which were made. On 30 November 1973, he called to say that he was taking the novel. As it happened, that day was the day Janet and I were married, and the call came just as the ceremony was completed.

The novel, *The Second Experiment,* was published in 1974 under the byline J. O. Jeppson. Janet avoided the use of "Asimov" (to which she was legally entitled) and expressly forbade Houghton Mifflin to mention the relationship to me in the flap matter or the advertising.

The book did reasonably well for a first novel. It earned back its advance on trade sales and went into paperback editions in the United States, Great Britain, and France.

Yet the inevitable happened. A reviewer in a science fiction fan magazine, having disapproved of the book thoroughly, went on to state that only nepotism could explain its publication.

Too bad. I had strained my relationship with Janet and we had hampered the Houghton Mifflin publicity department in order to remove the faintest suspicions of nepotism, and it hadn't helped.

Since then, Janet has written a mystery novel—which never sold—and another science fiction novel which, after revision, was sold to Houghton Mifflin and which appeared in the spring of 1980 as *The Last Immortal*, again by J. O. Jeppson. Again, I had refused to read the manuscript or to aid her in any way, however indirect.

Aside from her novels, Janet has in recent years sold a short story to *F & SF*, and a couple of nonfiction pieces to other markets. One of the latter was an article that appeared in the New York *Times* travel section in January 1979, and that received a great deal of favorable attention. In none of these cases did I lift a finger to help her.

Well then, some months ago, I came across the manuscript of a short story on her desk entitled "The Cleanest Block in Town." Intrigued by the title, I asked permission to read it. I did and was fascinated.

So, for the first time since I had met her, I suggested a collaboration. I wanted to rewrite the story, make it longer, add one or two of my own ideas, and then offer it to the world. Janet agreed and, eventually, we had a story that bore the byline of J. O. Jeppson and Isaac Asimov.

The next step was to decide where to send it. It seemed to me that it *had* to go to *Isaac Asimov's Science Fiction Magazine*. After all, I am *supposed* to write for it occasionally. In fact, any time I write a science fiction story, *Asimov's* must, by contract, see it first unless I get special permission to submit it elsewhere. Besides, I liked the story and thought it would look good in the magazine.

So we sent it to George Scithers—and he *rejected* it.

That's all right. He's supposed to do that if he doesn't like a story. He has the last word even if I openly disagree with him. Even if it's my own story that's in question, he still has the last word. So that was that.

Janet and I didn't exactly feel good about it. I myself felt particularly bad since I couldn't help but wonder if I had perhaps spoiled the story, and if she might not have had better luck sending it out in her own version. Just the same, we were both of us professional enough to accept the rejection.

After that, Janet wrote another short story and this time didn't welcome any interference from me. She sent it to George and, after asking for some small revisions, he agreed to take it. (This reinforces my feeling that she's better off on her own than with my help.)

One of these issues, then, Janet's story will appear under the byline of J. O. Jeppson, and we're making no secret of her identity. She's Mrs. Isaac Asimov.

However, her appearance in "my" magazine is, I hope you all see, *not* a matter of nepotism, since George has already shown that he is quite capable of rejecting her stories (and mine, too, for that matter) if he feels he should.

To summarize, being married to me has done Janet no good whatever in her longed-for writing career, but has, instead, set up considerable disadvantages in the way of psychological roadblock. Not the least of these disadvantages is her awareness of the impossibility of avoiding the unfair (and sometimes spiteful) suspicion that I've helped her, or used my "influence" to get her published.

But she loves me anyway, and I love her.

✦

AFTERWORD: Janet went on to sell a series of her Pshrinks Anonymous stories to Asimov's, though one or two were rejected. She also published a collection of them under the title of The Mysterious Cure (Doubleday, 1985). Also, since her solo competence was well established, we finally took to writing in collaboration, though in every such collaboration, she did 90 percent of the work. There are a series of stories about a robot named Norby, put out by Walker and Company for younger readers. So far, there are seven of them by "Isaac and Janet Asimov":
Norby, the Mixed-up Robot (1983)
Norby's Other Secret (1984)
Norby and the Lost Princess (1985)
Norby and the Invaders (1985)
Norby and the Queen's Necklace (1986)
Norby Finds a Villain (1987)
Norby Down to Earth (1988)

She has also sold a nonfiction book, *How to Enjoy Writing* published by Walker and Company in 1982, and has done two science fiction novels for Walker and Company all by herself, *Mind Transfer* (1988) and *The Package in Hyperspace* (in press). To our great relief, no further charges of nepotism have ever been raised. (And the one person who did so will, I assure you, live forever in my memory.)

57

Persona

THE ANCIENT GREEK ACTORS
wore masks when they played their parts. There were several reasons for this. I
have heard it said (but don't know if it's true) that the masks acted as voice
amplifiers, which in open-air amphitheaters, without the advantage of micro-
phones, might well have been necessary. Then, too, the masks were so formed
as to present the essential information concerning the character. The audience
was too far to see the minutiae of expression we can now see on a bloated
screen, so the mask told them what they needed to know.

The masks could be moving, too. In *Oedipus Rex,* the Theban king,
Oedipus, would surely have been shown with a mask that marked the noble,
serene regularity always found in the Greek representations of their gods and
heroes. When, however, in the last scene, Oedipus had plucked out his own
eyes (off-stage, of course), he would appear again in a mask distorted to show
tragedy, and painted to indicate blood coursing down from empty eyeholes.
The audience would then have all the grisliness it needed to get the catharsis
Aristotle thought true tragedy should give.

The Latin word for these theatrical masks (and we still see them representing the theater in two forms—the tragic with opened downturned mouths,
and the comic with open upturned mouths) was *persona.* The word is still used
to represent a public character carefully cultivated by someone in order to
mask the real "person" underneath.

Why should any such persona be developed? The most common reason is that of the Greeks—because one is playing a part for a living. Because one is in show business, in other words.

The most successful persona I know of (at least, in my own opinion) was that of Jack Benny. For decades, on radio, in the movies, and on television, he cultivated the persona of a vain person of no ability, distressingly self-centered, and impossibly stingy. He did this so continuously, so three-dimensionally, and so persistently that the persona was universally taken for the person. As a person in real life, he was forced to be unusually generous because he knew that everyone took it for granted he was cheap. He was actually a modest, warm character loved by all.

But then why did he choose a persona that seemed to be without redeeming value? Because he had made a discovery that few comedians seem to have found (or could bear to use if they had found it). Benny made himself the butt of the jokes. Everyone on the show got the better of him. Everyone else got the laughs—at his expense. The result? There was no way of being angry or annoyed with him, since he always got his comeuppance and didn't need anything else from us.

In fact, he got his so thoroughly that the audience had to balance the scales. For all his impossible vanity and abhorrent cheapness, they found themselves forced to love him.

What is all this leading up to? Well, rather to my astonishment I find that I am accused of having developed a persona. At least, I have received a letter of accusation, and where one person thinks so, others may concur.

The letter was inspired by my essay "The Little Tin God of Characterization" in which I maintained that in science fiction, at least, ideas were more important than characterization. Most of the letters I received as a result disagreed with me, but only one really startled me. That was by Michael T. Folie of New York City, whose letter I did not print because it was entirely too complimentary. (Yes, I know I'm supposed to lap up flattery—and I do, but only in secret.)

He scolded me for even bothering to answer those who criticized me, and for letting myself be brainwashed into thinking I was not good at characterization. He says, "I think that you have poured all of your considerable ability to create character into creating the one character that you will ever need. That character is, of course, the Good Doctor, Dr. Isaac Asimov. You have created this persona and it is one of the most vibrant characters in science fiction."

I wish I had created the Good Doctor, as accused. How clever that would have been of me. I would have repeated Jack Benny's feat of deliberately designing a set of characteristics that would force people to react to me in such a way as to enhance my career.

But I can only say, "Not guilty, my friends, not guilty."

The most obvious fact about me is that I am a prolific writer and seem to write with equal ease in fiction and nonfiction, for children and adults, and on almost every subject under the sun. This, however, is not something I can fake or pretend or assume as a deliberate persona. It is a fact and, let me tell you, it's the result of hard and unremitting labor. I enjoy writing and find it easy, but no matter how joyfully and easily I write, turning out 327 books is a very time-consuming and thought-consuming process. I'd hate to have anyone think all those books were merely a device to attract favorable attention.

There are other, more superficial qualities I seem to possess, however, that might be deliberately assumed. For instance, I never seem to grow tired of talking about myself and my writing (witness this essay). Have I purposefully adopted this pose of self-absorption or, if you like, vanity?

I don't think so. It comes with the territory. How can anyone be a professional writer without thinking highly of himself? A writer must believe *from the beginning* that publishers and readers will be willing to pay him for his thoughts and for his mode of expressing them. Consider what a piece of conceit this is! A modest writer is a contradiction in terms. If a writer were modest he or she would (like Emily Dickinson) hesitate to offer anything for publication.

The fact is that I know many writers and I don't think any one of them is modest about his or her writing. He or she may be modest about everything else, but not about his or her writing.

Of course, they may *pretend* to be modest, and cultivate the "aw, shucks" attitude, but then *they* are creating the persona.

I admit that I do more talking and writing about myself than anyone else in the field does and that I am more open about the fact that I like my stuff and more freely admit that I am a hotshot writer—but I just happen to be cursed by a complete lack of self-consciousness, and always have been. It does not embarrass me to say what I consider to be the truth just because it would sound conceited. To me, there is no attitude more tedious and useless than that of false modesty. It is unconvincing and irritating, whereas what I call a "cheerful self-appreciation," when it is well earned, as in my case, has at least the virtue of being open and honest.

So my self-absorption is me, not my persona.

How about my well-known quality of being "suave" with women? It's true enough. I am very fond of women generally, and I take advantage of my position as a minor celebrity and of my gray hairs to flirt outrageously. Believe me, there's nothing of pretense about it. That's me, not my persona.

Nevertheless, I have received the following letter from someone calling himself "Pro Bono Fandom." There is no hint as to the true identity of the writer and I will not speculate. To be sure, the stamp on the letter is from Sri Lanka but the only person I know in Sri Lanka is a minor writer named Arthur C. Clarke, whom I don't suppose anyone else has ever heard of. "Pro Bono Fandom" writes:

For years the Good Doctor has claimed to be one of the world's great lovers; it's time to put the record straight. At vast expense, considerable difficulty, and no small risk, a devoted group of private investigators has been following the G.D.'s trail of havoc at numerous science fiction Conventions, and interviewing the disappointed, distraught, or relieved victims of his machinations. Here are some of their comments:—

1. I fell asleep first.
2. He lectured me on genetics for two hours—then *he* fell asleep.
3. Isaac who?
4. The sonofabitch! He said he was John Norman.
5. I didn't notice: I was reading an Arthur Clarke book.
6. I had such a laughing fit he got worried and called a *real* doctor.
7. Autograph hunters knocked on the door, so he forgot me.
8. Janet had a spare key.
9. He had an idea for a short story.
10. Carl Sagan phoned.

Is it necessary to give any more examples to expose this *soi-disant* Don Juan? Let's hear no more of his preposterous claims!

—Well, how do I explain this bit of character assassination? Without trying to guess at his identity, I would suppose that "Pro Bono Fandom" is three years older than I am, thirty years balder, and three hundred years uglier —and is simply corroded with envy at the way the young ladies flock about me.

♦

AFTERWORD: I suppose not one reader of my essays (including the ones in this book) can fail to notice that I do a great deal of talking about myself. In fact, one reader canceled his subscription to *Asimov's* because he said he could no longer endure my ego (see Chapter 64). We were sorry to lose him but this extremely personal manner of writing happens to be my style. What can I do?

58

My Name

I RECEIVED A LETTER, RECENTLY, in which my name was mentioned at five separate points, and the name of the magazine at a sixth point. In all six places, my name was misspelled.

This is, alas, a common occurrence, but I have never really learned to adjust myself to it. I remain absurdly sensitive to such misspellings, and invariably (when I can) indicate my displeasure as politely as possible.

Oddly enough, it never occurred to me until this letter was received that misspelling my name means, automatically, the misspelling of the magazine's name as well. Whether you refer to the magazine in full as *Isaac Asimov's Science Fiction Magazine,* or, more economically, as *Asimov's,* questions concerning spelling and pronunciation remain. It occurs to me, then, that if I take up my name in full detail, the matter may be laid to rest.

The name Isaac is of biblical origin and comes from a Hebrew word meaning "laughter." The use of the name in the Bible is explained in three different places. When Abraham was ninety-nine years old, and without a son by his chief wife, Sarah, God promised that he would have a son by her. "Then Abraham . . . laughed, and said in his heart, Shall a child be born unto him that is an hundred years old? and shall Sarah, that is ninety years old, bear?" (Genesis 17:17).

On another occasion, the promise being repeated, Sarah overheard the discussion. The result was that ". . . Sarah laughed within herself, saying, After I am waxed old shall I have pleasure, my lord being old also?" (Genesis 18:12).

Both laughs were laughs of disbelief, but when the child was born, it became a laugh of pleasure: "And Sarah said, God hath made me to laugh, so that all that hear will laugh with me" (Genesis 21:6).

So the child was named Isaac. In Hebrew, it is Yitzhak, where the *h* represents the guttural sound of the German *ch*.

When the Bible was translated into Greek in the third century B.C. (its first translation) Yitzhak became Isaak (in Greek letters, of course). The Greeks didn't have the *tz* sound in their language and so an *s* was substituted. They did have the guttural *ch*, and the double *a* seems to have indicated it. Since Latin does not use a *k* in its words, the name became Isaac in Latin translations of the Bible. Latin does not have the guttural *ch* and though they kept the double *a*, its significance was lost.

In modern languages, it is Isaak in German, and Isaac in French, and in both cases is pronounced "ee-zak" (not too far from the Hebrew), with the Germans accenting the first syllable and the French the second. In English, which followed the French and Latin spelling, rather than the German and Greek, the initial *i* was given the long pronunciation and the name is "eye'zik," with the accent on the first syllable.

Under the circumstances, it is rather natural to have people who are not familiar with the name replace the *c* with a *k* or *ck*, or the *s* with a *z*. Since the *aa* combination is very unusual in English words it is also common to omit one of the *a*'s. That omission is even standard in some languages. The name is Izaak in Dutch, and Isak in Danish. (A famous Danish writer has, as her pseudonym, Isak Dinesen.) For that matter, it is Isacco in Italian.

The misspelling I find least forgivable (and most common), however, comes about when people dimly remember that there is a double letter in the name but are unwilling to accept the possibility of an *aa* combination. They, therefore, spell it Issac. In no language that I know of is there a double *s* in the name, and I consider it an abomination.

My own possession of the name came about through the Jewish custom of naming a child for a member of the family who is no longer alive. In this way, I suppose, the dead relative is honored and memorialized. In any case, my mother's father, already dead at the time I was born, had been an Isaac, and so I received the name.

As for my second name, that is of more recent origin. Under Tsar Nicholas I, a century and a half ago, the Jews of the Russian Empire were required to adopt family names. Until then, they had called themselves in biblical fashion as "Joshua, son of Nun," so that I would have been "Isaac, son of Judah."

The family names chosen were of different types of origin. For instance, the word for "winter" in Russian is *zima*. Winter grain (the kind that is sown in the fall, so that after winter dormancy, it ripens the following spring and summer) is therefore called *azimy*.

My ancestor in the time of Tsar Nicholas was a merchant who dealt in winter grain, among other things, so he was probably called Judah Azimy ("Judah, the winter-grain dealer") in any case, and he adopted that as his official surname, to be used on documents.

Eventually, this was modified to Azimov, in order to get the Russian ending and give it the sound of a higher social status.

That name was, of course, spelled in the Cyrillic alphabet that is used in Russian, and my father when the family arrived in the United States was faced with the necessity of spelling it in the Latin alphabet which English uses. My father was not familiar with the Latin alphabet but knew that the sewing machine in his house in Russia had the word Singer on it, in the Latin alphabet, and that this was pronounced (German fashion) as Zinger. He assumed, therefore, that *s* had the *z* pronunciation and he spelled his name Asimov. It has so remained ever since. The *s*, however, is still pronounced *z*.

For some reason, "Asimov" seems to represent an insoluble mystery to many people as far as its pronunciation is concerned. In Russian, the name is pronounced with the accent on the second syllable: "ah-zee'muv." In English, however, it is the *first* syllable that is stressed, and it becomes "az'ih-mov."

In fact, the easiest way of getting the correct pronunciation is to say the three simple English words "as," "him," and "of," one after the other, and drop the *h*, cockney fashion, in the second word. "As," " 'im," "of." That's it!

I can tolerate the substitution of a *z* for an *s* in my surname. After all, that is the way it should be, really (but isn't). I can even tolerate an *f* or *ff* in place of the *v*, but that's all.

The German *w* is pronounced *v*, so that when Russian names are transliterated into German, they routinely receive an *ow* or *owsky* ending. That's why the name of the composer Chaikovsky is sometimes written Tschaikowsky or Tchaikowsky, and pronounced by some Americans as though there were a *cow* somewhere in its middle. Under such conditions, my name would be Asimow and, indeed, there are, in California, some very distant relatives of mine who have that as their surname. This I would seriously object to in my own case, because it changes the pronunciation Tschaikowsky-fashion, and I do not want that to happen.

As in the case of my first name, so in the case of my surname, the most offensive misspelling is the use of a double *s*.

One odd point is this. For some reason, "Asimov" seems to evade some American tongues altogether. They cannot say it, but manage to get out the word Asminov instead. I simply can't understand it. It seems to me that Asminov is far more difficult to say than Asimov but so many people say the former that I feel there must be some legitimate linguistic reason for it, and it amuses me too much to allow me to get very angry.

I can tell you numerous tales of odd misspellings and pronunciations, but I will satisfy myself with only two.

The first was an occasion, about twenty years ago, when I lectured at a Jewish temple in Philadelphia. As I walked in, I passed a huge poster announcing the glad tidings of my talk, and my first name was spelled Issac. I had the pleasure of asking the rabbi, gently, if he ever read the Bible in English. He produced one indignantly, and I turned to an appropriate passage, indicated it, pointed to the poster, and watched him look appropriately horrified.

Better than that, though, was the occasion in 1977, when I received a Nebula for my novelette "The Bicentennial Man" from the Science Fiction Writers of America.

One would certainly expect that the various SFWA officials, whatever else they knew or did not know, would know how to spell one of the most familiar names in the science fiction lexicon. Of course, one would not expect that these officials would personally carve my name on the plastic award, but it is not asking too much that they give the workman the appropriate instructions, and that they proofread the results.

Ha! I received my Nebula with my name upon it as Issac Asmimov.

They offered to replace it, but I refused. I felt that they would spell it even worse the second time.

So there's the story; and now—all together:

ISAAC ASIMOV (eye'zik-az'ih-mov).

♦

AFTERWORD: It strikes me, after rereading the above essay in order to make sure it's in shape for publication, that there must be some readers who, when faced with a fourteen-hundred-word essay devoted entirely to the spelling and pronunciation of my name, might say, "Who cares?" To which the answer is *"I do, darn it."*

59

Bestseller

IN THE DECEMBER 1982 ISSUE OF *Asimov's* the first two chapters of my novel *Foundation's Edge* were presented as an excerpt, together with an essay of my own on the novel's genesis and some pleasant comments from my friends and colleagues. I agreed to all this under strong pressure from the editorial staff, who thought it would be a Good Thing and who overrode my own objections that readers would complain that I was using the magazine for personal aggrandizement.

As it happened, my fears were groundless. Readers' comments were universally friendly, and a gratifying number indicated their determination to get the book and finish reading it.

It may be that you are curious to know what happened after the book was published. (For those of you interested in Asimovian trivia, it was published on 8 October 1982.) I'd like to tell you, because what happened astonished me totally. The book proved to be a bestseller!

I don't mean it was a "bestseller" in the usual promotion way of indicating that it didn't actually sink without a trace on publication day. I mean it appeared on the national bestseller lists and, as I write, it is in third place on both the New York *Times* list of hardcover fiction and on the *Publishers Weekly* list for the same. Maybe by the time this essay appears, it will have disappeared from the lists, but *right now* it's there.

In the past, in these essays, I have promised to keep you up to date on my endeavors and I will do it now in the form of an invented interview:

Q. *Dr. Asimov, is this your first bestseller?*

A. For some reason, people find that hard to believe, perhaps because I'm so assiduous at publicizing myself, but *Foundation's Edge* is my first bestseller. It is my 262nd book and I have been a professional writer for forty-four years, so I guess this qualifies me as something less than an overnight success. Mind you, this is not my first successful book. Very few of my books have actually lost money for the publisher and many of them have done very well indeed over the years. The earlier books of the Foundation trilogy have sold in the millions over the thirty years they have been in print. Again, if you group all my books together and total the number of sales of "Asimov" (never mind the titles) then I have a bestseller every year.

However, *Foundation's Edge* is the first time a *single* book of mine has sold enough copies in a *single* week to make the bestseller lists, and in the eight weeks since publication (as I write), it has done it in each of eight weeks.

Q. *And how do you feel about that, Dr. A.?*

A. Actually, I have no room for any feeling but that of astonishment. After publishing 261 books without any hint of bestsellerdom, no matter how any of them might have been praised, I came to think of that as a law of nature. As for *Foundation's Edge* in particular, it has no sex in it, no violence, no sensationalism of any kind, and I had come to suppose that this was a perfect recipe for respectable nonbestsellerdom.

Once I get over the astonishment, though (if ever), I suppose I will have room for feeling great. After all, *Foundation's Edge* will earn more money than I expected, and it will help my other books to sell more copies, and it may mean that future novels of mine may do better than I would otherwise expect, and I can't very well complain about any of that.

Then, too, think of the boost to my ego! (Yes, I know! You think that's the last thing it needs.) People who till now have known I was a writer and accepted it with noticeable lack of excitement, even over the number of books I have committed, now stop me in order to congratulate me, and do so with pronounced respect. Personally, I don't think that being on the bestseller lists makes a book any the higher in quality and, all too often, it might indicate the reverse, but I must admit I enjoy the congratulations and all that goes with it.

Q. *Are there any disadvantages to all this great stuff, Isaac?*

A. Oddly enough, there are. For one thing, my esteemed publisher, Doubleday & Company, would like me to travel all over the United States pushing the book. (It was, as of this writing, their only fiction bestseller and they are as eager as I am to have it stay on the lists forever.) They are putting considerable money into advertising and promotion and it would only be fair that I do my bit as well. However, I don't like to travel, and so I have to refuse their suggestions that I go to Chicago, for instance. And it makes me feel guilty, and a traitor both to my publisher and to my book. I *have* made a trip to Philadelphia, though.

There is also a higher-than-normal demand for interviews through visits or on the telephone. This doesn't demand traveling on my part and I try to oblige (telling myself it's good publicity for the book), but it does cut into my writing time, and I can't allow too much of that.

Then, too, there's an extraordinary demand for free copies. This is a common disease among writers' friends and relations, who feel that there is no purpose in knowing a writer if you have to help support him. My dear wife, Janet, who is a shrewd questioner, has discovered the astonishing fact that some people think writers get unlimited numbers of free copies to give out. They don't! Except for a certain, very small number, they have to *buy* copies just as anyone else does. (Even if they did have unlimited numbers of free copies, giving them rather than selling them would ruin a writer, just as giving meat rather than selling it would ruin a butcher.)

What I have done is to resist firmly any temptation to hand out *Foundation's Edge*. I have told everyone they must buy copies at a bookstore. If they insist, I will give them copies of other books, but those sales of *Foundation's Edge* must be registered. Every little bit helps.

Q. *Do you see any importance in this situation aside from personal profit and gratification?*

A. I do, indeed. Soon after *Foundation's Edge* was published, Arthur C. Clarke's new novel, *2010: Odyssey Two,* was published, and it hit the bestseller lists, too. At the moment of writing it is in fifth place on the New York *Times* list. Earlier this year, Robert A. Heinlein made the list with *Friday* and Frank Herbert did so with *White Plague.*

I think this is the first year in which four different science fiction writers made the lists with straight science fiction books. I also think that in the case of Clarke and myself, this is the first time straight science fiction has landed so high on the lists.

This is gratifying to me as a longtime science fiction fan. It indicates to me that, finally, science fiction is coming to be of interest to the general public and not simply to those few who inhabit the s.f. "ghetto."

In fact, I wish to point this out to those s.f. writers who are bitter and resentful because they feel that they are shoved into the background and disregarded merely because they have the s.f. label on themselves. Neither *Foundation's Edge* nor *2010: Odyssey Two* makes any effort to hide the fact that it is science fiction. The publisher's promotion in each case utterly fails to obscure that fact. In the case of *Foundation's Edge*, the New York *Times* carefully describes it as "science fiction" each week in its bestseller listing. And yet it continues to sell.

To be sure, there is a trace of the "ghetto" just the same. There is one thing that Arthur and I have in common, aside from bestselling books. As of the moment of writing, neither *Foundation's Edge* nor *2010: Odyssey Two* has been reviewed in the New York *Times*. I presume the paper hesitates to bestow that accolade on mere science fiction. Oh well!

Q. *And what are your present projects, Isaac?*

A. Well, Doubleday has informed me, in no uncertain terms, that I am condemned to write one novel after another for life, and that I am not permitted to consider dying.

So I am working on another novel. This one is to be the third novel of the robot series. Both Lije Baley and R. Daneel Olivaw will reappear and will complete the trilogy that began with *The Caves of Steel* and *The Naked Sun*. The third novel is called *The Robots of Dawn*.

After that, I am afraid that Doubleday expects me to do a fifth Foundation novel; and, apparently, so do the readers. For three decades they badgered me for a sequel to the Foundation trilogy and when I gave that to them, the ungrateful dogs responded by badgering me for a sequel to the sequel.

I'd complain, except that I love it.

60

My Projects

I RECEIVE A SIZABLE NUMBER OF letters asking me what my next book will be, what projects I have in hand, whether I am working on this or that specific opus, and so on. I don't feel that my privacy is being invaded by letters of this sort and I do my best to answer all such questions, even if only by a brief postcard.

The number of such letters is increasing, however, and I see that it will soon reach the level where I simply cannot answer them all—and then I am likely to be forced to answer none of them, out of sheer dislike for playing favorites and answering some but not others. It occurred to me, therefore, to devote an essay to a discussion of some of the things that are on the griddle, in the perhaps hopeless dream that this will make some of the questioning letters I receive unnecessary. I won't do this often, I assure you, just once in a long while when the pressure gets heavy.

The question I am most asked, of course, now that *Foundation's Edge* is safely published (and *still* on the bestseller list after twenty weeks, at this moment of writing) is "When is the next Foundation novel coming out?"

The answer is: not for just a little while, please.

I'm sure it was Doubleday's notion, once they saw they had a bestseller going, that I begin a new Foundation novel at once, and they handed me another contract immediately. That was the feeling of my dear wife, Janet, too. Once she finished *Foundation's Edge*, she came to me and said, in her best tone of wifely command, "I want you to start the next novel *right now*."

However, it is one thing to order a book written, and quite another actually to write it. I might as well admit that writing *Foundation's Edge* was not something I did between yawns. It took me nine months of hard work (though I admit it might have taken a little less time if I hadn't been working on a dozen other projects as well) and it rather wore me out. I felt I needed time to let the well of inspiration refill.

Besides, now that I had finally acceded to innumerable requests for a continuation of the Foundation series, I felt that I would be bombarded with demands that I complete the Lije Baley trilogy.

I had, you see, written two novels dealing with the detective Elijah Baley and his robot sidekick, R. Daneel Olivaw. These were *The Caves of Steel* (Doubleday, 1954) and *The Naked Sun* (Doubleday, 1957). The first dealt with a crowded Earth in which human beings far outnumbered robots, and the second dealt with the nearly empty planet Solaria, in which robots far outnumbered human beings.

Incautiously, I let it be known that I was planning a third novel that would complete the trilogy and that would be set on the planet Aurora, on which human beings and robots achieved a reasonable balance. In 1958, I actually started the third novel and wrote four chapters before bogging down, partly because I was dissatisfied with the plot I had worked out, (see Chapter 45) and partly because (what with *Sputnik I*) I had become overwhelmingly interested in nonfiction.

So the decades passed and readers grew steadily more insistent on the matter of the third novel. Once the fourth Foundation novel had appeared and was successful, I knew that it would not be safe any longer to try to continue resisting the matter of the third Lije Baley novel. I got to work on 22 September 1982, abandoning my earlier effort altogether and taking off in an utterly new direction.

The new novel, *The Robots of Dawn*, is, as planned originally, however, the tale of Baley and Daneel on the planet Aurora. On this day of writing, five months later, first draft has just been completed and by the time this essay appears in print, the novel should be in press and well on the way to publication. Doubleday even hopes it will be out before the end of 1983.

The new novel will be longer than either of the first two Lije Baley volumes by a good bit; it will, indeed, be about as long as *Foundation's Edge*.

I cannot possibly guarantee that *The Robots of Dawn* will be as successful as *Foundation's Edge*, but my editors seem enthusiastic about it, and I've worked hard on it. We'll see what happens.

And what comes after that?

Well, the push for two novels, back to back, has forced me to cut down on other work. Specifically, I have had to suspend operations on at least four important nonfiction projects. There is, first, a long-overdue revision of *Asimov's Guide to Science* that I am doing for Basic Books; second, there is a massive question-and-answer book on science for Doubleday; third, a book on supernovas for Dutton; and fourth, a two-volume history of the world for Walker. I can't put all of these on the back burner forever. Each of these books has anywhere from fifty thousand to five hundred thousand words done and that's a large investment.

Unfortunately, I can't get sympathy from publishers by moaning about all the other work I must do. They tend to be stony-hearted, largely because of my well-known prolificity—which has its hellish side effects. (I wish I had a bestseller for every time a publisher has brushed aside my sad tale of other commitments and said, "You can just knock that off on a weekend, can't you, Isaac?")

So, if *The Robots of Dawn* does well, I know that Doubleday will keep asking me to knock off the four nonfiction books (including even their own) in four successive weekends and get on with more novels. And I suppose I will have to do at least some thinking about the matter.

Well, if my Gentle Readers don't mind (and how can they stop me?) I would like to do some thinking aloud on the matter.

The next novel I do will, inevitably, have to be a fifth Foundation novel. There will be absolutely no choice in the matter. But what *kind* of Foundation novel?

Consider! So far, all my Foundation stories have been written moving forward in time. The series starts just before Hari Seldon sets up the Foundations, in the year 1 of the Foundation Era (F.E.), and the most recent novel, *Foundation's Edge*, takes place in 498 F.E. Furthermore, this most recent novel ends with a clear indication that there is still some mystery about the long-forgotten birth-planet of the human species, Earth.

The assumption then is that the fifth Foundation novel should continue the story and take up the search for the Earth with all that might entail. Indeed, it had been my casual intention to begin at the precise point where *Foundation's Edge* left off and to continue—though exactly what the nature of the plot is to be in that case, I haven't yet the faintest notion.

Recently, however, it has occurred to me that there is a second alternative. I can do another kind of Foundation novel.

In *Foundation's Edge*, I made a point of referring to various non-Foundation novels of mine and indicating how they might fit into the Foundation universe. (A few of the critics disapproved of this, but I'm darned if I know why. They are my books and I can do as I wish with them, I should think.)

A major embarrassment were the Lije Baley novels, which can in no way be fitted into the Foundation universe. The Lije Baley novels contain societies based on strains of humanity with life spans of up to four centuries and supported by elaborate systems of robots. The Foundation novels have ordinary short-lived strains of humanity only, and no robots at all.

In *Foundation's Edge*, I finally mentioned robots, and in *The Robots of Dawn* I amused myself by letting the plot serve the function of pointing the Lije Baley universe in the direction of the Foundation universe.

Well then, might it not be possible to write additional novels within the interval between *The Robots of Dawn* and *Foundation*? Might I not have "pre-Foundation" novels, in other words?

I could have a novel in which the conversion from the Lije Baley universe to the Foundation universe is half complete, with considerable friction between the two types of societies. I could also have one that takes place still later, in the latter days of the Galactic Empire with Hari Seldon still in the full vigor of early middle age and founding the science of psychohistory. Then, after I have done one or, at most, two of these pre-Foundation novels, I can turn back to the sequel of *Foundation's Edge*.

I don't expect any of these novels will be easy to write and every one of them may present me with insuperable problems when I try to fit them into the framework that already exists, but I keep thinking about it. And if any of the readers have ideas about whether I should move strictly forward or take some backward steps as well, please let me know.

In the end, I'll have to go my own way, I suppose—but I'd love to hear your opinions just the same.

✦

AFTERWORD: Now that you've read the above essay and the one before, let me bring you up to date. *The Robots of Dawn* was published as scheduled in 1983. I followed that with a sequel, *Robots and Empire*, published in 1985. Both did very well, though not as well as *Foundation's Edge* did. After that, I finally did the fifth Foundation book, *Foundation and Earth*, which was published in 1986. It starts right where *Foundation's Edge* leaves off. Then came *Prelude to Foundation*, published in 1988, which takes place fifty years before the start of *Foundation.*

As for the nonfiction books I mentioned in the above essay, two have been finished. *Asimov's New Guide to Science* was published in 1984 by Basic Books and *Exploding Suns* was published in 1985 by Dutton.

61

My Autobiography

HAVE A RAPPORT WITH MY READ-
ers. It was something like twenty years ago that I began speaking directly to
them in my nonfiction essays, and even in forewords and afterwords in my
fiction collections.

This had (and has) both its advantages and disadvantages—as everything
does. The advantage is that it works both ways. If I am clearly friendly and at
ease with you, you become friendly and at ease with me. I doubt that there's
another writer so many of whose readers habitually think of him by his first
name. This spills over onto *Asimov's*, which is also perceived by its readers (on
the whole) to be warm and friendly.

The disadvantage is that this relationship among ourselves is apt to be
puzzling to those who are outside the fold. Then it requires explanation. There
is, for instance, the case of my autobiography, which seems a most peculiar one
when one doesn't understand the rapport between myself and my readers.

The autobiography is in two fat volumes. The first is *In Memory Yet
Green*, published in hardcover by Doubleday in March 1979 and in softcover
by Avon in March 1980. The second is *In Joy Still Felt*, published in hardcover
by Doubleday in April 1980, and in April 1981, it will be in Avon softcover.

The first volume, which is a little over seven hundred pages long, covers
the first thirty-four years of my life (1920–1954); the second, which is a little
over eight hundred pages long, covers the next twenty-four years (1954–
1978). That's 640,000 words devoted to a rather quiet life. (It can't help but be
quiet. Having published well over two hundred books and innumerable

shorter pieces, I do precious little other than sit at the typewriter, and there's not much drama in that.)

Well then, why have I written so *much?*

Almost all the reviewers have been very kind to me, but that is what they wonder. Even when they admit they liked the books and didn't find them tedious, they tend to refer, with both amusement and bemusement, to my insistence on describing *everything.* Some call the book a laundry list; some say, as kindly as possible, that it tells more about me than anyone would care to know.

Yet surely I'm not an incompetent writer and can be supposed to know what I'm doing. Then why did I write such a peculiar autobiography?

Let me explain—

I know something others don't know, because I'm the one who gets the letters from my readers. I'm the one who knows the questions I am asked. I'm the one who knows how often someone will write and ask me for a complete list of every book I've written on any and all subjects. I'm the one who knows how often a reader wants to know where a particular article appeared or if I had written on a particular subject, or how many times a particular item was rejected and so on. Apparently, my writing career is sufficiently out of the ordinary to warrant this sort of detailed curiosity, and my open friendliness to the reader is such as to make me seem accessible to such questions.

Therefore, I deliberately planned to make my autobiography a complete and very personal literary reference book. I give details on every piece of fiction I wrote: when I wrote it, how I wrote it, who accepted (or rejected) it; how much I was paid for it; in which issue of which magazine it appeared; and in which of my books it could be found. Some of my nonfiction pieces (there I was somewhat selective—or the book would have been impossibly long) are similarly treated.

Every book without exception is mentioned. For every year from 1950 onward, the names of the books and the publishers are given in the order in which they appeared in that year, and each is given an overall number.

At the end of the book there is an appendix in which all my books are listed in nineteen different categories. For each book, the overall number is included, the publisher, and an asterisk if it is for children. Finally, there is a title index in which every single piece of writing (even if it is an item that was never finished, or a title that was never used in the actual published form) is listed and the pages on which it is referred to are given.

It sounds like egomania and I'm accused of it frequently enough, but I am attempting to supply a need. My readers want to know these things and I am willing to tell them. It is physically impossible for me to tell each reader all he or she wants to know by detailed individual communication, but the autobiography supplies it instead.

Once it appeared, I could answer most questions by referring the reader to my autobiography. And no, this is not a device to push sales and get rich. Readers know very well they can get the books at lower prices from the Science Fiction Book Club, at still lower prices as a paperback, or at no price at all from the public library.

A second feature of the autobiography is that I have gone to some trouble to include every foolish and silly thing I have ever said and done that I can remember. (Ben Bova pointed out that that alone accounts for the length of the autobiography.) Why do I do that? Well, to begin with, such stories generally make for funny reading. More important is the fact that they tend to puncture the all too frequently held opinion that I am incredibly smart and that I know everything.

I'm no dummy, of course, and I know a great deal, but I do not wish to be overestimated and made better than I am. Such overestimation is uncomfortable for me and it makes it impossible for me to avoid disappointing people. What's more, I don't wish to accumulate the dislike that often adheres to people who seem to glory in their own perfection. For that reason I am perfectly willing, even eager, to display my shortcomings and to establish myself as an ordinary human being who, like all human beings, is a mixture of bright and dumb, nice and not so nice.

Finally, my autobiography is, in some ways, an experiment.

I have an excellent memory and, from 1 January 1938, I kept a diary (and I'm still keeping it). It was therefore possible for me to write the book in a great deal of accurate detail as far as dates, names, and even actual conversation are concerned.

Not only, then, did I attempt to write a strictly objective and factual account (to the limits of my fallible humanity) but I endeavored to make it absolutely chronological. I did not skip here and there across the years in order to make some point. I did not make use of foreshadowings. At every point in the autobiography, I tried to reveal no more than I knew at that moment in my life. The reader knows only what I know and lives my life along with me.

Ideally, I hoped that the reader would pause now and then in the tale and wonder, "Say, is he going to make it?"

For all these reasons, I wrote the autobiography the way I wrote it. And yet some things I left out. I tried not to include things that would hurt the feelings of others or invade their privacy. I also omitted all philosophical rumination. I didn't try to gather together the "wisdom" of a lifetime. I didn't try to analyze or interpret what I had done, find motives, trace consequences, or, in general, indulge in autopsychiatry.

I felt that such things were bound to be self-serving. As soon as I started to interpret myself (beyond what was absolutely necessary) I would begin to find excuses for myself and would work to put the best face on everything.

I didn't want to do that. Rather, by merely presenting what I did, and what I thought at the time I did it, I left it to each reader to supply the interpretation, if he or she wishes. Interpreters may disagree with each other, but that is their problem, not mine.

Of course, my life is not yet over. Perhaps I will be given a chance to write a third volume. (I already have a title—*The Scenes of Life.*) If so, I will stubbornly write it along the lines of the first two, following the same system.

And I will feel justified in doing so. Aside from my own inner approval, which is essential, I am backed by someone whose opinion I respect.

Algis Budrys, who reviewed *In Joy Still Felt* in the Chicago *Sun-Times* of 13 April 1980, said, "Once again, Asimov has gauged his audience correctly. If you were to ask a board of experts how to write an autobiography, the resulting prescription would look nothing like this. But this *works.*" (Italics his.)

AFTERWORD: Ideally, I would want to publish the third volume of my autobiography in 2000, when I would be eighty years old, but it seems questionable whether I will make it. My dear wife, Janet, wants me to write it year by year as I go along, but do I have the time for that? Also, Janet wants me to be philosophical and dish out the wisdom of age, and I hate the mere thought of that.

62

What Makes Isaac Run?

MY GOOD FRIEND HARLAN Ellison openly requests that no one bother sending him letters telling him how great he is because he just tosses them away without reading them.

That is an example of stoic nobility that I would follow if I could, but for me it would be hopeless to try. The sad fact is that I love letters telling me how great I am and I read them very carefully so as not to miss a single precious word.

You can imagine, then, how annoying it is to find in my mail, every once in a long while, a letter that does *not* tell me how great I am but, on the contrary, finds fault with me. When that happens, I look all about me carefully to make sure no one is watching, and if I am indeed unobserved, I tear up the letter and snarl and chafe.

And just the other day there came a letter that accused me of the crime of writing too much. This, apparently, was offensive to the letter writer for two reasons, as nearly as I could tell. First, it showed in me an unlovely ambition and a despicable grasping for money and fame. Second, it was an artistic crime since, if I had the common decency to write less, or more slowly, or both, I might perhaps write good literature instead of the miserable stuff I crank out.

I sent my critic a polite note suggesting that he might suffer less if he stopped reading me, and I hope he follows my advice, for I don't like to be the cause of misery for someone who may just possibly be a human being.

Yet it occurs to me that he may not be alone in his thoughts and that some of you, who don't write me, nevertheless have the feeling I write too much or too quickly or both. What you think of me, of course, matters only to me, but some of that impression you have may overflow onto the magazine that bears my name and such an overflow is another matter altogether. For the sake of the magazine I will have to explain myself.

To begin with, while I am a prolific writer, there are many prolific writers, especially among those who grew out of the pulp tradition as I did, and I set no records in that respect. There are a number of writers who have not only written more than I have—but have written more than I can possibly write if I live to extreme old age and carry on my present level of production to the very end.

(If you're curious about figures, I have published about 20 million words in my lifetime altogether, but there are some writers who have published, in their lifetimes, anywhere from 40 million to 100 million words. There's no way in which I can approach these marks and, believe me, I have no ambitions to try.)

Then what gives me my unusual reputation for prolificity? Partly (perhaps entirely) it is because I spread my net wide. I not only have this series of monthly essays, but I have a monthly science essay in *F & SF,* a monthly essay on the future in *American Way Magazine,* a monthly essay on science history in *SciQuest,* and a monthly mystery in *Gallery.* I appear less regularly in scores of other magazines, too. Then, too, my books, which are numerous in themselves, appear in a score of categories, so that one librarian told me she found at least one book of mine in every major division of the Dewey decimal classification.

The result is that people who are used to seeing me in one place or having me deal with one subject are very likely to run into me somewhere else, unexpectedly, dealing with something completely different. This astonishes them and makes them feel surrounded.

Under such circumstances, naturally, people get the impression that I'm setting a world record for writing and that I'm some sort of unbelievable prodigy. But I'm not! I'm just your garden variety of prolific writer.

That, in itself, is considerable. By the time this book appears, the number of my books should be pushing 400—and even that relatively modest number (the world record, by some South African writer I've never heard of, is about 900) seems to puzzle people.

Why do I do it?

It does take considerable application of seat to chair and fingers to typewriter keys to turn all that out, and I do write every day, including Sundays and holidays, unless circumstances physically prevent me from doing so. Well then, why?

Is it truly unlovely ambition and a lusting for money and fame? —Not so, and I can prove it. If I were desperate for money and fame I would channel my efforts into steamy sex novels or semi-mystic horror, or go to Hollywood. I could then do a lot less and get a lot more. To be sure, I might lack the talent for that sort of thing, but if I wanted filthy lucre at all costs, I would at least *try* to do these things and the fact is, I never have.

Well then, if not that, what else? What makes Isaac run?

The answer is so simple that it always surprises me that no one guesses it. It surprises me even more than when I do tell people the answer, they find the utmost difficulty in believing it.

Here it is— I *like* it! I *enjoy* writing! I would rather write than anything else.

What's more, I write exactly what I like to write in exactly the way I like to write and the fact that it has brought me money and fame (to some extent) is a fortunate accident. I neither scorn the money and fame, nor refuse to accept it, but that's not what I was after.

I have lost count of the number of times people have said to me, "You must have *enormous* self-discipline to be able to stick at the typewriter day after day."

My answer is "Not at all! If I had self-discipline I would move away from the typewriter now and then."

Once someone asked me, "If you had to give up either writing or sex, which would you choose to give up?"

My answer, delivered without hesitation, was "I can type for twelve hours at a time without getting tired."

Barbara Walters, refusing to believe that I really liked writing all that much, asked me (off-camera), "What would you do if the doctor gave you only six months to live?"

My answer was "Type faster!"

So in the end, they all say, "Well, you're a workaholic!"

Why? If I loved to play golf or tennis and did so every chance I got, I would be considered a good sport and a very loyal American. If I had a woodworking shop in my basement and amused myself in every idle hour turning out gadgets and furniture for the house, I would get medals.

63

More Asimov?

EVERY ONCE IN A WHILE, WE RE-
ceive a letter which contains a sentence something like this: "Another thing
that I'm curious about is why, since it is *Isaac Asimov's Science Fiction Magazine,* Isaac Asimov doesn't appear more often in the magazine."

Of course, I *do* appear in every issue with an essay, but apparently that is
not quite enough for them. What the letter writers are after is my science
fiction.

One answer to this question is that you can't really go by the title. That
just means that the magazine is put together in the spirit of Isaac Asimov, and
need not contain my stories. Ellery Queen appears in the magazine which has
his name in its title even more rarely than I appear in "my" magazine, and
Alfred Hitchcock never appeared in his magazine at all, even when he was
alive.

Somehow, though, I have a feeling that this sort of argument cuts no
ice. I can almost hear my loyal readers telling me that they're not interested in
other magazines, only in this one.

What's more, Kathleen and Joel are totally on the side of those particular readers who want "more Asimov." (I say "those particular readers" because
I don't want to imply that this is a unanimous demand.) They would like to
have something by me in every issue, and they don't mean an essay, either.

So how about it, Isaac?

I have no objection to thinking aloud on this subject. We're all friends

But because what I like to do is *paid for,* I'm a workaholic.

If I typed and typed and typed and *didn't* get paid for it, then it would just be a hobby and that would be all right no matter how much I worked at it, provided I also had some job which earned me a living and which I hated and did as skimpily and as sloppily as I could. Then I would be a worthy human being whom it would be an honor to know.

(I'm sorry if I sound a little bitter, but I *hate* being called a workaholic, or being described as "compulsive.")

But how about the speed with which I write? Have I no feeling for my art? Don't I want to do a good job and wouldn't I turn out better stuff if I thought about it and considered it and weighed it in my mind and brooded over the first draft and revised it eighteen or nineteen times and compared the different versions carefully?

Maybe. I don't know. I've never tried it and I'm pretty sure I'm never going to try it. I can't.

Why can't I?

Let me ask you a question. Have you ever experienced an itch on your forearm? Am I correct in assuming you promptly scratched it?

Has it ever occurred to you that perhaps if you considered the itch, weighed carefully its location and intensity and thoughtfully took into account the various ways in which you might scratch it and the various instruments with which you might scratch it, you might end up—after fifteen or twenty minutes—doing a more efficient and artistic job in removing that itch?

I'm sure nothing like that has ever occurred to you. You just scratch—as quickly and as thoroughly as you can.

Well, for me the desire to write is an itch. And I scratch.

AFTERWORD: I think I sound defensive in the above essay, but there are times when I can't help being defensive. I would like to be praised for my industry and hard work, instead of being looked at as some kind of nut.

Incidentally, eight years after the above essay was written, the total number of my published books is now at 393.

and I would like to thrash out the problem as well as I can and to solicit your opinions on the matter.

The points in favor of "more Asimov" are strong ones. I like to please the readers if I can, for one thing. Then, I have a feeling that life will become difficult for me if I don't make at least an honest effort to please Kathleen and Joel, for though both of them are kindly people who show every sign of being fond of me, they get a kind of chilled-steel look in their eyes, at times, that imparts a definite chatter to my teeth when I see it.

What's more, I would be an obvious hypocrite if I tried to pretend that I didn't know I was a good writer. And since I do write good science fiction, even now in my late youth, what right have I to deprive the magazine, and its readers, of this writing?

With all that, can there possibly be any arguments against what demand there is for "more Asimov"?

Absolutely!

1) I feel more than a little nervous about using *Asimov's* as a showcase for myself. I won't really be doing so, of course, for Kathleen is perfectly capable of rejecting any story of mine that doesn't pass muster. As I've said on a number of occasions, *Asimov's* has, in the past, firmly rejected an occasional story of mine—something which always strikes my friends as hilarious when I tell them about it.

"Do you mean to say even your own magazine won't print your stories?" they ask in delight.

And I have to explain to them that it's not really my own magazine and that the editor has a higher duty than that of pleasing me—but they're usually too busy laughing to listen.

The trouble is that even though the magazine is not a showplace for me, it might *look* like one. For instance, the special *Foundation's Edge* issue bothered me. It contained not only the first two chapters of the novel, but a lot of talk about it, and it certainly looked as if I were drumming up business for the book. Still, Kathleen was convinced that the readers would be interested, and she said that it was an event—the first new Foundation novel in thirty-two years—and it was simply essential for a magazine with my name on it to celebrate, so I nervously let her have her way. Well, at the time I'm writing this, that issue has not yet appeared, and all I can say is I hope she is right, but I'll bet New York City to South Succotash that I get letters talking about my giant ego.

2) I'm nervous about taking up the room. We can only print so many words of fiction per issue and we have hundreds of times that many submitted to us. Over 99 percent of the stories we get must be rejected, and a few of them are marginal and *almost* make it. If I publish a story in the magazine, then some story that might have made it if I weren't there might *not* make it.

Have I the right to lose some writer a sale? I have no great need of money or of exposure or of fame, and the other writer may well have a need for all three.

You might say, of course, that my story is better than the story that was rejected to make room for it. You might say that *every* story printed brings about the rejection of some story that might otherwise have been accepted. Granted, but can I be sure that a rejectee might not feel particularly hurt if he imagines that his story has been rejected just so that *mine* can be printed, feeling that with my name in the title, I have an unfair advantage? I know this is not really so, but even if I don't take an unfair advantage, I might be *appearing* to take one.

3) There is really a question of time. I do have a great many commitments and in some directions they are getting worse. For instance, Doubleday, having waited three decades, finally lost patience and insisted I write a new Foundation novel over my loudly expressed fears that I couldn't.

So I wrote it and when I finally brought in *Foundation's Edge*, my editor, Hugh O'Neill, grew seriously annoyed. He had tended to believe my protestations, but he was only partway through when he said, "Now I'm *really* mad, Isaac. Why haven't you been writing science fiction all along?"

You might say that that is only Hugh (a very gentle and kindhearted young man) buttering up a peculiar author who is past his prime, but while you might butter an undeserving person with words, you don't do it with money. Not if you want to stay in business for very long. Yet not long after the novel was brought in, Hugh placed a contract for another novel in my hands, and the first half of an even larger advance than *Foundation's Edge* had gotten me and said, "Don't say anything. Just sign where I'm pointing."

This new contract is for the third Lije Baley/R. Daneel novel, the sequel to *The Caves of Steel* and *The Naked Sun*. Doubleday has been waiting only twenty-five years for this one, so it's clear they're increasingly unreasonable.

Hugh said I could start it when I felt ready, but today he wanted to know if I had started it yet, and he also said in an offhand manner, as though he were just thinking out loud, that it might be a good idea if I pushed aside all other commitments and just wrote novels—one—after—the—other.

It makes my blood freeze. It really does!

There *are* other writing projects I want to undertake. —And yet Doubleday, more than any other publishing firm, has made me what I am today, and somewhere in my misspent youth, I got hooked on a thing called "gratitude." It's very inconvenient and it gets me into a lot of trouble, but there it is. And if I oblige Hugh, will I have time to write lots of stuff for *Asimov's?*

4) I can hear you all say, "Sure you will, Isaac. How long does it take *you* to knock off a story, for goodness' sake? You can do it during lunch hour."

I admit I can write monthly columns for extended periods of time. I've kept up one series thirty years without faltering. These columns are not science fiction, however. They're science essays—in one case, mystery fiction. Those are no problem.

Science fiction is harder to do, and if I tried to churn out s.f. stories when there wasn't adequate time, I would surely turn out below-par potboilers, and I don't want to do that, either.

—Well then, Gentle Readers, what do you think? Please consider what I have said concerning the very real problems that bother me, and let me have your conclusions. I want to know.

AFTERWORD: You might be interested in knowing what response I got to the plaintive question in the last paragraph of the above essay. By a large majority, the readers said, "Do exactly what you want to do, Isaac." Their faith in me is touching, but the fact remains that I only have so much time available. I do my best, but I continue to fail to satisfy the magazine.

64

Superstupidity

SOME MONTHS AGO, A READER
sent me a sulfurous letter, one that charred the paper it was typed on, to the
effect that he was canceling his subscription to *Asimov's* because he was sick
and tired of reading essays in which Asimov talked about Asimov in his
swollen-headed, egotistical way.

I couldn't think of any way of keeping him within the fold, for I knew
very well that Asimov would continue to creep into my essays and, for that
matter, into almost anything else I write in essay form. It's part of the infor-
mality of my style of writing and I console myself with the thought that most
of my readers don't mind.

Of course, the size of my ego is taken for granted even by many people
who don't find themselves offended by it. I was interviewed on National
Public Radio recently and the interviewer said, in a perfectly friendly way, "It
is frequently said, Dr. Asimov, that you lack false modesty. What about it?"

I responded cheerfully, "Most people, when told that I lack false modesty, would respond, 'Or any other kind, either.' I admit it, but what I'm not
modest about, I have no reason to be modest about."

Yet some things shake me. The other day I picked up the January 1985
issue of *Asimov's* and settled down to read the "Viewpoint" essay, "Superintelligence" by Tom Rainbow (may he rest in peace!).

First came the nasty shock of seeing the introductory illustration to the
article. It showed little men opening the skull and studying the brain of

someone who was a virtually photographic representation of myself. What's more, throughout the essay, Tom kept using me as an example of superintelligence and seemed to take the attitude that this was so self-evident that no one would argue the point.

My heart sank. I don't mind being considered vain, but I hate to have people come to that conclusion because of false assumptions.

You must understand that the beauteous Shawna McCarthy has a completely free hand in organizing *Asimov's*. She is not compelled to ask my advice on purchases or to show me anything in advance—unless she is uncertain about something and *wants* my advice, and that doesn't happen often.

Well, Tom didn't consult me in writing the essay, and Shawna didn't consult me in purchasing and publishing it. I received no hint of its existence until I opened the January 1985 issue and, in all innocence, settled down to read the article.

Someone might say something like "Oh, well, maybe that swellheaded bum didn't insist on being called 'superintelligent,' but Shawna must know which side her bread is buttered on, and she feels compelled to flatter him."

And that someone would be wrong. You should have watched Shawna, about half a year ago, hand back an essay I had submitted. "Not for us, Isaac," she said, stifling a yawn. "Peddle it elsewhere. Don't try to stick *me* with it."

Well, maybe she didn't use those exact words, but she certainly rejected my essay, so she doesn't feel at all compelled to flatter me.

All this doesn't mean I'm now going to insist I'm modest and demure. I'm not. —But, as I told the National Public Radio interviewer, my immodesty is legitimate. I *know* that I'm a prolific, facile, and excellent writer of science fiction, mysteries, and nonfiction of many varieties; and I know that I'm one of the best off-the-cuff after-dinner speakers in the world.

I'd be a liar if I denied these things, and a posturing fool if I pretended I didn't know it.

But my immodesty ends there. Were I really vain, I'd insist I was great in directions in which I am untalented—and I don't. I am perfectly willing to point out that I was never good at sports, that I can't play any musical instrument, that I sing only moderately well, can't dance, can't ride a bicycle, and am physically clumsy at activities that require deftness (with some exceptions, such as typewriters and women). I'll even admit, cheerfully, that there are some kinds of writing I can't do. I can't write books on economics, psychology, art, or higher mathematics, and I can't write for the visual media since I lack the talent for it.

But that brings us to the question of whether I am intelligent, let alone "superintelligent," as Tom pretended to take for granted. I say "pretended" because Tom was well known to be a joker and may well have been making straight-faced fun of me.

Intelligence is, I have always thought, an elusive abstraction that is hard to pin down. To be sure, it would be hard to argue that anyone who writes and speaks as well as I do can be unintelligent, but is intelligence a simple thing that can be measured in a simple way?

I don't think so. I am convinced that what we call "intelligence" is a property of the mind that is as complex as is the mind itself and has as many facets. If you take any given person, you will find that the extent of his intelligence varies according to what aspect of his behavior you are considering. I imagine it would be possible for a person to seem a moron in every possible way until you (let us say) put cards in his hand and discover, to your sorrow, that he is very intelligent about playing poker. As a matter of fact, the current play/movie *Amadeus* rests its psychological point upon its contention that Mozart was a transcendent genius in composing music and was a dunce in every other way.

And so it is with me. People who concentrate on the quantity, quality, and diversity of my writing are liable to feel certain that I am superintelligent, while people who know me socially are always surprised when I go for two hours without doing something stupid.

Thus, my various editors at Doubleday & Company, who feel completely secure about my writing and who know that I can be counted upon to meet my deadlines with items that are publishable and profitable, nevertheless have had occasion to tell me, now and then (in the most loving possible way), that I "need a keeper."

Let me give you a very recent example of what I mean, something that my beloved younger brother, Stan Asimov (vice-president in charge of development at *Newsday*), would have no compunction in calling an example of my "superstupidity."

Newsday, a large and flourishing newspaper based in Long Island, was introducing a new weekly science section, and Stan phoned me to ask if I would give an address on the occasion to a group of *Newsday* officials and key advertisers, and I agreed. Furthermore, Stan said he would arrange to have me paid four thousand dollars for my trouble. (This is well below what I usually gouge out of people who want me to give a talk for them, but blood is thicker than water.)

Months later I gave the talk and, by that time, I had forgotten all about the promised payment.

Then, months after the talk, late on a Friday afternoon, I received a call from *Newsday* and this is the conversation:

Newsday: "May I have your social security number, Dr. Asimov?"

Asimov (suspiciously): "Why?"

Newsday: "So we can write out a check for you."

Asimov (surprised): "A check for what?"

Newsday: "For the speech you gave about the science section."

Asimov (totally astonished): "A check? For how much?"

Newsday (now puzzled itself): "For four thousand dollars."

Asimov (flabbergasted): "But wasn't I doing it for nothing?"

Newsday (shocked): "You mean you don't want the money?"

Asimov (recovering): "No, no. If you're offering it, then I'll force myself to take it."

I hastily gave *Newsday* my social security number and did a little thinking. I knew that the person who called me would get in touch with my brother first thing Monday morning and say something like "Stan, your brother was under the impression he was giving the talk for nothing. Do we really have to pay him?"

I decided I had better talk to Stan first, so a little later in the evening, I phoned Stan at home.

I said, "Stan, remember that talk I gave a couple of months ago for the science section?"

He did, and I thereupon told him the entire story of the phone conversation as I have given it here. "Please," I said, "be sure and tell them I was supposed to get the money, if they come to you and ask."

At this, Stan said, in a very testy manner, "Why do you tell me this on a Friday evening, Isaac?"

I was taken aback at his evident annoyance and asked, "What's the difference *when* I tell you?"

And he said, "Because now I have to wait until Monday morning to tell

everybody at *Newsday* the latest 'my stupid brother, Isaac' story, and having to
wait will ruin my entire weekend."

So much for superintelligence!

AFTERWORD: I have many other stories of this kind. You'll find a number of
them here and there in my autobiography.

65

Autographs

I HAVE NEVER BEEN AN AUTO-
graph hound myself and, to be perfectly frank, I do not understand the fascination that people find in them.

Suppose you have a signature written by Abraham Lincoln. You can
stare at the dim line of curving ink and say to yourself, "My goodness, Honest
Abe wrote that with his very own hand." It seems to me such a thought would
be good for ten seconds' worth of contemplation, and then the whole notion is
used up. The next time you see it, what else is there to think of?

And why should there be something special about his *name?* If he had
written "General Grant" or "yes, indeed," wouldn't that still be something he
had written with his very own hand?

I have the feeling that the awe that a signature inspires dates back to a
time when literacy was quite exceptional. In those days, signatures that ordinary people encountered were very rare and, when encountered, were usually
those of officials and were affixed to laws, orders, pardons, excommunications,
and other documents of note, so that the idea grew that names were *powerful.*

Without going into matters of religion or demonology, we get a whiff
of this mysterious power of a name in the familiar folk tale of "Rumpelstilts-
kin."

What has all this to do with science fiction?

I don't think you'll have any trouble guessing. With the increasing
popularity of science fiction comes the increasing demand for autographs from
its practitioners.

This is not in itself a problem. Indeed, it is flattering. Even though I am not interested in autographs myself, I am rather pleased that people should seek mine. In fact, it is a source of particular pleasure to me that the very first time I was ever asked for an autograph (over forty years ago), it was from a young and unknown fan named Damon Knight. (Yes, *the* Damon Knight, who eventually founded the Science Fiction Writers of America.)

However, the requests for autographs have been increasing in sheer number (not only in my case but, I'm sure, in those of other established writers) and, however flattering this may be, it does begin to pose a problem.

For instance, at the 1955 World Convention, at which I was Guest of Honor, the attendance was three hundred. If 10 percent wanted autographs, that could have been taken care of in a few minutes. At the 1980 World Convention, however, the attendance was six thousand and when an autograph session was arranged, I signed steadily for an hour and a half. Toward the end, I grew less aware of the flattery implicit in the long line, and more aware of my aching fingers.

It does strike me, therefore, that there might be some points of etiquette that could well be developed for such occasions.

1—Autographs in Public Places

a) Don't hand a closed book to a writer and leave it to him to find a place to sign. Open the book to the title page (or wherever you wish it signed) and present that to him. This is a simple courtesy that saves autographing time, and is considerate of others, if you are part of a line.

b) Be reasonable in your demand for personalization. When there is a long line, I merely sign my name over and over. When there is less pressure, I ask for a first name and write "To John." If there is still less pressure, I add "best wishes" and the day's date. It is kindest to allow a decision on such matters to be made by the autographer.

Unfortunately, many people wish to dictate the details of the autograph. They will sometimes ask for a personalization although there is a line stretching to the crack of doom, so that I am forced to ask them to come back when the line is done—and they sometimes act irritated at that. Or, if I ask the first name, they say firmly, "Jonathan, Ethelfrieda, Bonaparte, and Fido Schnellenhammer" (Fido is the dog, of course). This is not really fair to the writer's cramping tendons.

Sometimes a little mash note is demanded, and you are asked to write "To Morris, with best hopes for a happy bar mitzvah that will make your mother very proud of you" or "To Clinton, with full confidence that you, too, will be a great science fiction writer some day if you do your homework carefully and listen closely in school."

Mind you, I never refuse, but these things I do not reckon as part of the joy of authorship.

c) Please recognize that not all autographs are alike to the fellow scribbling his name. I have heard fellow writers announce, very firmly, that they will sign only hardcover editions of their books. I have never been able to bring myself to do this, alas, which means that I must sign, quite indiscriminately, everything that's handed to me (including blank checks—on which I carefully write "Harlan Ellison").

Yet even I recognize that paperbacks represent a lower grade of flattery than hardcovers, that program booklets are still lower in the scale, and that a scrap of paper hastily torn out of a notebook produces almost no feeling of chest inflation at all. I sign scraps, yes, but I can never make myself believe that an odd piece of paper is going to be saved for long. Someone who presents a scrap for a signature is just being caught up in the mass hysteria; or else, it seems to him that since something is being given out for nothing, it is only fair that he get a sample—no matter what it might be.

2—Autographs in the Mail

a) You have every right to expect an autograph for nothing, since the flattery might be regarded as sufficient return, but surely it isn't fair to *charge* the writer. It is very common for an autograph request to come through the mail without the inclusion of any provision that would make life a bit easier. The writer must find a card, sign it, find an envelope, address it, then put a stamp on it. It is something that can be shrugged off where one person is concerned, but as the number of autograph requests increase, it becomes steadily more troublesome.

The proper way to ask for an autograph in the mail is to send along a card you wish signed, together with a stamped self-addressed envelope. I don't insist on that, you understand, especially when the request is from a preteen who lacks the sophistication to think of such things, so I invest steadily in cards, envelopes, and postage. Nevertheless, I can't help but dream of a better world in which there was just a little more consideration.

b) You ought to indicate some personal interest in the writer whose autograph you request. If you have read something he has written, say so. Name the piece you have read. Say you liked it (if you did). It is rather deflating to get a letter that simply says, "Dear sir, I collect autographs. May I have yours?"

Well, at least that's polite. The other day I got a form letter, without salutation, which said, "Sign the enclosed and return to the following address." Enclosed were five cards, and no return envelope or postage. I finally rebelled. I did not do as requested, but put the cards aside so that I could use them for people who were just a little more courteous.

c) Don't mail books for signature, unless you write first and ask permission to do so. I know writers who say they keep any book sent them for signature and add them to their own libraries. I can't do that, so that I am forced to sign those I receive, package them, figure out the postage (or go to the post office). It is an enormous imposition on a writer. If you *do* send a book, send along a stamped self-addressed mailer as well.

My own feeling is that it is far better to send a stick-on label or a bookplate, have the writer sign and return that, and then paste it in the book. That is much easier for everyone, and you don't have to trust a book you value to the tender mercies of the post office.

(I was once asked by a distant bookstore if I would sign "a few" books. I agreed, not wishing to offend a bookstore. I received *sixty* of them. I signed them all, packaged them, and trundled them to the post office. But I sent along a furious letter as well, because I was beyond caring if they were offended.)

3—Signed Photographs

In recent years, I have been receiving an increasing number of requests for signed photographs.

I draw the line at that. The notion arises because people in show business find that recognition of face and person is the key to success. They arrange to have a flattering photograph taken and reproduced in thousands of copies, then have some secretary send them off (all signed by stamp or by the secretary) to anyone requesting them.

That doesn't fit my case. I'm not in show business. It's not my face I'm selling but my writing, and I'd rather people had my books than my photograph. So I don't have any photographs and I don't send any out. When someone requests a signed photograph, I explain and sign the letter of explanation—which I think is better.

◆

AFTERWORD: Since the above essay was written, five years ago, a new wrinkle has been added. People write to ask for autographs and say, "Could you also include a favorite passage from one of your stories in your own handwriting?" I *never* do that. I have difficulty sending them the autograph alone. Such presumption!

66

Irritations

IN THE PREVIOUS ESSAY, I EX-
plained how anyone who wants an autograph can make life a little easier for
an aging, hardworking writer.

On the whole, the effect was good. To be sure, the number of people
writing for autographs increased markedly, since a number of readers who had
never thought of asking me for an autograph were inspired to do so by the
essay. (This made the beauteous but heartless Shawna laugh, for she had predicted that would happen.) However, almost all the new autograph seekers
sent along specific objects for me to sign and (as I had gently suggested)
included a stamped self-addressed envelope. After all, if I just sign what they
send me, stick it into the envelope, lick it, seal it, and put it on the pile to mail,
that's really very little trouble, and I don't mind at all.

It is time, then, for me to get a few more irritations off my chest in the
hope that it will help ease my life in other ways. Even if it doesn't, I know I
will feel better for having aired the matter, for if I go about with my bosom
surcharged with repressed annoyance over little things, it tends to make me
snap at my loved ones whose soft eyes then fill with unshed tears, and I don't
want to do that.

What currently annoys me the most is what is going on in grade schools
the country over. There are, apparently, teachers of sixth-grade students who,
in their anxiety to stimulate the kids into reading worthwhile material, come
up with what seems to each to be a novel idea. What they actually say, I don't

know, but in my fevered and overstimulated imagination, this is what I hear them say:

"Now, children, I want each one of you to choose something you've read that you liked. Write down the name of the author and I will get his address out of Who's Who. I then want each of you to write a nice letter to that author. Tell him the name of the story you read and how you liked it. Then ask him some questions about his writing, and ask him please to answer your letter because it is a school assignment."

One of the kids is bound to raise his hand at this point and say, "Miss Fritzenheimer, what kind of questions are we supposed to ask?"

The teacher says, "Well, why don't you ask him how he got started writing, and if he likes writing, and what made him write whatever story or book you mentioned, and if he is writing another book, and things like that."

The teacher then sits back and thinks what a marvelous idea she has dreamed up, for everyone knows that writers have practically nothing to do and would welcome the chance to take a break from the boredom of just sitting around all day long by answering questions about how they started writing and so on. Not only do the kids get to do a little homework, but the writers get to do a little homework, too. What fun!

Most of the kids, perhaps, write to the estates of Franz Kafka and James Joyce, but some do write to me.

The letters all sound the same. This is a very typical (imaginary) example:

"Dear Mr. Azminav, I am a 6th grade student at P.S. 1728 of Rock River, Rhode Island, and I am doing this for a class assignment. I have read a book of yours about Lucky Starr and I liked his name very much. I would like to ask you how you got to think of the name Lucky Starr. How did you start writing about Lucky Starr and why are there two r's in the last name? Did his parents really name him Lucky? Are you writing another book about Lucky Starr? Is his name going to be on the new book, too? Could you send me something about your life and please answer right away as Miss Fritzenheimer is in a hurry. [signed] Jeremy Indecipherable."

It is clear to me that all the kid read was the word Lucky Starr in the title of the book, and with great ingenuity made a school assignment out of that. Pleased with his cleverness (and remembering some episodes in my own grade-school career in which I successfully met the requirements of a school assignment with a minimum of real work) I answered the letter as best I could.

Along about the 722nd letter of this sort, however, I grew tired of sweating away at all those school assignments even though it was now well over a half century since I got out of grade school, and I let myself be goaded into the following answer.

"Dear Jeremy, Thank you very much for your nice letter. If you will ask Miss Fritzenheimer to write me a letter telling me how she got started in teaching, and how she likes teaching, and if she expects to continue teaching next year, and all about her life, I will then answer your questions."

I did not expect an answer, but, rather to my surprise, I got one. Miss Fritzenheimer wrote me two pages telling me how many siblings she had and how much she weighed and a few other intimate facts and asking me what was so hard about answering in that fashion.

My conscience hurt me and I was considering a letter of apology when I got a second letter from the head of the library of the school. Miss Fritzenheimer must have showed the correspondence to the library head—clearly an older and more muscular specimen—and she must have said (if my imagination is to be trusted),

"Why, that unmitigated brute. Why did you write such a milk-and-water letter to him? Here, now, you leave it to me. I will take the hide off him."

And she promptly wrote me a letter telling me how far I had fallen in the esteem of all right-thinking people and how some of the gloss had been rubbed off me because of my treatment of hardworking students who read and loved my books and wrote to me with such hope in their hearts and were so bitterly disappointed at my unfeeling answer.

I took all these blows with philosophical stolidity; and then came her concluding remark which went something like this: "If ever you should be in this position again, I hope you will behave more decently."

If *ever* I should be in this position *again???*

That was too much. I sent off a letter which was undoubtedly the most plainspoken she ever got in her life from an infuriated and supremely articulate person.

Did she honestly think that I had gotten exactly one letter of this type in my life and that it might be fifteen years before I might get a second one? I let her know that I received no batch of mail without at least one letter of this type in it, and it was by no means an unusual week in which I received as many as twenty, all asking the same tedious questions, and all demanding a quick answer.

So let me make my position clear.

I get many letters from enthusiastic youngsters who have read some of my stuff and liked it, and who have gone to the trouble of writing me to tell me they liked it (giving clear evidence of having actually read it), and who do not hesitate to point out flaws, and who then ask me questions out of honest interest and curiosity.

I answer *all* such letters, if there is a return address I can read, and I answer the questions, too.

However, any letter that starts "I am a sixth-grade student and my teacher has asked me to write to you . . ." I intend to tear into four pieces and toss into the wastebasket.

And, while I'm at it, here are other letters that get unceremoniously dumped—

Once long ago, I got a letter pleading with me to send a manuscript, or a signed book, or an unneeded article of clothing, or anything personal to the undersigned. It would be used in a "celebrity auction" to be raffled off for money for some useful and worthy cause. I signed a paperback and sent it off. Then I got another letter of the same sort and again I signed a paperback and sent it off. With time, I realized that there were fifty celebrity auctions being carried on in various parts of these United States every single day, and that they all used the same computerized sucker list and that my name was on it. They would clearly consume every paperback I have and I would have to start sending off all my old socks. So now every letter bearing the magic words "celebrity auction" gets thrown out.

This is also true of all letters and (sometimes) bulky packages containing someone's solutions to all so-far unanswered problems in science, detailed demonstrations of the invalidity of Einstein's theories, careful proofs—pages and pages of it—of Fermat's Last Theorem, or of the trisection of the angle, or of the true meaning of the Great Pyramid. If a return envelope, stamped and self-addressed, is included, the material is sent back. Otherwise, my wastepaper basket gets filled to the brim at one stroke.

If all this makes me sound curmudgeonly, consider—

My writing and speaking schedule is enormous and surely that should come first. The time I have left is short and growing shorter, and I don't want to use it on grade-school assignments and on useless correspondence. Shouldn't I spend my time on my work, instead?

What do you think?

♦

AFTERWORD: Here's another one that has cropped up lately. Someone is in the hospital, someone is getting married, someone has just been made eagle scout, someone has just had a baby—*therefore* a scrapbook of mementos is being made up and would I please send a beautiful handwritten message of congratulations/condolences/inspiration to be included in the scrapbook. Sometimes I do it, if I feel touched by the situation, or if a child is involved. And when I do, do you think I get a letter of gratitude in response? Heavens, no! *Their* time is valuable.

ABOUT THE AUTHOR

Born in Petrovichi, Russia, in 1920, Isaac Asimov emigrated to New York with his parents in 1923. It was during his childhood in Brooklyn that he developed his lifelong love of books by reading the volumes in his local library, shelf by shelf. Accepted to Columbia University at the age of fifteen, Asimov earned his bachelor of science degree, and went on to receive his Ph.D. in chemistry in 1948. He taught biochemistry at the Boston University School of Medicine until 1958, when he turned to writing full-time.

Dr. Asimov began writing science fiction at the age of eleven and had his first short story published in 1938. His first book-length work of science fiction, *Pebble in the Sky*, was published by Doubleday in 1950, and he soon branched out into nonfiction as well. Asimov has written on nearly every subject under the sun, ranging from math and physics to the Bible and Shakespeare, and currently has over 390 published books to his credit. He has received numerous honorary degrees and writing awards, including a special Hugo Award honoring his internationally bestselling Foundation trilogy as "the best all-time science fiction series." And he was recently named Grand Master of Science Fiction by the Science Fiction Writers of America.

Not content with specializing in his first field of expertise—the sciences —Dr. Asimov has proved a successful essayist, mystery writer, editor, journalist, biographer, humorist, and all-around exponent of the written word. Happiest working in the seclusion of his two-room office, lined with more than 2,000 books, Asimov lives in Manhattan with his wife, writer Janet O. Jeppson.